Central Organizations of Defense

Westview Special Studies in Military Affairs

Central Organizations of Defense
edited by Martin Edmonds

Defense and strategic studies traditionally have paid little attention to the structure and administrative context within which policy decisions are made. This volume fills that existing gap, focusing on the principal actors in the defense decisionmaking field, their relationships to one another, and the statutory and legal provisions governing the spheres of responsibility and competence among military, civil, and paramilitary institutions.

The book is designed to assist scholars and policymakers in comparative analyses of complex organizations and institutions and to identify similarities and differences among the central administrative structures of the major industrial states. Toward this end, each contributor concentrates on his or her own transnational analysis. The authors are all respected experts on defense issues in their own countries, and their analyses conform to a common framework developed to compare central organizations of defense around the world and to define what states can learn from each other's experiences and what developments can be expected.

Martin Edmonds is senior lecturer in higher defense studies at the University of Lancaster. He previously taught at the University of Manchester and the University of Southern California and has been a research associate at Columbia University. His publications include *War in the Next Decade* (coedited with Roger Beaumont, 1975), *International Arms Procurement* (1981), and over fifty articles on defense and military studies. He is the editor-in-chief of a major new journal, *Defense Analysis*.

Central Organizations of Defense

edited by Martin Edmonds

Routledge
Taylor & Francis Group

LONDON AND NEW YORK

First published 1985 by Westview Press

Published 2018 by Routledge
52 Vanderbilt Avenue, New York, NY 10017
2 Park Square, Milton Park, Abingdon, Oxon OX14 4RN

Routledge is an imprint of the Taylor & Francis Group, an informa business

Copyright © 1985 by Taylor & Francis

Library of Congress Cataloging in Publication Data
Main entry under title:
Central organizations of defense.
  (Westview special studies in military affairs)
  Includes index.
  1. Military policy—Decision making—Addresses, essays,
lectures. I. Edmonds, Martin, 1939– . II. Series.
UA11.C45 1985   351.06   85-3191
ISBN 0-86531-684-8

British Cataloguing in Publication Data
Central organizations of defense.
  1. Defense departments
  I. Edmonds, Martin
  351.06   UA10
ISBN 0-86187-507-9

ISBN 13: 978-0-367-01485-8 (hbk)
ISBN 13: 978-0-367-16472-0 (pbk)

In fond memory of my parents,
Wallace and Phyllis Edmonds

Contents

Tables and Figures

Preface

The notion of compiling and editing a volume on central organizations of defense had been with me for several years—in fact, since I began teaching civil-military relations in the mid-1960s. Each year I took the easy way out and gave my students general outlines of the countries that seemed most relevant at the time. But as the years passed and as defense expenditures everywhere mounted, I perceived an increasing need for a volume that spelled out the issues associated with the making of defense policy and described the context within which it was made. The last straw came about two years ago when discussions of Soviet and U.S. strategic policy and of European responses to plans for strategic stability in Europe were articulated and analyzed in highly personalized terms, with no recognition of, or apparent reference to, the interplay of political, bureaucratic, military, scientific, and economic forces that constrain options and shape preferred solutions.

The time had come, I felt, to remind everyone that the defense policies of nations and states are the product of the interplay of powerful interests, all operating within well-defined structures, according to generally recognized and prescribed processes and within a wide range of different political systems. Furthermore, the interaction of these powerful forces takes place within the wider context of domestic and international economic, political, and social considerations.

The volume seemed to be an important contribution to the ongoing discussions of defense and strategic issues, but it also offered a rare opportunity to encourage a fresh look at the problems associated with comparative political analysis, in particular the comparison of a major department of government across a variety of states in an area of central political concern.

Once the commitment to embark on the project had been made, two further decisions were necessary. The first was to ask contributors to work within a common analytical framework, which is outlined in Chapter 1; the other was to ask for contributions from "indigenous" authors. The common framework was meant to create some semblance of analytical commonality and to facilitate the highlighting of contrasts and similarities; the local authors were to ensure that the nuances of central organizations of defense would not be overlooked because of a lack of immediate and intimate familiarity.

But neither objective was wholly achieved. Several contributors pointed out that the political systems and historical contexts of their particular state did not lend themselves to the comparative framework I had given them; their compromise was to employ it where appropriate and depart from it where necessary. The second objective foundered on the rocks of the reluctance of relevant authorities, but in most cases our authors succeeded. To them I owe a debt of gratitude for their great efforts, especially those who wrote for an essentially foreign audience in a foreign language.

This was not possible in all cases, and I must record my most sincere thanks to all those who helped me to translate and get the best from those contributions that were not in English. In no specific order of relevance I thank sincerely and warmly Michelle Fournier, Anne Mandeville, Bob Baker, and Fiona Knowles-Lote for their linguistic help and support and for their kind forbearance when I insisted on altering their more elegant prose, and colleague David Weston for his reassurance that I was not always too far off the mark.

To Lynne Rienner and Deborah Lynes at Westview Press and to Frances Pinter, I wish to record my appreciation of their respective support for and confidence in the pertinence of this volume and of their quite remarkable patience. To Christine Arden at Westview I owe a particular debt of gratitude for her exceptional copy editing, which improved the volume immeasurably. And to Valerie Mingay, for typing, retyping, word processing, and generally enduring my irascibility throughout the project, I give my special thanks.

Martin Edmonds

1
Introduction

Martin Edmonds

Almost without exception—and the exceptions scarcely warrant close attention in any case—every state in the world possesses armed forces. There is wide variation in composition, type, function, role, capability, and size of armed forces. In some cases the emphasis is more on the domestic arena and in others, the international; but in all instances there is, within the structure of political authority of each state, a government department, ministry, organization, bureau, or directorate—the titles are as multifarious as the types of armed forces—that is charged with the responsibility for, and the direction, use, and control of the activities of armed force. More often than not, there is more than one such government institution. This fact alone offers the opportunity, if not the challenge, for comparative analysis, with the promise at the end, *ceteris paribus*, of a better understanding of how and why different states are more or less successful in exercising control over their armed forces and of an answer to the ever-relevant question, *Quis custodiet custodes*?

Why choose the central organizations of defense as the vehicle for comparative institutional and political analysis? Two considerations stand out. The first is the truism that the armed forces of any state constitute bodies of men and women who are organized, equipped, and trained to be able to bring physical coercive force to bear as a means—an option—at the disposal of those in political power to resolve national or international political disputes. For the most part, armed forces are established principally to meet or deter perceived external threats to the interests of the state and its citizenry, both at home and abroad. The majority of states differentiate between the armed services and the police, whose primary responsibility is, if the occasion warrants it, to bring coercive force to bear in disputes that are perceived to constitute a threat to the stability and domestic order of the state. The distinction, of course, is neither universal nor customary, and examples abound, on . the one hand, of the involvement of the armed services and paramilitary forces in the maintenance of domestic order and, on the other, of the use of police and parapolice abroad (although this is less common).

It stands to reason, therefore, that armed forces, by dint of their specific functions and the coercive power they possess, constitute a

1

potential independent political force. Alternatively, they can be a tool at the disposal of a nongovernmental domestic political faction, a course of action that would be inimical to constitutional order and customary political practices. As S. E. Finer so appositely pointed out in his pioneering study of the military, the pertinent question is not so much why the military intervenes in politics, but why it does not.[1] In the same vein, but from a different ideological perspective, C. Ackroyd and J. Margolis noted that the armed forces at the disposal of state authorities are no more neutral than the state itself; on the strength of this premise, it is fallacious to assume that the coercive power of the police and the armed services will not be employed in defense of the existing political regime, defined here as both the holders of political power and authority and the political system itself.[2] It is thus a matter of paramount importance to know and understand both the constitutional provisions for the existence of organizations and institutions that can exercise coercive power within any state and the statutory provisions for their control.

If the first reason for focusing our attention on central organizations of defense were not enough, the very magnitude of spending on armed forces, within individual states (whether expressed as a percentage of the gross national product—GNP—or in absolute terms) and throughout the world, should give cause for proper consideration of the provision of adequate means of their control. But the sheer magnitude of spending on armed forces today, together with the effect of that expenditure on national economies and its opportunity cost, is not the only consideration: Since World War II, spending on armed forces has also inexorably risen at an almost exponential rate. This fact, however, pales almost to insignificance when compared to the phenomenal increase in the destructive power of modern weapons systems, their extended range of effectiveness, their greater reliability and accuracy, and—as a consequence of complexity, production lead times, and labor intensiveness—their constant state of readiness. Nowhere is this consideration more critical, and the question of control more imperative, than in the provision for the effective and, as far as possible, guaranteed control over those who are responsible for the deployment, protection, state of readiness, and, ultimately, use of nuclear weapons. Contemporary public concern in European states over the control of U.S. nuclear weapons stationed in Europe and a more general worldwide concern over the control of nuclear weapons by the nuclear powers—as the consequences go far beyond the parties immediately involved—highlight this problem.

The potential influence of armed forces and the wider effect today of meeting their perceived requirements in terms of money, men, and materiel are two clear reasons for which a close scrutiny of the central organizations of defense among, at least, the major military powers in the world is pertinent. Indeed, within the central organizations of defense of all states is found the very essence of civil-military relations within any society, and the core of the relationship between armed force and society. It is that locus where the armed forces, as both the executors of policy and the institutions reponsible for the operational functions for the security system of the state,[3] meet and work in conjunction with the political representatives of the population, who, depending on the state, have been either elected, delegated, or mandated to prosecute approved and legitimate policies concerned with the external and internal security of the state and the "protection of internal values."[4]

In some states the relationship is clearly one of the armed forces' subservience to their political masters, with the inevitable qualification that the former—as professional bodies possessing a virtual monopoly of experience, expertise, and information in matters, especially, of physical defense and deterrence against external threat—must exercise influence over security policy. In other states, this is less obviously the case; at one extreme, there are those in which the armed forces, or an element of them, have taken over the government and hence the differentiation between political and police/military authority no longer applies, and, at the other, there are those that constitute single-party or totalitarian systems in which the armed forces and the government authorities are both subservient to and, in a practical sense, under the control and direction of a single-party leadership.[5] Nevertheless, even in this second category the central organization of defense remains the forum in which the determination of policy and the management and execution of that policy is deliberated and, finally, decided.

An analysis of central organizations of defense necessarily raises many conceptual and definitional problems, particularly when comparisons are drawn between one state and another. It is not sufficient to assert that, to a large degree, the armed forces and their functions— defined by Morris Janowitz as the constrained management of violence[6]— are elements that all states have in common, partly because differences in the size, composition, and technical complexity of the armed forces of states are in such orders of magnitude that to draw comparisons would be tenuous, and partly because not all states differentiate between armed forces designed and trained specifically for defense against external threat and armed forces exclusively employed in the domestic arena. Customarily, the distinction is one drawn between the armed services and the police force, although many states also have paramilitary and parapolice forces, and many others equip, deploy, and staff their armed services specifically for operations in the domestic arena.

Two examples may be used to illustrate this point: One concerns Britain, which differentiates between its armed services and its police force, both in the structural arrangements for each set of institutions and in the provisions for their respective accountability to the legislature. It is also worth noting that, with a few exceptions, the British police do not carry arms; moreover, the British Army has been used since 1969 in Northern Ireland, for which role it has been specially equipped and trained. The other concerns France, whose Gendarmerie Nationale is as much a fourth armed service as it is a national police force; this duality is reflected in its accountability to three political masters: the

Departments of Defense, Interior, and Justice. Further complications are associated with the degree of inconsistency that exists even in those states that diffentiate quite clearly between the armed services as the agencies responsible for external defense and the police as that for internal law and order. Then there is the number and type of organizations classed as "armed services." Most states possess armies, navies, and air forces; Britain, Spain, and Germany are clear examples. The Soviet Union, however, has found it necessary to have five, and the United States and France, four each.

To some extent, these distinctions between different states are secondary to the central issue, even though it is prudent to bear them in mind. Central organizations of defense are directly concerned with the defense of the state against external threat, and consequently they are not concerned entirely with the broader issue of national security. Assuredly, defense is nevertheless the most important, and arguably the most dominant, element in national security, but the two concepts or objectives of state policy are not synonymous. For this reason, the analysis of central organizations of defense is concerned with those agencies—for all intents and purposes, the uniformed armed services— for which it is politically and publicly accountable. Other armed forces, as with the police, special task forces, bureaus of investigation, and so on are excluded, unless they are directly accountable to constitutionally and legally defined organizations, ministries, or departments of defense.

For this reason, the point of departure for the study of central organizations of defense is the constitutional and legal standing of the relevant department of government and of the armed services and other defense-related agencies for which it is responsible, as well as the procedures that prescribe both the relationship between these two elements and the way they go about their business. The juridical principles upon which the political systems of different states are based vary significantly, and contrasts between the states' central organizations of defense will be immediately apparent on these grounds alone. Take, for example, those states in which Marxist principles prescribe the constitution and the organic laws outlining the powers and functions of state institutions: In the Soviet Union and the People's Republic of China, a foundation has been firmly established that integrates the administrative structure of government, including defense, with the structure of the Communist party. Britain, with a political system based on common law principles and lacking any single formal constitutional document, stands in marked contrast with its European continental partners whose constitutions are both written and founded on the principles of Roman law. The United States, constitutionally a mixture of both British and European influences and traditions, is different again, for which reason it is significant to note that the constitutions and structural arrangements for the central organizations of defense of both Germany and Japan were established with strong U.S. influence after World War II.

Constitutions do not determine the policies of governments or the behavior of officials; nor do they necessarily prescribe who should decide policy. They do, however, define the parameters and structure of formal authority within the state and the responsibilities, duties, and authority that are vested in the institutions and offices of state. Those who hold positions within those institutions ostensibly may exercise power only within the terms of the constitution and as defined by law; reality would suggest, however, that such considerations as expediency, custom, and opportunism are sufficient reasons why this is not always the case, even in states with a "mature" political culture, and why departures from constitutional and legal norms not only frequently occur but also go unnoticed, unchecked, or unremedied.

Constitutions exist as a codification of the structure of the political system; moreover, in prescribing and defining both the powers that office-holders may exercise within the law and the processes of decisionmaking in matters affecting the state as a whole, they serve as guidelines and guarantors of democracy, and of popular sovereignty, in the sense of ensuring provision for public participation in political processes, government accountability, and access to information and authority. These legal prescriptions apply not only to questions of the selection of individuals to hold public office, but also to matters associated with the formulation and execution of public policy. Generally speaking, they relate in liberal democratic societies to universal suffrage and to the sets of arrangements concerned with the election of public representatives to legislatures. Public participation in central government decisionmaking is much less evident for purely practical reasons, and such involvement as exists is conducted through political parties, interest articulation and pressure groups, and, to an increasing extent in modern advanced industrial societies, a more corporate approach of governments to policymaking.[7]

But democracy is much more than public involvement in elections and accessibility to those in authority. The hallmark of any effective democratic system is the degree to which governments and those who exercise political power are accountable and answerable to those whom they ostensibly serve, and in whose names policies are formulated and executed. Depending on the nature of the political system, its philosophical and juridical foundation, and the particular structural arrangements codified in the constitution and in statutory law, so the mechanisms of accountability differ.

In parliamentary democracies, where the elected legislative assemblies are assumed to be sovereign in that they are the only source of legislation, one form of accountability is manifest in terms of the public's participation in elections. The government forms the executive branch, which, for the most part, seeks legislative endorsement of and financial backing for the policies it feels necessary to pursue in the nation's interest. Among such policies is that of defense, for which legislative endorsement is generally required in relation both to the policies the government wishes to pursue and to the resources required to turn those policies into effective action. It is central to notions of democracy under these sorts of arrangements that governments should be accountable to legislative assemblies not merely for their policies, but also for the efficiency and fiscal propriety with which they implement them.[8]

In the field of defense, the accountability of the government and of those of its departments responsible for the formulation and execution of defense policy raises one critical issue in particular—the right and the need, respectively, of the public to know what the details of defense policy are and how those responsible have gone about their duties and with what degree of fiscal propriety. Assuming legislative assemblies to be paramount in these matters as the institutions that reflect popular sovereignty and, therefore, popular will, the issue should be clear: Governments, by definition, should be fully accountable. But the issue of defense raises the question of national security and the protection of the state and its citizens against external threat; consequently, open access to government information on defense policy, operational planning, military weapons, intelligence appreciation, and so on can itself constitute a threat to those very institutions established to protect the state and its citizens. Different societies place different emphasis on access to defense and military information, a fact invariably reflected both in the opportunities to raise relevant matters before the government in public and the degree of comprehensiveness with which explanation and answers are given.

In nonparliamentary democracies, particularly one-party states or those with specific philosophical underpinnings to their constitutions, processes of accountability, especially in defense matters, are significantly different from those characteristic of liberal democratic societies. The latter case is not necessarily one of less accountability in a practical sense; rather, accountability operates and is expressed through mechanisms parallel to the formal administrative structure of the state, invariably the constitutionally recognized single political party. On the premise of one party, and of one philosophical principle upon which the state is based, accountability therefore becomes as much an issue of the conformity of government behavior and policies to prescribed philosophical tenets as one of responsiveness to the public at large, which holds or reflects alternative, and opposing, values, preferences, and demands.

The relationships between central organizations of defense and governments, and between the government as a whole and its department of defense as well as the sovereign legislative bodies of the state, are essential to the understanding of how defense policies are formulated and implemented over time. Defense and foreign policy has been defined as "high politics" in the implied sense that they are areas too complex, too central, too sensitive, and too fundamental to be comprehended by the public at large and too important for the survival of the state to be subject to the vagaries and vicissitudes of popular fashion, opinion, or whim.[9] Conversely, there are policy areas that, in some cases, carry with them implications for the very survival of mankind, if not the whole of that country's society, in that they involve massive investment of human, material, and financial resources of the state and have an impact that stretches far into the future—all of which would suggest that an imperative of any democratic political system is the existence of effective mechanisms for public accountability regarding defense policy and the availability of adequate information on strategic, security, defense, military, and foreign affairs matters with which to formulate a balanced judgment.

The question of who should be accountable, and for what, turns attention directly back to the central issue area here—that of the central organization of defense. Defense accountability and answerability is concerned, respectively, with (1) policies (the defined ends of any state's defense and military efforts); (2) programs (the choices exercised among many alternative options with which to achieve policy ends); (3) processes (the management efficiency with which governments and their agencies execute these programs); and (4) proprieties (the assurance that the resources allocated to the defense effort have been expended according to the amounts and terms agreed by the legally constituted authorities, that is, the legislature). Within the central organizations of defense of states, the apportionment of responsibility for those aspects of government action for which the four dimensions of accountability apply is not always clear, and constitutional and statutory provisions do not always satisfactorily point to or provide the answer.

Military and party dictatorships aside, the responsibility for formulating defense policy is the exclusive concern of governments, which act on behalf of the people; it follows that such responsibility is a civilian matter that reflects the generally accepted principle of all democracies that the military and other defense forces should be subservient to such a political authority. Structurally, this is usually the case in most states, such that the prime minister or minister of defense (or his or her equivalent) serves in the name of the government as a whole as the top authority in matters concerning defense. Subservient to this post are its departments and the armed services of the state. In some instances, the armed services are directly subject to the head of state, who is either a president or a monarch (in a titular sense), although defense policy itself and the appropriation of funds and resources often fall within the realm of government authority.

In short, line charts of authority may be relatively easy to determine in most states, but they invariably give a misleading picture of what really goes on and whose influence prevails at any one time. One explanation for this is the distinction between the responsibility for formulating defense and military policy on the one hand and the responsibility for its execution on the other. The former principally pertains to politicians, who, almost by definition, are not experts in military and defense matters; the latter responsibility is, by law, exclusively that of the senior staffs of the armed services. The complexity, cost, and magnitude of military command, operational planning, and service operations—separately, on land, by sea, and in the air, and together in combined operations—are such that the importance of expertise and experience in defense matters is heavily weighted on the side of the service professionals. In the forums of decisionmaking within central organizations of defense, the balance of influence between political power and authority, on the one hand, and service expertise and responsibility in time of war or military action, on the other, is a delicate and potentially vulnerable one.

In many states, questions are continually being raised as to how political authority can be exercised over the armed services without at the same time jeopardizing their morale, commitment, and cooperation, or how it can be exercised without appearing to disregard legitimate professional advice from the services. The issue is more complex still in those instances in which the services operate institutionally independent of one another and enjoy a greater degree of autonomy than would be the case if they were incorporated either into a single defense force (as in Canada), or had a single defense department, to which they are all accountable, in place of separate service ministries (as in Great Britain).

The debates over the appropriate structure and processes of central organizations of defense have, in different states and at different times, emphasized more than just the central question of political supremacy over the military. In recent years, defense spending has almost universally increased, and the costs pertaining to men and materiel have risen significantly. With the abandonment, in some cases, of conscription as a source of manpower to be replaced by permanent all-volunteer professional forces, manpower has become an expensive and highly qualified element in modern defense budgets, and even in those states that have retained conscription, the proportion of conscripts and full-time professionals has changed with increasing technology in the direction of the latter, especially in the more capital-intensive services such as the navy, the air force, and missile-based forces. Weapons costs have risen exponentially not merely among the advanced industrial nations but also among those states whose political and military leaders are not prepared to accept either second-hand, obsolete, or relatively unsophisticated weaponry from the major weapons-producing states.

The overall result of these rapidly rising defense costs has been to put pressure on defense policy planners, not just to ensure cost-effective solutions for defense policies, goals, and commitments, but to effect management efficiency also among those who administer the central defense machinery, those who train and prepare the armed services for operations, and those who research, develop, and produce defense materiel. The supposition widely held in most advanced industrial states is that adjustment to the defense decisionmaking policy processes, the wide application of analytical techniques as a part of that process, structural alterations to prevent duplication and waste, vigilant central financial control, and functional costing will have the desired effect of combining operationally rational planning with a strengthened central, and therefore political, financial management and control.

Then there are the debates that revolve around the appropriate command structure of the armed services and the distinction between peace and war. Ideal structures and processes in time of peace, which are geared to the constrained control over the armed services and optimal forward defense planning at minimum cost, are not necessarily (and as the past record of many states would suggest, probably are not) the most appropriate basis of higher defense command in time of war. Peacetime objectives place an emphasis on defense structures and decisionmaking processes that is different from those of war. To begin with, time scales are different. Moreover, decisionmaking must often be delegated, given the exigencies of war, to those commanders in the field with a full intelligence appraisal of the situation, rather than retained by politicians and civilians who are distanced from the conflict in time, place, and knowledge. It is recognized in most states, however, that the major decisions—those of declaring war and terminating it, and of certain military strategies and tactics that carry with them longer-term political implications—have to be the responsibility of those with political authority, and this is provided for in constitutions. However, the command and control of forces engaged in war as a matter of expediency are likely to be delegated, with a relatively high degree of autonomous authority, to senior service staff. Not all central organizations of defense provide for wartime defense planning and control; the final arrangements (unless a supranational body such as either the North Atlantic or Warsaw Treaty Organization is present) tend to be ad hoc, according to the specific circumstances.

In recent years there has been much debate in several advanced industrial states about the relationship between the defense industries and weapons producers with central organizations of defense. The main questions raised concern the extent to which weapons procurement and the management of defense research, development, and production should be incorporated within central defense structures, merely monitored by them, or delegated to private industry under contract. The dilemma between close supervision and surveillance leading to duplication and extra cost, and delegation of responsibility to defense-oriented enterprises working under contract to meet the needs of the armed services, is one that everywhere must still be resolved. In most states the structure is mixed between centrally owned and controlled defense-oriented industries with procurement agencies or directorates responsible for their operations and products, and government contracting agencies responsible for placing contracts with defense industries on behalf of the armed services. As a general rule, fundamental, or pure, defense research and development tends to be assumed by government institutions under the direction and control of the central defense organizations.

Whether or not central organizations of defense emphasize central control and planning and the treatment of defense as a single aspect of government policy or perceive defense as a coordinated activity between the principal armed services operating almost independently, all incorporate within their structures certain departments charged with the responsibility to coordinate the diverse elements that today make up the defense efforts of most advanced states. For example, in addition to separate armed services intelligence agencies, there are combined intelligence departments, joint operational requirements for the services, and joint research, development, and operational planning centers. Sensibly enough, these joint agencies are located in the given central organization of defense at a point within the hierarchical structure where their influence can have most beneficial operational and economic effects.

As the aforementioned contextual developments take effect, whether they are of a political, economic, technological, or military nature, so central defense organizations adjust accordingly. Although it might appear that the consistency of defense as a basic responsibility of government should determine that it is unlikely that the provisions for central organizations of defense should change very much, if at all, the opposite has been the case in most states, whether economically advanced or not. Indeed, the histories of central organizations of defense are replete with examples of structural changes, acrimonious debates over policy procedures, institutional battles for influence and, sometimes, power and prestige. Attempts to ensure the political control and accountability of the armed services, and efforts to impose strict financial management and control over a complex and multifarious set of institutions, organizations, agencies, and departments, have invariably been confronted with powerful service opposition. For this reason, the development of central organizations of defense, in the period since World War II, at least, when the phenomenon of large and expensive standing military forces became a feature of both the modern state and the international system, is essential to an understanding of defense policy and the central organization responsible for it in any state. The debates concerning the control over defense policy today are in no small degree the legacies of past debates and of previous structural and procedural changes.

Although no general prescription or ideal model for central organizations of defense exists that could meet the needs of all states, a comparative analysis of the history, legal foundations, political context, structural arrangements, decisionmaking procedures, and behavior of those immediately concerned with defense at any one time in a number of states does help to highlight the extent to which there are similarities and differences, and the ways in which these in turn help to point to those features and approaches that have proven the most successful. Such comparisons also help to identify and anticipate potential problems, as constructive a process as finding possible solutions, and to demonstrate that the issues associated with the comparative analysis of central organizations of defense provide indicators of the nature of civil-military relations in a given state as well as of the general attitudes of the public toward defense policy issues and the armed services as institutions. Both factors are significant in the light of the size and the scope of the defense sector, the potential consequences of defense policies, and the increasing internal use of the armed services in a domestic political role.

Assuming, then, that the comparative analysis of central organizations of defense is a purposeful pursuit and lends itself to drawing some lessons from which defense planners and their political masters can benefit, the critical decision concerns which states might most fruitfully be included in the analysis. The choices largely determine themselves, insofar as any analysis that failed to include the two superpowers would be found wanting in its attempt to be relevant. China, the other major world Communist State, is a further clear choice mainly as a point of comparison and contrast with the Soviet Union. The major European states each offer a distinctive dimension: Britain, given its distinctive constitutional arrangements; the Federal Republic of Germany, given that its central defense organization was constructed from scratch with the benefit of both experience and hindsight; France, given its deliberate attempts to rationalize its central defense structure in a manner compatible with the strong executive and presidential style of government introduced under the Fifth Republic; and Italy, given its recent experiences with attempts by the military to exert its influence over government policy and, not so long ago, over the government itself. All are examples of states with relatively large indigenous arms industries and extensive alliance and external security interests.

Spain offers a particularly promising opportunity for comparative analysis given the significant constitutional changes that occurred there, following four decades of military dictatorship and its gradual emergence from a period of military isolation to one of increasing involvement in the international arena. In 1981, however, Spain witnessed an attempted military coup d'etat that highlighted the importance of effective arrangments for central control over armed forces. Almost diametrically opposed to Spain's experience has been that of Norway, whose external defense is bound to a regional military alliance (NATO) combined with an extensive militia-type defense system based on reservists and an obligatory period of military service for certain sections of the population. In short, Norway represents the typical model of a modern state with militia-based defense arrangements; the neutral states of Switzerland, Austria, Sweden, or Finland can, of course, provide similar examples.

Spain, Germany, and Japan have in common the development of new constitutions and newly structured central organizations of defense. It was partially by virtue of this commonality that the central organization of defense in Japan was included in this volume, but more especially because the Japanese Armed Forces are designed only for self-defense. It is important to examine whether and how a defense system based on a policy of self-defense alone is reflected in a central organization of defense—an analysis that offers a rare opportunity to investigate the contrast between Japan and those other states that maintain armed forces with the potential capability of projecting military power beyond their immediate boundaries. Japan also shares with Germany the experience of military defeat in World War II, Allied occupation, and a strong antimilitary sentiment among the population when the question of rearming was first raised. Under the close supervision of the United States in particular, the architects of Japan's new defense system and central defense structure had to give close attention to the question of political control and the provision of adequate checks against a resurgence of Japanese militarism. Today, large segments of the populations of both Germany and Japan continue to exhibit strong opposition to the existence of defense and security forces at the service of the state.

In one sense, all states are unique, both in time and space, and each should be examined *sui generis*. The same argument might also apply to their respective central organizations of defense. Ideally, the list of central defense organizations under analysis in this volume would have been inclusive of all states in the international system, but some criteria for selection had to be imposed, given the limitations that such a course of study would introduce. Accordingly, only those states known to have advanced economies and perceived to have some impact on the world's security arena were selected. Third World states, for all their intrinsic interest, had to be excluded, as were those states whose interests fall largely outside the main international focus of military and security interest. In the final analysis, that is, the states of Europe, North America, the Asian land mass, and the Far East were included, but such potentially interesting and instructive states as Israel, Brazil, India, Argentina, Canada, Pakistan, South Africa, and Australia were excluded.

Given the salient factors for analysis and the approach that the authors were invited to adopt in their examination of central organizations of defense, it is pertinent to ask what conclusions, generally, might be drawn from the exercise. There are several, although three stand out in particular. First, and above all, the clear impression is given that there exists in each state, irrespective of its political complexion, a clear civil and military divide with regard to defense policy formulation and the appropriate means with which to execute that policy. Because of the requirements to plan ahead, sometimes for periods well in excess of the operational life of existing military weapons and certainly over the gestation period from research to production of new weapons systems, military influence, backed invariably by the interests of the weapons manufacturers, has increased significantly relative to that of politicians. In some cases, this trend is particularly acute: Italy, for example, is a state in which political advancement is closely associated with accessibility to defense- and military-related offices. In other states, such as France, the influence of a strong executive branch and a marked tendency toward personalized systems of government and administration have tended to close the gap between civil and military personnel, but with the effect of enhancing military power and influence. With a strong commitment to an independent defense and foreign policy, military influence is likely to continue in France, especially given the relative weakness of its legislative assemblies.

In Britain, Spain, and Germany, the converse has tended to be the case, with increasing assertion of civil authority over the military. The reasons for this vary, however. Prompted by attempts at internal defense rationalization as Britain's Empire and commitments declined, and by the need for reductions in overall defense and public spending, successive British governments, regardless of their political persuasions, have worked to limit the autonomy and influence of the armed services, and to contract their separate spheres of competence to a relatively low level while strengthening control at the center. The same pattern can be seen in Spain, although for reasons that have less to do with organizational streamlining and economy than with efforts to avoid a repetition of the attempted military coup in 1981. Germany's constitutional and defense arrangements continue, as do those in Japan, to avoid any suggestion of excessive military influence over government or defense policy. Although Germany has recently been promoted to the status of major European partner in NATO, at least in the eyes of the United States, and has established and developed an advanced weapons-manufacturing industry, the provision of strong political control over defense and the armed services has continued to be emphasized, as has the concept of its *innere fuhrung*.

The Communist states are not immune from concern for military influence over defense policymaking. As demonstrated in the chapter on the Soviet Union, the period of personalized power under Stalin and Khrushchev, in which the military played an influential role, has been replaced with more rational structures in which the definitions of authority and competence between party and government institutions are clearer.

Nevertheless, as the unexpected and precipitate departure of the Soviet chief of general staff, Marshal Ogarkov, recently revealed, the influence of the military cannot be underestimated; speculation has it that he had exceeded the bounds of his authority to the disapproval of his political masters. Much the same is true of China, which also experienced a period of excessive military influence in the late 1940s and early 1950s until its central Military of Defence was established in 1954. Since then there has been a steady consolidation of party control over the military to the point where it can now be described as "stable." Given the pressures for defense modernization, however, the near future may well see the Chinese People's Liberation Army playing a more prominent role.

Literature on the military in the United States is replete with references to excessive military influence and the lack of any effective constraint, despite the checks and balances that were so carefully written into the U.S. Constitution. It was, indeed, the United States that gave the world the concept of the military-industrial complex and set the pattern that many have followed by introducing central departments of defense and decisionmaking and management systems into defense policy and procurement planning. Analysis of the Pentagon, a virtual symbol of central organizations of defense, is a daunting challenge, given its size alone, but surfacing from the morass, nonetheless, is evidence that the division of power and authority between the military and the political leaders is one that has not been resolved—nor is it likely to be resolved at any time soon under the present Reagan administration.

A second conclusion to be drawn from the present analysis is that all the states reviewed in this volume manifest a desire for improved efficiency and expanded central financial control over defense spending. The pressures of spiraling defense costs for modern weaponry, full-time professional forces, and the requirements to maintain minimum levels of preparedness have necessitated certain structural changes within central organizations of defense. Furthermore, the emphasis on administrative and planning efficiency has resulted, to a varying extent in different countries, in the introduction of combined and joint planning staffs, and a heavy emphasis on the use and application of managerial and analytical techniques. These elements, in turn, have been incorporated into new decisionmaking processes, administered and, for the most part, controlled from the center—again a trend that tends to increase the power and influence of civilian bureaucrats and politicians at the expense of the armed services.

Most indicators seem to suggest that in the balance of influence within the central organizations of defense of advanced industrial states, the armed services, despite their expertise and operational functions, are less politically significant now than before. This would suggest cause for optimism, particularly among those who feel that undue military influence in defense policymaking is both dangerous and expensive. But the overall picture is not all that encouraging, for one clear conclusion to be drawn from the chapters that follow concerns the decreasing degree of accountability of politicians and governments to legislative assemblies and the electorate. In other words, political control at the center of defense organizations has not kept pace with increased political accountability. Much of the problem arises from limited right of access to information, but in some cases it also involves a strong reluctance on the part of political leaders to feel any obligation to keep their public fully informed on issues of defense policy or its content.

As a third and final conclusion, it must be said that defense is a serious business with potentially devastating consequences. Control over defense policy and over the armed services of a state is a critical and fundamental consideration for all concerned with the wider issues of peace and war, defense spending, and democracy. In the central organizations of defense of the advanced industrial nations, control at the center is considerably greater now than it had been in the past, and political power over the military has increased significantly, except in the area of future equipment planning—the constraints of economics, technical feasibility, and political acceptability notwithstanding. Political control over the military in time of war also requires attention. Decisionmaking processes and the structures of central organizations of defense are more rational than before; each such organization is now geared toward the matching of objectives with cost-effective capabilities. The great challenge today is to make these central defense structures and those who head them more accountable to the people they serve.

Notes

1. S. E. Finer, *Man on Horseback*, 2d ed. (Harmondsworth: Peregrine Books, 1976), p. 4.

2. C. Ackroyd, J. Margolis, et al., *Technology of Political Control* (Harmondsworth: Penguin Books, 1977), p. 58.

3. M. Edmonds, "The Function of Armed Forces," in University Service Study Group, *European Military Institutions: A Reconnaissance* (Edinburgh, 1971), pp. 1–5.

4. A. Wolfers, "National Security as an Ambiguous Symbol," in A. Wolfers, ed., *Discord and Collaboration* (Baltimore: Johns Hopkins University Press, 1967), p. 163.

5. R. Kolkowicz, "Toward a Theory of Civil-Military Relations in Communist Systems," in R. Kolkowicz and A. Korbonski, eds., *Soldiers, Peasants and Bureaucrats* (London: Allen & Unwin, 1982), pp. 231–249.

6. M. Janowitz, "Military Organisation in Industrial Society," in M. Janowitz, ed., *Military Conflict* (Beverly Hills, Calif.: Sage, 1975), p. 130.

7. See P. Schmitter, "Still the Century of Corporatism?" *Review of Politics* (January 1974), pp. 85–131.

8. David Robinson, "Government Contracting for Academic Research," in B. L. Smith and D. C. Hague, eds., *Dilemma of Accountability in Modern Government* (London: Macmillan, 1972), pp. 110–113.

9. See S. Hoffmann, *The State of War* (New York: Praeger Publishers, 1965).

2
China

Gerald Segal

China's central organizations for defense are both clearly defined and confusing—clear because China is a communist state and the Chinese Communist party (CCP) is in charge; confusing because the realities of the Chinese revolution produced a political structure more complex than the model of unified, one-party rule would suggest. It follows that power in China does not flow through smooth conduits. China is not only a communist state; it is also a Third World nation and a great power and is ruled by a regime that came to power in a protracted and violent revolution. These and other factors contribute to the complexity of Chinese defense policymaking.

In order to assess how the central organizations for defense function, three overarching elements must be considered. First, as Chairman Mao Zedong noted, "political power grows out of the barrel of a gun." The revolution in China, and the establishment of CCP rule, was due primarily to the success of the People's Liberation Army (PLA). Thus the CCP recognized that the armed forces play a central role in maintaining its power, both against foreign pressures and by ensuring domestic order. Second, as Mao also noted, "the party controls the gun," and the gun must never be allowed to control the party. Therefore, despite its recognition of the centrality of PLA power, the CCP also remained vigilant in controlling the use of that power. The revolution in China was made not purely to take power, but rather to take power so as to implement social revolution.[1] Yet the definition of the CCP's ideology has frequently been the subject of internal debate, leading some to seek support from the PLA against their comrades in the party. Party-army relations are therefore crucial, but also confusing.

Third, as China is poor, populous, and largely a peasant society, the nature of the PLA and its military doctrine is naturally different from that of any communist army in the more developed world.[2] The relative absence of sophisticated technology, the reliance on massed infantry, and the military strategy of "people's war" (under modern conditions) all developed naturally from the realities of China's predicament.

The interaction of these three distinctive elements of Chinese defense politics takes place among three institutions. The CCP, as the guiding force in Chinese politics in general, also maintains its influence through political cadres in the armed forces down to the lowest level. Second, the PLA itself, as an institution, interacts with both party and state, not only in its professional military pursuits but also in its fulfillment of roles in civilian politics. Third, the state machinery of the Chinese government nominally implements CCP policy, including that for the PLA. These state functions include not only the Ministry of National Defense (MND), but also the various military industries that supply the PLA. Thus the picture is already a complex one of three-way interaction. Party-army relations are affected by party-state ties, and both in turn are influenced by PLA-state relations. What is more, the CCP, the PLA, and the state are far from unified institutions. More often than not, the three-way politics is complicated by cross-cutting cleavages as alliances are established across institutional lines.[3]

In order to untangle some of the essential lines of power and policy, it is best to begin with a brief résumé of how power was first consolidated by the CCP and PLA and of the emergence of the first state institutions. Then, following a formal analysis of contemporary central organizations for defense, three major policy questions will be studied to illustrate the complexity of institutional politics.

Party, Army, and the Chinese Revolution

Post-1949 defense policymaking has deep roots in the origins of the CCP and the PLA. Most of the basic dilemmas of the present were set in the revolutionary era. First is the problem of identifying where the PLA ends and where the CCP begins.[4] The dividing lines of civil and military power were necessarily blurred in the Chinese case because for more than twenty years before the establishment of the People's Republic of China in October 1949, those who led the PLA tended to be those in charge of the CCP.[5] Mao's initial success in taking charge of the CCP lay in his recognition that military power was crucial to revolutionary success, but the power had to be wielded in a way better suited to the relative backwardness of China and the weak CCP position.[6] Thus in the Long March to the northern caves of Yanan, and then in the drive south against Chiang Kai-shek's Guomindang, Mao ensured a primary role for the PLA. But the consequence of this close cooperation was an inevitable mix of party and army leaders. Not surprisingly, in a revolution made possible by a protracted armed struggle, it was largely impossible to identify separate party and army leaders. This mix of party and army leaders made good sense during the making of the revolution, but it became a problem in the context of consolidating it.[7]

Hand in hand with recognition of the importance of PLA power was Mao's desire strictly to control the evolution of the armed forces. Military power had to be used to further the revolution and, in particular, Mao's view of the revolution. Thus Guomindang and Soviet visions of the

CCP's future were rejected by Mao as he took charge of the CCP. For Mao, revolution was to be protracted, and made essentially by organizing the countryside to rise up in revolt against the existing social order. The urban areas were then to be seized by means of encirclement. The early phases of guerrilla war in the countryside were part of a longer-term strategy of people's war. But basic problems in managing the PLA soon emerged. For example, it was often unclear whether the revolution should be directed from the CCP central headquarters, or whether the guerrilla bands should be granted greater autonomy. The compromise solution was to ensure CCP influence down to the lowest PLA levels as the "institutional conscience" of the army.[8] Yet this parallel power structure often resulted in arguments over tactics at various levels, and most often was resolved on a case-by-case basis.

This dilemma for the CCP of central control by regional representation was often resolved through rectification campaigns. The most thorough one, in 1942–1943, was not aimed primarily at the PLA, but it obviously had an important impact on party-army relations.[9] The purpose of rectification for the PLA was to reeducate the soldiers with revolutionary values so they could grasp the ideological purpose of their struggle. Needless to say, friction was created among those PLA members who wanted to leave the "red" out of their lives and concentrate on the "expertise" of their professional duty.[10] The dilemma was not acute at this stage of the revolutionary struggle, but it would become so after 1949.

Apart from the regular emphasis in the PLA on politics over professionalism, some members of the armed forces were also not pleased with the great stress placed on ensuring close relations with "the people."[11] It was one of the strengths of the PLA that its members earned support from villagers by establishing friendly relations on a personal level. But parts of this process involved helping in the fields and carrying out nonprofessional tasks in the village. While it is true that much of this "civilian support" was in keeping with traditional Chinese military practice, it became a source of disagreement with PLA professionals when it was carried out after 1949.[12]

By 1949, the very victory of the PLA was bringing further problems. The quick collapse of the Guomindang toward the end of the civil war meant that the PLA was for a time the only effective organization in the liberated territory.[13] The extent of this period of de facto military rule varied from place to place. It was of course understandable for this transition phase to be lengthy, as the problems left by the Guomindang were immense. But the transfer to civil power was often accompanied by rapid demobilization of the PLA.[14] The sometimes hurried pace upset some PLA men, and it certainly caused dislocation in China as a whole.

The demobilization was suspended with the outbreak of the Korean War and China's entry into combat in late 1950. It is no exaggeration to say that the Korean War came as a shock to the PLA and the CCP.[15] Following its initial battlefield success, which was achieved largely by surprise, the PLA soon found it was facing a far better armed and trained enemy than it had fought in the civil war.[16] Rapid changes were brought into the PLA, essentially with the assistance of the Soviet Union.

The Soviet Union sent equipment and, above all, a "model" for the development of the PLA and of China as a whole.[17] The change essentially meant greater emphasis on professionalism, improved military hardware, training, and the establishment of ranks and a professional officer corps. The contrast to the revolutionary experience was huge, and it set the scene for major policy debates. Greater professionalism meant less emphasis on the intervention of party authorities, and it enhanced the role of the new state authorities through the Ministry of National Defense.

The MND was only formalized in the 1954 state constitution as part of a general move away from the ad hoc relationships in the revolutionary era. Thus a new tier of control in defense policy was established. As the state assumed new powers, including the various ministries of military machine building, the making of defense policy became a three-ring rather than a two-ring circus. But as if matters were not already complex enough, new problems set in after 1956. The Soviet model was seen by some in China to be inappropriate, and the trend toward professionalism in all spheres, including the PLA, was challenged.[18] As China grappled with the problems of routinizing the revolution, defense policy became one of many spheres in which debate and change took place. The twists and turns of this process are too numerous to describe here, but by 1982 there did emerge a new pattern that held out some hope for greater stability. What are the contemporary institutions in defense policymaking, and how do they deal with pressing questions of policy?

Formal Institutions

In principle, a chart of Chinese central organizations for defense should be so clear as to need no elaboration. Unfortunately, Figure 2.1 provides only vague outlines of how and where power flows. It is inevitably simplistic and certainly requires elaboration, only some of which can be provided here.[19] But, first, some caveats are in order. It is almost axiomatic that in the study of closed societies, the absence of reliable information makes the analyst's task difficult. Indeed, even in comparison to the Soviet military, the Chinese case is poorly understood. This is true in part because of the peculiarities of Chinese politics, a notable one being that numerous leaders hold more than one office at a time. Hence the bureaucratic axiom of "where you stand (on policy) depends on where you sit" becomes hopelessly simplistic.[20] Furthermore, in the Chinese case the role of personal ties among officials seems to be far more important than institutional alliances.[21] To understand the

Figure 2.1   People's Republic of China Central Organization of Defense

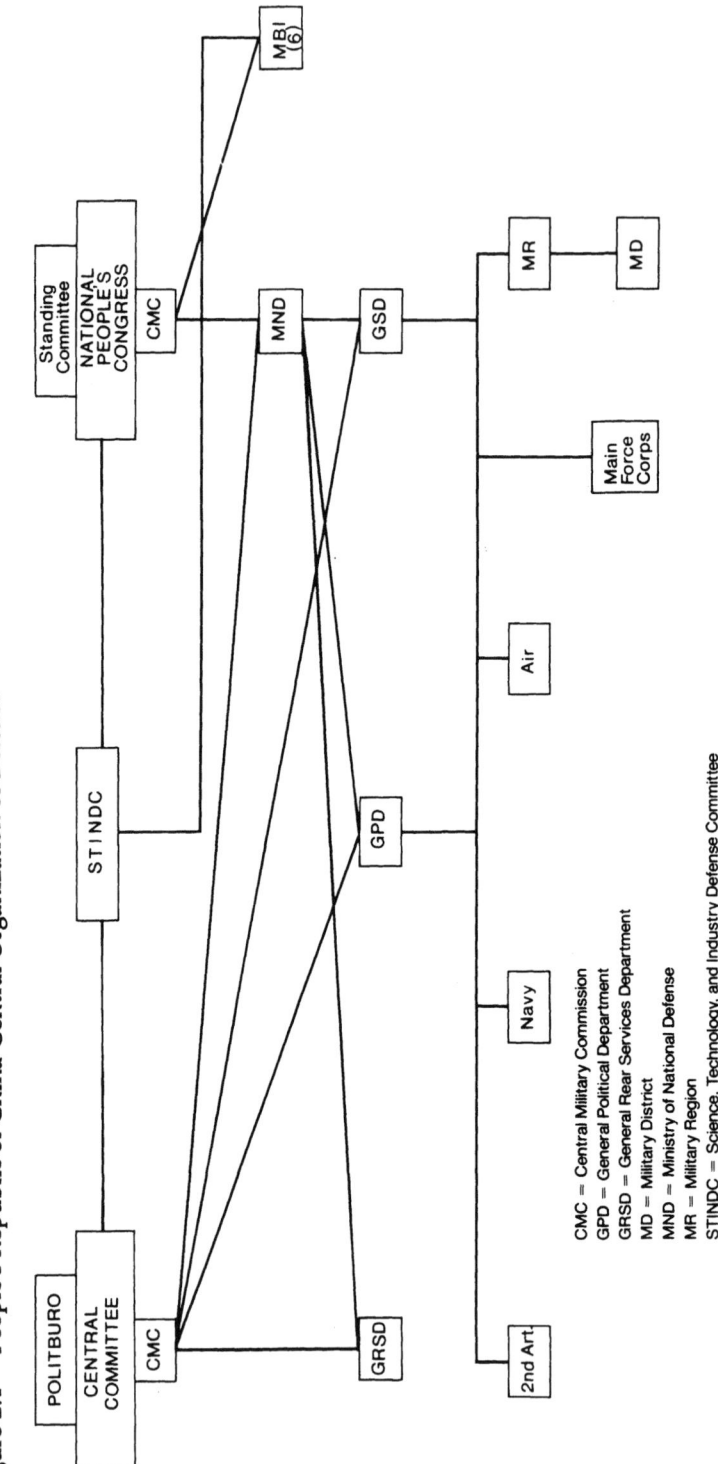

CMC = Central Military Commission
GPD = General Political Department
GRSD = General Rear Services Department
MD = Military District
MND = Ministry of National Defense
MR = Military Region
STINDC = Science, Technology, and Industry Defense Committee

Chinese case requires a good grasp of the factional politics and personal ties that have developed over decades. Nevertheless, there is some point in analyzing the institutions of Chinese defense policy. In brief, the following primary institutions and major relationships can be identified.

The Politburo and the State Council

There can be no doubt that of the two parallel authorities, party and state, the former is dominant in almost every important way. That is not to say that the State Council is unimportant or that the premier is powerless, but rather that the Politburo and the secretary general of the CCP are more important. The 1982 state constitution is perfectly clear about the "leading role" of the CCP in guiding government work.[22] While the party sets policy guidelines, the state implements them. While the party supervises implementation, the state enacts corrections if they are needed.

To be sure, such a simple division of tasks is less straightforward in practice. The fact that state officials tend to hold important party positions means that the lines are always fuzzy. For example, the first that Premier Zhao Ziyang would hear about the restoration of ranks in the PLA would probably be in the Politburo, although the issue might also be considered in the State Council. In any case, the PLA is not given special treatment in this regard, for the CCP's "leading role" affects all aspects of the government of China.

The Central Military Commission

Obviously the Politburo cannot deal with all aspects of the PLA, and for that reason a special body in charge of defense issues exists—the party Central Military Commission (CMC), also known in some Western analyses as the Military Affairs Committee.[23] There has been little doubt among observers of China that the CMC is the real locus of control over the PLA. In 1982 the state set up a parallel central military commission, and at first there was some confusion as to whether real power was being transferred to the state. The 1982 Constitution specified that "the CMC of the PRC directs the armed forces of the country." However, it soon became apparent that not only were the two CMCs composed of the same members, but also that, in keeping with the "leading role" of the PLA, Chinese officials openly gave primacy to the party CMC. "Since its founding, the PLA has always been under the leadership of the CCP, and the leadership of the CCP over the army has not changed even since the establishment of the Central Military Commission of the state." It was noted that the two CMCs had parallel membership, and "therefore there is absolutely no difference between the state's leadership over the army and the Party's leadership over the army."[24] In essence, as the party guided the state, so it guided the army.

The importance of the CMC is clearly shown by the type of people who have served as its chairman. Mao held that post from 1935–1976 and was replaced by Hua Guofeng, who also took over as party chairman upon Mao's death. When Hua was ousted in the early 1980s and the post of party chairman was abolished, Deng Xiaoping took for himself the key CMC chairmanship (1981) and installed Hu Yaobang as party secretary general. The broader membership of the CMC has not always been clear. The heads of the main departments and/or military elders have held the second-tier post of vice-chairmen of the CMC and formed the powerful standing committee of the CMC. Although some regional commanders and service chiefs make up the final tier of the CMC, power resides overwhelmingly with the inner circle.[25]

The CMC's writ runs far and wide, bypassing the Ministry of National Defense if it chooses and reaching down to the services and districts directly. The CMC has a large, independent staff, which undertakes investigations of its own and passes commands through its own channels. It is relatively safe to say that whoever controls the CMC controls the PLA—namely, the same person (or group) who leads the CCP.

Ministry of National Defense

The Ministry of National Defense (MND) is ostensibly a state body, although it clearly takes direct orders from the CMC. Its responsibilities, in any case, fall primarily in the realm of administration.[26] In fact China's Ministry of Defense is probably one of the world's least important such ministries, especially considering the size of the armed forces concerned. Its MND has no command function, and for many years the ministry itself was superseded by some of the nominally lower institutions such as the General Staff Department.

The minister of national defense is, of course, an important figure, but more because of his seniority as first vice-chairman of the CMC than by virtue of his MND post. The contrast to the Soviet case is instructive. There have been only six Chinese ministers of defense since 1949, and until 1971 there had been only two. All have been military professionals with the exception of the fifth, Geng Biao, who held the post for the shortest period and apparently upset the professional lobby. But, overall, those ministers who have fallen from grace did so because of their role in wider politics and not by reason of their PLA connections.

The General Political Department

Of the three departments nominally under the MND, the General Political Department (GPD) is least involved in professional matters. Its task is threefold: to supervise the ideology of the PLA, to ensure discipline, and to maintain morale.[27] Ideological tasks are primarily concerned with establishing the CCP's leading role, and thus it is not surprising that the CMC directs the GPD work. The ideological role is visible at the top in the army's paper, *The Liberation Army Daily*, and all the way down to the company level, where a parallel pyramid of political commissars supervises the CCP line.

The true extent of this nonprofessional power in the PLA has, of course, changed from time to time as the general CCP line has shifted. Clearer still is the fact that this parallel chain of command has played a crucial role in sorting out the extent of party politics and professionalism in the PLA. This role has not always been a pleasant one. Professional officers tend to resent interference in their work, and yet the GPD does become involved in the promotion of these officers.[28] As the major security organ, the GPD can obviously have a damaging impact on an aspiring officer if he crosses the political powers that be.

But by and large, the GPD has done an efficient job. It has maintained very high morale, especially considering the poor level of equipment available to the PLA. The PLA has also proved itself to be highly reliable, even when called upon to take part in civilian politics. To the extent that the political role of the PLA has changed, it has been due to factional politics within the CCP leadership. The PLA has largely been a faithful executor of policy. While at present there are signs of PLA opposition to aspects of CCP policy, they tend to come from individuals in the PLA leadership who also hold top party posts.[29] Their complaints have more to do with sitting in a civil seat than in a military one.

The General Staff Department

The General Staff Department (GSD) is the chief executive and main administrative body of the PLA. Its orders nominally come from the MND but, in effect, are guided by the CMC, to which it reports. Its main task is to translate CMC policy into action for the services below it. Its pyramid of power extends down, further than that of the GPD, to the lowest levels. Thus it obviously carries the heaviest responsibility, especially now that the PLA concentrates more on professional matters.[30] What is more, the GSD can generate some of its own commands, albeit only those of lesser importance and concerned exclusively with professional matters.

Considering the importance of the GSD, it is not hard to understand that its leader, the chief of staff, holds a dangerous position. On the top of the professional pyramid, and feeling the cutting edge of CMC policy, he is always vulnerable to being toppled as the higher-level policy shifts. There have been nine chiefs of staff in the past thirty-five years, with the present holder, Yang Dezhi, in the post since 1980. Many of his predecessors have been removed as part of a general political shakeup. For the time being, Yang's position seems relatively—if unusually—stable.

The General Rear Services Department

The General Rear Services Department (GRSD), like its Soviet counterpart, after which it was modeled, is responsible for ordering and distributing the logistics requirements of the PLA. Although it has a pyramid of power parallel to the GSD, its officers are under the direct command of the military professionals at various levels. The GRSD, clearly the least influential of the three main departments, is primarily a service department for the other two.

This is not to suggest that the GRSD has a simple task. Its role involves liaison with the State Council and the various machine-building ministries in order to obtain PLA equipment.[31] This connection inevitably ties it into the requirements of changing domestic politics, but the GRSD seems to lack the political clout possessed by its Soviet counterpart. In fact, most of the GRSD work is decentralized and thus reliant on local production reminiscent of the revolutionary days of PLA self-sufficiency. Obviously it engages in less sideline production now than it did in 1949, but some clearly does take place above and beyond what one would generally expect from most established armed forces.

The Services

The picture of the PLA below department level can become quite complex. There are essentially ten service arms: the navy, the air force, the artillery and the armored, signal, engineer, antichemical warfare, and railway force headquarter units (units that essentially support the infantry).[32] The two remaining services are the second artillery (nuclear weapons) and the public security forces. The services are all directly responsible to the CMC, but most orders come down from the GSD. The engineers, railway, and part of signals seem to be run through the GRSD.

It is notable that no specific infantry service exists. Given the PLA's heavy bias toward the infantry, such a service would be unwieldy. Therefore, command is more diversified than it would be otherwise, and sometimes rather confused as well.[33] Most soldiers are contained in the thirty-seven main force infantry corps. They are subject to commands from Beijing, but the military regions (MR) and military districts (MD) play a major role in administration. Obviously the potential for changes in the locus of power, from the center to the eleven regional commands, is great. The balance has indeed shifted several times, with regional commanders sometimes playing major roles affecting Beijing politics. However, these commanders actually control few troops, and most of their power seems to be derived from their extensive local influence built up over time. Therefore, in recent years, after central control had been reestablished, the main weapon used regularly by Beijing was to shift the regional commanders to different regions.[34] But so long as the PLA remains essentially an infantry force, the potential for regionalism will continue to be a threat to central authority.

The three other important services are less complex. Both the air force and the navy are highly centralized and constitute the elite of the PLA. The air force is now organized into eleven air districts, which match the eleven military regions, but it retains a high degree of independence of command. The navy has only three fleets and is even more independent of the main forces and regional controls.[35] The Second Artillery (2nd Art) is the most special case. As the most centralized service, it is also dominated by public security and scientific personnel.[36] In fact, little is known about the operation of the Second Artillery, but it does appear to be a useful tool in the hands of central authorities for bypassing professional military interests.

Military Industry

The PLA, like other armed forces, requires weapons and thus has some sort of military industry. But to call the Chinese industry a military industrial complex would be an extreme exaggeration.[37] In its present configuration, there are six ministries of machine building supplying the PLA. Basic decisions concerning the required weapons are taken in the CMC in conjunction with the State Planning Commission and, presumably, the state CMC. Following the several changes that have occurred, there also seems to be a state commission in charge of Science, Technology, and Industry for National Defense, which coordinates resources for the machine-building industries.

Much of this decisionmaking process is shrouded in secrecy and, in any case, has undergone so many changes in recent years that it is difficult to establish many clear patterns. Much clearer is the fact that the policy arguments must be complex at the point where state, party, and army come together. It is also clear that, in recent years, PLA professionals have given up control of the machine-building industries.[38] As stability returned to the domestic political scene, the PLA became more confident that its needs would be met. This was certainly not the case during and immediately after the Cultural Revolution. But by 1984 the PLA no longer had a direct hand in the state realm of industry, even military industry, and thus exists in stark contrast to its colleagues in the Soviet Red Army. The reasons for these changes, and indeed much of the preceding institutional framework, can best be understood by turning to an analysis of key issues in PLA politics.

Institutions in Action

Institutions as represented on charts can be very different from institutions in action. There is nothing like the pressure of high policy questions to bring out the primary features of how the institutions really operate. In the Chinese case, any number of issues could have been analyzed, but three topics stand out as being of greatest importance.

Professionalism: Between Red and Expert

To the extent that the PLA can be seen as a group with identifiable interests, it is most concerned with two issues: the extent of professionalism and the size of its budget. How are these concerns dealt with in the hierarchy of central organizations for defense? The answer is not a simple one.

Various phases have occurred in which the pursuit of professionalism in the PLA has risen and fallen. But the process has not been one dominated by a party-army struggle. It is notable that all the changes have mirrored changes in Chinese politics as a whole, and have not merely been the result of civil-military dispute.[39] In the 1950s, the rejection of the Soviet model in favor of more Sinified politics led to the Great Leap Forward. In the PLA, professionalism was minimized in favor of a more ideological and less technology-dependent path. But this shift was taking place all across China at the same time and did not represent a special problem confined only to the military.

In the 1960s, the PLA carried on a mixture of red and expert that was eventually to find favor with Mao. The Great Helmsman seized upon the PLA as an institution to be "learned from," and then he used it to help purge the CCP of "revisionists" in the Cultural Revolution.[40] Professionalism in the PLA obviously suffered at this time. But the PLA was not locked in a party-army dispute on this matter. Rather, the PLA was being called upon by one element of the CCP to intervene against other civilian party leaders. Professionalism began to return to the PLA in the 1970s when the general political balance tilted away from the radicals. But the 1970s were also years of radical-moderate conflict, and the PLA was pulled in different directions as the variable winds blew from the Politburo.[41] With the purge of the radical Gang of Four after 1976, professionalism once again was the vogue in China, and naturally the PLA was pleased to follow suit.[42]

To suggest that professionalism was largely not an issue in dispute between party and army is not to say that the issue was unimportant. Far from it: The issue was, indeed, important for the nation as a whole. China struggled to define the proper balance between red and expert in the postrevolutionary generation, and the PLA was only one of several spheres in which these struggles were played out. The complexity of the debates is clear, with divisions along institutional lines but also by generation and personal faction.

The main battleground for these debates was not so much the CMC, where one might expect to find it if the split were simply that between party and army. In fact, the arguments seemed to take place higher up in the party, and preeminently in the Politburo. The CMC would naturally mirror the Politburo shifts but did not seem to stake out an independent path.[43] Political careers were made and broken in these times, but once again fates seemed related more to broader political issues than to party-army disputes over professionalism.

Defense Minister Peng Dehuai was ousted in 1959, along with a few top colleagues, but his purge was related more to his opposition to Mao on economic policy than to the issue of professionalism. It is notable that the PLA was not subject to a wholesale purge, as one might have expected if the issue of professionalism was either so crucial or confined to the military.[44] In 1965, Chief of Staff Luo Ruiqing was toppled by one of the opening shots in the Cultural Revolution, but less for reasons of professionalism than because of his strategic debate with Mao and other military men.[45] In 1976, Zhang Chunqiao was removed as head of the GPD, but because he was a member of the Gang of Four and not because of his policies within the PLA. In 1982, Defense Minister Geng Biao was shoved aside (but not purged) for a number of reasons, but a dispute over professionalism seems to have played only a minor role. As the first "civilian" defense minister he was not "trusted" by the PLA, but in general the issue of professionalism was not under challenge at the time. Deng Xiaoping and PLA professionals share a belief in greater professional expertise.

If the red and expert issue transcends normal party-army relations, can the same be said about the issue of the PLA budget? It does seem that, although the PLA remains concerned about its level of funding, the issue has not been one of major debate with the party. Military spending has been remarkably constant in China, thus suggesting some sort of fundamental consensus agreeable to a wide variety of leaders.[46] The choice on allocations seems to be made at the Politburo level, in conjunction with wider economic discussions with the state apparatus. The military budget is divided into its constituent parts at the lower CMC level, where demands from the services and regions are undoubtedly well aired.

The specific division of funds does not seem to be related to any shifts in factional politics. Although China's economic pie does seem to be growing, the PLA is getting less than its share of the growth.[47] Once again, there is little evidence of deep dissatisfaction. The reasons for this, and, indeed, for the previous quiescence, seem quite complex. Not only is the PLA made up of different services with varying needs for equipment, but in the end the PLA remains a labor-intensive army. Accordingly, expenditures on technology either have to be massive if the millions are to be armed in a comprehensive way, or else they must be gradual, allowing for long-term planning and spreading of costs. The latter path seems to have been consistently pursued in China, given its refusal to buy military equipment off the western shelf as only the latest evidence that China tends not to believe in quick fixes. Furthermore, in recent times, the PLA has compensated for the limited funds by means of other savings and ingenious schemes.

The steady improvement in PLA fighting power, despite financial limits, seems to be due to several factors:[48] (1) Greater efficiency has been found in organizational reform; (2) improved doctrine has increased combat effectiveness; (3) limited investment in new, inexpensive, defensive technology has filled some of the more glaring gaps; and (4) a new military export drive has earned hard cash and models of the latest Soviet equipment to be copied back in China.[49] These improvements have obviously involved a number of institutions, from the foreign ministry (arms sales) to the GSD and the military regions (greater professionalism and better logistics). They mirror changes under way in China as a whole, and signify no new party-army relationship. The causes of this new policy are to be found in the changing balance of power in the Politburo, for, as with most policy issues in China, the top of the CCP is the main locus of authority.

Civilian Politics

The twin issues of professionalism and budget are primarily those in which the civil authority shapes the military. But what about the shaping of the civil authority by the military, especially by means of intervention in civil politics? China seems to have had a military in politics, but not a military in charge of politics. The reasons behind their initial involvement in politics, their restraint while in control of important political positions, and their willingness to withdraw to the barracks say a great deal about the PLA leaders.

The PLA willingly surrendered power in the early 1950s as the CCP established stability and consolidated the revolution. From then until the mid-1960s, the PLA stayed out of civilian politics, accepting the dictum that the "party controls the gun." But in the Cultural Revolution the PLA was taken out of the barracks by Mao and cast into the fray, first in support of radical groups and soon after to restore order and smash the same radicals.[50] These were obviously special times in China, when the army was used by part of the party to destroy its enemies. The PLA did not grasp power; rather, power gravitated to it.

The decision to involve the soldiers in running China was not taken at the Politburo level, primarily because it was precisely in the Politburo that Mao found his most entrenched opponents. Here the CMC and various ad hoc Cultural Revolution groups came into play. The Cultural Revolution was preeminently an anti-institutional struggle, intended to destroy "revisionists" in the party. The result was an absence of regular institutional lines of control. Not only was the party torn apart, but the PLA itself had different factions, with some regional commanders flexing their new muscles and ignoring central commands.

As one of the few institutions to emerge relatively intact from the upheaval, the PLA held a dominant position in the provinces and at the center by 1969. But it was not a position of control that most military men desired to retain. To be sure, Defense Minister Lin Biao was apparently involved in some sort of attempt to retain power, but he was defeated in murky circumstances by Mao's coalition, which included many powerful regional PLA commanders and some PLA figures from the center.[51] Following the Lin Biao affair, the PLA was pleased to shuffle back to the barracks. But the steps back were halting and in the end only partial, because the stability that the PLA had initially intended to bring to civil politics was not emerging. In the early 1970s, the squabbles between radicals and moderates were ended only by the purge of the Gang of Four after Mao's death. Only then, when moderates proved that order was returning, did the PLA properly return to professional pursuits.

This exit from civilian politics was largely welcomed by the PLA as the natural thing to do. Soldiers had remained in various regional and central offices for close to a decade, and, to a certain extent, politics also entered the military, just as the military had entered politics. There was no going back to the pre–Cultural Revolution days. Not only had many PLA men acquired new expertise in civilian politics, but the already blurred lines resulting from one man holding more than one position ensured that civil-military lines in general would remain unclear.

The surrendering of power was most complete in the regions where, after a series of shifts of commanders, entrenched power was undermined and civilians could be put back in charge. At the center, the process has been less complete, with the military forming an important segment of the CCP Central Committee and, above all, the Politburo. To be sure, the PLA's power, even at the center, has been much reduced and is likely to be cut back even further.[52] But there are several reasons for continuing PLA involvement in civilian politics. First, politics has in fact entered the PLA to a certain extent, and many top leaders have become used to the notion of intervention in high policy. Second, the legacy of the past fifteen years has left an even greater overlap in office-holding, making any identification and clear-out of military men more difficult. Third, stability has by no means been fully assured in China, and to the extent that guaranteeing stability was a prime motive for PLA involvement, it remains at least partially relevant.

Thus contemporary Chinese politics continues to see an important role for PLA figures. This is not because of some basic party-army split, or because the PLA does not trust the CCP to govern. Rather, it seems to be due to a legacy of past intervention and to the serious blurring of institutional lines. But because this involvement is not the result of party-army disputes, but instead is one internal to the top CCP leadership, the combat is likely to take place in the Politburo rather than in the CMC. In any case, disagreements are likely to continue.

Foreign Policy

The extent to which any armed force is involved in making foreign policy is notoriously difficult to assess.[53] For example, in the case of the Soviet Union it is now generally accepted that the Red Army "participates" in the process.[54] It has been delegated certain areas of expertise, controls others by virtue of its monopoly of information, and advises as one of several voices on matters of high policy. In the Chinese case, the PLA has no such wide role.

Foreign policy seems to be made primarily in the Politburo, with implementation left largely to the Foreign Ministry. The extent of PLA infuence varies from minor to nil. Even in matters involving the use of force by the PLA to support Chinese policy, the military's input appears to be minimal.[55] Unlike the Soviet case, in which the armed forces play a central role, all foreign conflict in China has been seen primarily as a political problem, such that the military is considered an instrument to be used.

The reasons for this state of affairs are numerous, if not always clear. Not only does the PLA have no single institutional preference, but it also has no pressing need to protect interests in the realm of foreign policy. With the exception of the "Soviet threat," China's international standing is not really related to its military power. In the Soviet case, the relationship is largely the reverse.

Yet the PLA undoubtedly has some effect on foreign policymaking. For example, in considering Sino-Soviet relations, one of the major concerns for China has been the extent of the threat posed by Moscow.[56] An assessment (such as the one seemingly made in 1982) that the Soviet Union is less threatening now than before hinges in large part on how the power of the PLA is viewed by the Chinese leadership. Any decision on whether and how to bolster the PLA would naturally involve the military, at least indirectly, in any given foreign policy question.[57]

Second, to the extent that Chinese foreign policy is generally dependent on a sense of effective military deterrence, the readiness of the PLA is of major importance. If the civilian leadership should decide that deterrence can be achieved at least in part by the cheaper route of nuclear weapons, then this will have an impact on PLA politics. Similarly, if a decision is taken that "people's war," if adapted to "modern conditions," will suffice to defend China, then there will be no need for massive spending on conventional arms. Either decision or both would naturally provoke a response from various elements in the PLA. While the initial decision would probably be taken in the Politburo, the problems of implementation would most likely surface in the CMC.

Third, although China's arms sales program is far from the superpower scale, it has assumed greater importance since 1980.[58] The transfers are apparently directed by the GRSD, with the equipment being produced under the guidance of the military machine-building industries and the State Planning Commission.[59] The profits are probably shared between the PLA and the state, thereby funding overall modernization but also military modernization in particular.

Fourth, military men are represented abroad in Chinese embassies and aid missions. Their assessments of the military and strategic dimensions of policy no doubt have some impact.[60] In the Soviet case, the military view is inevitably more hostile to opponents. Evidence on the Chinese case is scarce, but it seems that the PLA has a less distinct view. If the involvment of the Chinese military should become more extensive in the future, its views may become more distinct. With greater professionalism, a wider role, say, in arms sales, and more effective military reach, the PLA may come to control more information vital to foreign policymaking. Under such circumstances the PLA may assume a role more comparable to that of their Soviet colleagues. But for the meantime, at most they provide a different emphasis rather than a different policy.

Conclusions

Peering through the dim light, we find that Chinese central organizations for defense appear Janus-like—on the one hand, simple and straightforward; on the other, complex and changing.[61] On balance, four main themes have emerged from the analysis just concluded. First, the dominant organization in China, as indeed in any communist state, is the Communist party. Although it exists parallel to an equally extensive state structure, the CCP is dominant in every sphere. In military policy, it dominates both at the top and at the lower levels of authority. The preeminence of the main institutions for decisionmaking on military policy, the Politburo and the Central Military Commission, has remained virtually unchanged. What *has* changed are the policies adopted by both bodies, but their ability to make policy has not been weakened.

Yet a knowledge of where the decisions are taken tells one very little about how or why they are taken. Thus the essential complexity of the Chinese case proceeds from the peculiar way in which institutions are manipulated in China. It appears that the mere existence of an institution counts for less in China than in most states. Considering that these are the people who invented bureaucracy, the Chinese seem peculiarly willing to ignore or bypass the regular channels. Indeed, the primary factors involved in assessing how the institutions work are personal relations and policy disagreements. The reasons for the importance of these aspects is a mixture of the revolutionary legacy by which one person sits on more than one institutional seat, the inheritance of a political culture primarily concerned with personal relationships, and an economic and geographic reality that minimizes expertise and specialization.

Third, this complexity of intra-institutional politics encourages a breakdown of inter-institutional barriers. In the language of the political scientist, the cleavages are cross-cutting. Therefore, it seems relatively easy to build coalitions that cut across institutional lines yet will not necessarily hold as the issues change. Those who are bound by the notion that a political stand will be taken on the basis of "where you stand depends on where you sit" will miss the far more complex reality of Chinese politics.

Fourth, there are signs of change, perhaps in the direction of greater importance for institutional structures. As professionalism becomes more entrenched in the PLA and in society as a whole, there may well develop a greater reliance on group views and concern for the needs of an institution. As the new generation of leaders emerges, less accustomed to multiple office-holding, organizational lines will become less blurred. If this is indeed the vision of the Chinese future, then China shows signs of evolving more closely to the present Soviet case. But China will always be different, even if it shares common characteristics of communist organization and the needs of professional soldiers. As a poor, Third World power based on a Chinese political culture, the mother of bureaucracy will always have unusual children.

Notes

1. Alexander Atkinson, *Social Order and the General Theory of Strategy* (London: Routledge & Kegan Paul, 1981).

2. Dale Herspring and Ivan Volgyes (eds.), *Civil-Military Relations in Communist Systems* (Boulder, Colo.: Westview Press, 1978).

3. Gerald Segal, "The Military as a Group in Chinese Politics," in David Goodman (ed.), *Groups and Politics in the PRC* (Cardiff: Cardiff University Press, 1984).

4. Harlan Jencks, *From Muskets to Missiles: Politics and Professionalism in the Chinese Army, 1945-1981* (Boulder, Colo.: Westview Press, 1982).

5. William Whitson, *The Chinese High Command* (New York: Praeger Publishers, 1973); John Gittings, *The Role of the Chinese Army* (London: Oxford University Press, 1967).

6. Stuart Schram, *Mao Tse-tung* (London: Penguin, 1967).

7. Jencks, *From Muskets to Missiles.*

8. Gittings, *Role of the Chinese Army.*

9. Mark Selden, *The Yenan Way in Revolutionary China* (Cambridge: Harvard University Press, 1971).

10. Jencks, *From Muskets to Missiles.*

11. Ibid.

12. Gerald Segal, *Defending China* (London: Oxford University Press, 1984), ch.3.

13. Gittings, *Role of the Chinese Army.*

14. Whitson, *Chinese High Command.*

15. Ibid; Gittings, *Role of the Chinese Army.*

16. Segal, *Defending China,* ch.6.

17. Ellis Joffe, *Party and Army* (Cambridge, Mass.: Harvard University Press, 1971); Franz Schurmann, *Ideology and Organization in Communist China* (Berkeley: University of California Press, 1968).

18. Ibid; Roderick MacFarquhar, *The Origins of the Cultural Revolution,* vol. 1 (London: Oxford University Press, 1974).

19. Based on Jencks, *From Muskets to Missiles,* pp. 136-137; see also Harvey W. Nelsen, *The Chinese Military System: An Organizational Study of the Chinese People's Liberation Army* (Boulder, Colo.: Westview Press, 1981).

20. Harry Harding, *Organizing China* (Stanford, Calif.: Stanford University Press, 1981).

21. Lucian Pye, *The Dynamics of Chinese Politics* (Cambridge, Mass.: Oelschlager, Gunn and Hain, 1981).

22. State constitution, in *Beijing Review,* no. 52 (December 27, 1982).

23. Jencks, *From Muskets to Missiles;* Nelsen, *Chinese Military System.*

24. Peking, Zhonggou Qingnian Bao, July 23, 1983, in *BBC: Summary of World Broadcasts,* FE/7398/BII/1-2.

25. Jencks, *From Muskets to Missiles.*

26. Nelsen, *Chinese Military System.*

27. Gittings, *Role of the Chinese Army.*

28. Jencks, *From Muskets to Missiles.*

29. Ellis Joffe, "Party and Army," in Gerald Segal and William Tow (eds.), *Chinese Defence Policy* (London: Macmillan, 1984).

30. Jencks, *From Muskets to Missiles.*

31. David Shambaugh, "China's Defense Industries," in Paul Godwin (ed.), *The Chinese Defense Establishment* (Boulder, Colo.: Westview Press, 1983).

32. Nelsen, *Chinese Military System.*

33. Jencks, *From Muskets to Missiles.*

34. Ellis Joffe and Gerald Segal, "The Chinese Army and Professionalism," *Problems of Communism* (November-December 1978).

35. Bruce Swanson, *Eighth Voyage of the Dragon* (Annapolis, Md.: Naval Institute Press, 1982).

36. Gerald Segal, "The Nuclear Forces," in Segal and Tow, *Chinese Defence Policy.*

37. Sydney Jammes, "Military Industry," in ibid; Shambaugh, "China's Defense Industries."

38. Jammes, ibid.

39. Segal, "The Military as a Group."

40. Ellis Joffe, "The Chinese Army Under Lin Piao," in John Lindbeck (ed.), *China: Management of a Revolutionary Society* (Seattle: University of Washington Press, 1971); *Current Scene,* no. 18 (December 7, 1970); John Gittings, "Army-Party Relations in the Light of the Cultural Revolution," in John Lewis (ed.), *Party Leadership and Revolutionary Power in China* (Cambridge: Cambridge University Press, 1970).

41. Ellis Joffe, "The Chinese Army After the Cultural Revolution," *China Quarterly* (July-September 1973).

42. Joffe and Segal, "Chinese Army."

43. Jencks, *From Muskets to Missiles.*

44. Segal, "The Military as a Group."

45. Harry Harding and Melvin Gurtov, *The Purge of Lo Jui-ch'ing* (Santa Monica, Calif.: Rand, R-548-PR, 1971).

46. United States, Central Intelligence Agency, National Foreign Assessment Center, *Chinese Defense Spending, 1965–79* (July 1980).

47. Ellis Joffe, "Party and Military in China," *Problems of Communism* (September-October 1983).

48. Gerald Segal and William Tow, "Introduction," in Segal and Tow (eds.), *Chinese Defence Policy.*

49. Yitzhak Shichor, "The Middle East," in ibid.

50. See Note 40.

51. Joffe, "Chinese Army Under Lin Piao."

52. William deB. Mills, "Generational Change in China," *Problems of Communism* (November-December 1983).

53. Gerald Segal, "The PLA and Chinese Foreign Policy Decision Making," *International Affairs* 57, no. 3 (Summer 1981).

54. Timothy Colton, *Commissars, Commanders and Civilian Authority* (Cambridge: Harvard University Press, 1979).

55. Segal, *Defending China.*

56. Gerald Segal, "The Soviet 'Threat' at China's Gates," *Conflict Studies,* no. 143 (1983).

57. Gerald Segal, "Sino-Soviet Relations After Mao," *Adelphi Paper* (forthcoming).

58. Shichor, "Middle East."

59. Nelsen, *Chinese Military System.*

60. Segal, "The PLA."

61. Paul Godwin, "Towards a New Strategy?" in Segal and Tow (eds.), *Chinese Defence Policy;* see also Godwin, *Chinese Defense Establishment,* generally.

3
The Central Organization of Defense in France

Jean-Pierre Marichy

Study of the relationship between politics and the military at the center is essential from the point of view of scientific methodology and political analysis. From a scientific perspective, the study of decisionmaking is an important area of modern political science; the classical constitutional approach regarded decisionmaking merely as an exercise in rationality, legitimized by the adherence of the proper authority to legal procedures and by the compatibility of the decision with established norms. Political science now emphasizes the complexity of decisionmaking by drawing attention to the intricacies of causes, of preparation and conception, of formulation and development, and of implementation and outcome. Instead of focusing on one decisionmaking point, it is necessary to refer to a continuous process with varying, ill-defined boundaries. "A decision does not rest with one man or a team, at a precise moment in time in a specific place."[1] A decision is the outcome of a fluid, cybernetic system. In the defense area it is especially important to understand these processes.

Defense is a fundamental issue confronting society: The survival of society and the protection of its core values compete with personal aspirations—all perfectly legitimate—for life, happiness, and peace within that tragic dialectic between the interest of the individual and that of the group—between being and having. This competition leads to difficulties in generating a commitment to defense as a public good in today's hedonistic and affluent societies. These difficulties should not be underestimated, especially when we are faced with the threat of nuclear apocalypse.

Defense planning still requires intuition, art, experience, and above all, determination and resolve. Today, it also relies on the prudent use of the applied sciences, which combine more or less sophisticated mathematical approaches (factor analysis, linear programming, game theory, graph theory, catastrophe theory, and so on) with the extensive power of data processing. The sand tray has been replaced with the computer, completely altering the subtle art of the headquarters' "Kriegspiel."

Although the classical distinctions regarding the implementation of policy seem to be maintained—political, financial, military, administrative, strategic, tactical, logistic—the sheer complexity of the defense system causes overlap and complications. It is also difficult to distinguish between authoritarian and democratic styles; most defense decisions are the result of compromise and negotiation, and personal authority, even in the privileged area of military command, often defers to the consultative process. Finally, the preparation, issue, and execution of a decision constitute a series of cybernetic processes from which it is difficult to isolate and identify both the level of authority of the agencies concerned and the point where the civil and military, political and administrative, and technical and financial interact.

The analysis of defense processes can therefore offer a significant case study of decisionmaking theory; to a greater extent, the study of the central organization of defense affords an excellent insight into the nature of the political system as a whole. Given the geostrategic nature of the contemporary world, the political authorities are linked more closely than ever to the military at the highest level. The challenge is to determine whether or not the relationship between the military and the political authorities reflects the political system in the sense that it represents an essential element in the exercise of power, or if, on the contrary, the specific nature of defense preparation necessitates particular structural arrangements that are unrepresentative of the political system as a whole.

This question is not an easy one to answer. Indeed, the central organization of defense is at the interface of two systems that, though different, are nonetheless integrated. The political system encompasses the military, which is judicially subordinated to it. However, the functional, corporate, and ethical specificity of the military system is such that it cannot reproduce exactly the characteristics of the political system to which it belongs. The relationship between the two systems will therefore be affected by both the tendency toward convergence with respect to the dominant characteristics of the political system and the tendency toward divergence with respect to certain traits of the military system.[2] Convergence can result not only from the "civilianization" of the military system, but also from the reverse process—if not by the militarization of society, stricto sensu, then at least by the establishment of a more concentrated and efficient authority structure.

We can approach the problem of the central organization of defense in France from this perspective insofar as the present institutions, set up in 1958 by General de Gaulle, reflect both the French liberal-democratic tradition and a preoccupation with the need to strengthen the political regime following the progressive weakness of the Fourth Republic. Other features of the French system help to demonstrate the relevance of this approach. First, France's geostrategic position as a medium-sized European power with a nuclear capability as well as a resolute policy of national independence, despite its attachment to the Atlantic Alliance, enables it to approach defense problems from a variety of angles. Second, although there is an undoubted tradition of military subservience to civil authority in France, neither the frequent rise to political prominence by famous military leaders, from Napoleon to de Gaulle, nor the unquestioned influence of the military on the emergence of the Fifth Republic—whether this is seen as the result of the pressures that brought de Gaulle to power in 1958 or the failed putsch against him in 1961—should be forgotten.

In order to integrate all these points, a three-part approach has been adopted. First, the problem of the analysis of the central organization of defense will be considered from a theoretical and methodological standpoint; then the chapter will move to a detailed analysis focusing on the salient characteristics of the relationship between the political and military leadership; and, in conclusion, the effectiveness of the system will be assessed, with an identification of both its strengths and its weaknesses.

The approach to defense decisionmaking differs according to different disciplines: The political scientist sees it as a complex and continuing process; the lawyer, as the outcome of a given set of procedures; and the "praxeologist," as that tragic moment in time when the decision, once taken, becomes irrevocable. This last approach is worth emphasizing: According to President Mitterrand's formula, "the key to French deterrent strategy is the Head of State, who is me. Everything depends on his judgement. All else is immaterial, at least until the decision; and the decision must consist absolutely in making sure that it is of no use."[3]

The approaches of the political scientist, the lawyer, and the statesman can be reconciled by bringing together the extremes of the sudden and drastic decision by the head of state to order the use of nuclear weapons, on the one hand, and the whole complex process that led up to it, on the other. Although the president himself determines the general direction of policy and makes final decisions on the basis of his own assessments, such decisions are nonetheless based on a close network of organizations and agencies along with a set of procedures designed to convert diverse information into action at different levels. To better understand these mechanisms, three different approaches will be adopted: the systemic, the procedural, and the structural.

From a systemic standpoint, decisionmaking is a function of several interactions between the system and the environment—both global and specific.[4] To oversimplify somewhat, an understanding of the global environment now includes ecological, economic, international, and cultural considerations, especially public opinion. The defense environment must also include the expanding and interdependent strategies of modern warfare, as well as the different modes of modern warfare including political and military, nuclear and conventional, direct and indirect, economic and demographic, ideological and psychological, revolutionary and reactionary, global and limited, and so on.

In addition to the problems that address the point of decision, there is the effect of the defense system itself and the points at which political and military systems interact. B. Chantebout has pointed out, with regard to the former, that the essential consideration is the nature of the responsibility vested in the political authorities;[5] this in turn is part of the complex relationship between the political and the technocratic. Given that the military system forms a large and important technocracy, then its relationship with the political system will be conditioned by the responsibility exercised by its leaders. With reference to three models of political systems, the following situations can be identified.

1. In very rigid, authoritarian regimes, where responsibility is not clearly defined, it is rare for those in authority to survive a military setback. The examples of the collapse of General Leopoldo Galtieri after the Falklands (Malvinas) defeat and of the Greek colonels after their Cyprus adventure might be added to the classic cases of Napoleon, Mussolini, and Hitler. In the absence of more precise arrangements, responsibility tends to become more total and increasingly based on military power when the regime loses its authority. Consequently, the head of state will tend to assume complete military responsibility, leaving only secondary roles to the military leaders themselves.

2. The opposite case, paradoxically, is the parliamentary system, in which political authority can be challenged on a daily basis. In this situation, the political leaders could not gain from assuming military responsibility. Lacking the necessary technical competence, they would not have adequate control over military affairs and could do little more than endorse the decisions of the military professional experts. Under these circumstances the autonomy of the military would be even greater. In the event of defeat, the political authorities would probably be treated with indulgence by their competitors, whereas the military would be viewed as a potential scapegoat. The direction of the war in Indochina by the governments of the Fourth Republic and the 1939–1940 government in the Third Republic serve as examples.

3. Finally, there is the intermediate situation in which a democratic regime is coupled with a strong executive; such is the case in the United States, the French Fifth Republic, and, unquestionably, modern Spain. In these instances, the head of state is not directly answerable to the nation and in military matters will be more inclined to assume such initiatives and responsibility for military affairs as his personal authority will permit.

The essential feature of military systems is that they are professional organizations with a high level of technical expertise. Their development poses delicate problems for the modern state, particularly with respect to interservice rivalries and competition between weapons and military units. These are seldom personal rivalries or "button quarrels" arising from a basic esprit de corps; they reflect instead a necessary delegation of authority within a vast system and the specialized nature of its various elements. These two features generate relatively autonomous units on the strength of their separate functions and needs, which in turn further divergent interests, particularly those related to budgetary matters. Moreover, such bureaucratic compartmentalization makes the coordination task of the headquarters staff simultaneously both harder and more indispensable.

In the French case, the problem exists at all levels. First, there is the conflict between the central organization and the armed forces themselves, such that the former emphasizes management and the latter, operational effectiveness. Second, there are the conflicts among the services themselves: France's air force and navy, both more technological but with fewer personnel, clearly separate themselves from its army. And finally, within each service, there are conflicts among the different arms (the infantry, artillery, and cavalry in the army) and among types of unit (elite corps—Legionnaires, Paras—and specialist forces—Marines, Alpine troops, Gendarmerie). The central organization of defense should have the means to unify and coordinate a very heterogeneous force and, at the same time, cope with both the multiplicity of environmental influences and factors as well as the constraints associated with the internal characteristics of the system itself.

The purpose behind a given procedural approach is to demonstrate how, following the introduction of a rationalized system of support to decisionmakers, the traditional divisions of responsibility (as between stages and levels) tend to break down and consequently make it difficult to locate the precise place and time of any decision. The growth of rational approaches to decisionmaking can be seen to apply at three different levels: that of the budgetary process, that of military program preparation, and that of assistance to the decision itself. Regarding the budgetary process, it is clear that France, like the United States with its Planning-Programming-Budgeting System (PPBS) procedures, has chosen defense as one of the areas in which to experiment with new approaches. Within the financial budget, which is only a paper presentation indicating the objectives of public spending divided under broad functional headings, the defense budget was one of the first for which a precise estimate was given of the cost of each of the services and their supporting forces. For example, the 1984 Defense Budget breaks down as shown in Table 3.1 (in percentages of the total defense budget). It is also possible to allocate costs according to certain categories of expenditure (see Table 3.2).

The "Rationalization of Budgetary Choice" (RCB) is widely used in defense matters to clarify a number of essential options, such as types of equipment, recruiting methods, and so on. Once alternatives have been identified and accorded priority, a list is made of the means by which they might be achieved through the application of cost-benefit analysis. The final selections are included in an overall five-year program, which is divided into annual budgetary slices. The execution of the

Table 3.1
France: 1984 Defense Budget, Armed Forces and Logistics (in percentages)

	Operating Costs	Equipment Costs	Total
FORCES	35	39	74
Nuclear forces	3.5	16.5	20
Army	10.5	8.5	19
Air force	5.0	7.0	12
Navy	6.0	6.0	12
Gendarmerie	7.5	0.5	8
Forces overseas	2.5	0.5	3
LOGISTIC SUPPORT	18.35	7.65	26
Research and development	1.5	3.5	5
Logistic support	5.6	2.4	8
Personnel support	4.75	0.25	5
Equipment support	3.25	0.75	4
Administration	3.25	0.75	4

Table 3.2
France: 1984 Defense Budget, Operations and Equipment (in percentages)

OPERATIONS		EQUIPMENT	
Pay and other charges	35.9	Research and Development	12.1
On-going costs	11.8	Production	23.9
Total	53.1	Capital costs	4.4
		Total	46.9

program is systematically controlled in order to check for discrepancies, provide opportunity to reevalute other options, and, if necessary, adjust the program. To cite a recent example, a choice had to be made between the Boeing AWACS, the Grumman Hawkeye, and the French Transall C-160 (equipped with British electronic equipment) for the next generation of France's early air-warning system. Eventually, the Boeing was selected because it was already in operation and immediately available, which, despite its higher cost, meant that fewer orders could be placed.

The introduction of program planning also fulfilled an urgent need for rationalization. Two examples can be given. The first concerns the preparation of the Defense Bill, which was last voted by Parliament in 1983; the other, more specialized, concerns the planning of defense research and development. Medium-term planning has to address itself to the desirable, which is a long-term consideration, but it must also take into account such current realities as the annual budget. It deals as well with the realms of possibility, which have to be defined in terms of political preferences, economic constraints, and technological estimates. Consequently, the content of the Defense Bill is the product of several successive planning phases—each more precise and more rigorous than the one preceding—which are directed toward balancing government strategic objectives, the operational capability of the armed forces, and other various constraints with the requirements of the armed forces in equipment and resources needed to fulfill those objectives.

Within the military, the chief of staff (CEM) plays an important role as arbitrator; at the political level this function is performed by the minister of defense. The final decision regarding the structure and content of the defense program is taken by the president in the Defense Council. The result is sent to Parliament for approval and represents a financial and binding guarantee of the amount of funding available for the next five years of the program. With it is a report outlining both the materiel and financial appropriations earmarked for each of the services.

Research and development have expanded within the integrated framework of the Ministry of Defense because the defense minister's powers have expanded to include, simultaneously, the coordination of both the manufacturers, through the Délégation Générale pour l'Armament (DGA), and the service customers, that is, the Service Headquarters Staffs. These expansions have facilitated the move from pure research to prototype development and the planning of basic research policies in advance, thus avoiding mistakes at the development stage along with all their associated financial penalties.[6]

Under the initiative and impetus of the Conseil des Recherches et Etudes de Défense (CED), which comprises all those responsible for defense R&D under the chairmanship of the president, an overall defense research policy is formulated. One branch of the Ministry of Defense— the Direction des Recherches, Etudes, et Techniques (DRET)—is responsible for the conduct and coordination of research and has initiated two separate basic programs: the Programme Pluriannuel de Recherches et Etudes (PPRE), which covers pure research, and the Programme Pluriannuel des Développements Exploratoires (PPDE) for equipment testing and evaluation. The definition of research objectives and their relevance to defense policy is facilitated by the Centre de Prospective et d'Evaluation (CPE), a ministerial thinktank that is standing in at present for the Groupe de Planification et d'Etudes Strategiques (GROUPES).

Although the CPE's technique cannot be detailed, it can be described as the application of graph theory. This technique enables any decision to be broken down into separate elements, each involving a different

Figure 3.1   The CPE Method of Analysis

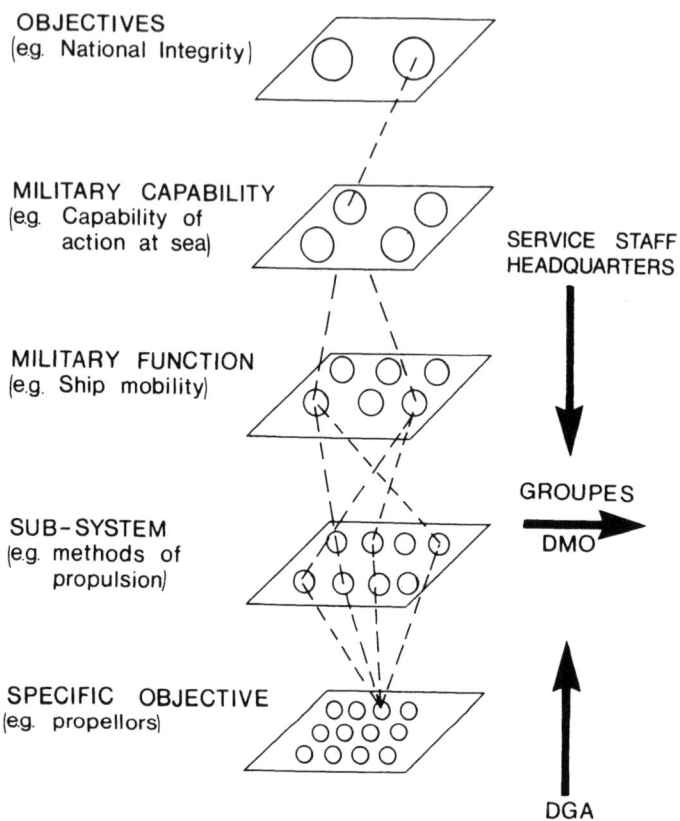

OBJECTIVES
(eg. National Integrity)

MILITARY CAPABILITY
(eg. Capability of
    action at sea)

SERVICE STAFF
HEADQUARTERS

MILITARY FUNCTION
(e.g. Ship mobility)

SUB-SYSTEM
(e.g. methods of
    propulsion)

GROUPES

DMO

SPECIFIC OBJECTIVE
(eg. propellors)

DGA

level of analysis. Each level can also be seen in relation to the level above, thus making it possible to aggregate them and to evaluate the aims of each in relation to the defense effort as a whole. The synthesis is undertaken by the GROUPES formulation known as the "directive ministérielle d'orientation des recherches" (DMO), which acts as the basis for specific projects.

Concerning support for the decision itself, the problem can be seen at three levels. First there is the tactical command level (of no relevance here),[7] which essentially takes responsibility for processing from various sources a large and important amount of information requiring immediate action. On the basis of the principles of command, control, and communication (C^3), the technique ensures the rapid transmission of information, a clear appraisal, and a variety of considered options with recommendations for action. The development of these techniques has reached an advanced level within all three services.[8] First introduced to the services some time ago (although not in effect as yet within the army, where it is still being reviewed), the technique has proved effective although it operates at a relatively low operational level.

At the highest military level, that of the Service Headquarters, data processing relevant to command decisions in real time is much more difficult. The current system, Systic 1, uses only automatic data processing when information, gathered from a wide variety of sources, is taken from a data bank and used to elaborate or clarify specific issues or problems. This information is not of direct use in decisionmaking, however; nor are sophisticated communication systems like Jupiter, which links the president to the commander of the Strategic Nuclear Forces, or Transit, which links the Headquarters Staff (EMA) with the commander of the 1st Army and the Tactical Air Force. The requirement for a genuine system to aid decisionmaking is nonetheless recognized, if only as a linkup with comparable systems of the Allied forces.

A new project, code-named EMTAME, is under review and has to meet many stringent requirements. At best, it might be conceived as an amalgam of the main information systems already in existence, which were originally introduced and developed with specific purposes in mind.

Lastly, the problems of decisionmaking support assume a different nature at the political level. For the top decisionmaker the problem is essentially one of extending contact with subordinates in order to control information while at the same time retaining his own freedom of action. In this respect, too much information—and associated pressures such as character, personality, and other human qualities—constitute the main obstacles.

The procedural approach, however, enables attention to be given to the interrelationships between salient actors in the decisionmaking process and helps prevent them from becoming distanced from the core of a complex structure. It is, of course, impossible to apply a structural approach to defense decisionmaking in such a short space; nonetheless, some of the concepts associated with it can be used to throw light on the problem.[9] Whatever is included forms part of an interrelated structure and operates on different levels. Each of these levels can have its own rationality and its own set of objectives, but the integration of the whole mixes them up to such an extent that they are hard to separate. Take, for example, the specific working of the French political system. The Constitution of 1958 can be interpreted in different ways. First, there is the traditional view of the "parliamentary liberal," who sees the accountability of the government to Parliament as the reason why the prime minister is responsible for national defense; and then there is the Gaullist who would attribute the same responsibility to the president of the Republic as to the head of the armed forces. Two interpretations must therefore be considered, employing different signals and symbols (to use the structuralist's vocabulary), although there is only one Constitution. In the same way, several different interpretations will exist with respect to the decisionmaking process, the significance of which will have to be assessed in the light of interpretations based on perceptions, the facts, and the actor's interpretation of the facts.

Every decision is based on an interpretation of the environment. Where defense is concerned, this interpretation is based first and foremost on perceptions of the external threat, the nature of the international situation, and international relationships. Public opinion also influences perceptions given the ambiguous demands of the public for both security and freedom, collective power and individualism, and international peace and national prestige. The politico-military system must necessarily keep in close contact with public attitudes; hence the Service d'Information et des Relations Publiques des Armées (SIRPA) is an agency that not only disseminates information on defense matters but, more important, continually measures the state of public opinion.[10] Finally, perceptions of economic constraints are particularly important today. Two examples will suffice. First, the scheme to reduce military service to six months, which had been canvassed during the 1981 election campaign, was postponed *sine die* on the pretext of fighting unemployment; and second, in a similar vein, the emphasis in the current five-year military program on major spending has been placed toward the end of the period (e.g., the order for the nuclear aircraft carrier) in the expectation of an improvement in the state of the economy by that time.

Any policy is conditioned by ideas and ideologies—and no more so than in defense matters. Today in France several such instances can be identified. The Socialist government's defense policy, which has been marked by a number of contradictions, is a case in point: Through the influence of the antimilitarist Left, some decisions—more symbolic than of substance—have reflected a desire to reduce military influence in specific areas, as in the decision to suppress the Tribunaux Permanents des Forces Armées (TPFA) and thereby give matters concerning military discipline, supposedly an instrument of ideological repression within the military, a more liberal status. Conversely, the strong nationalism within the Socialist party, combined with a distrust of totalitarianism, has led to opposing decisions, as with the clear support for NATO's position on the deployment of the Euro-missiles and the concern to encourage support for national defense within French society.[11]

More generally, the confrontation between a liberal philosophy and the military ethic continues to pose problems for all armed forces within any democracy, particularly with regard to the rights of servicemen relative to those of civilians. Legally, the hierarchy of norms and juridical formalism set out the ideal structure within which authority and subordination are defined, both within political and military systems and between them. Arising from the influence of the military based on its professional expertise, its overall function, and its own particular set of values, the one-sided subordination of the military to the political system is often substituted for a more flexible, if ill-defined, system of control.[12]

Ideas and ideology condition policy, but to these the language and logic of the participants themselves must be added. Military reasoning must be distinguished from political reasoning. The latter tends to be artificial, marshaled to persuade public opinion, and it emphasizes collective values when the realities of a complex world after a decade of mass movements are more individually perceived. The former, though largely symbolic, is the language of professional efficiency. In content and argument the three ideal types defined by Morris Janowitz—the heroic, the technological, and the managerial military leader—can be identified, and each has his own reasoning and emphasis both within the military and in connection with the political system.

An analysis of central organizations of defense reveals how political and military factors relate structurally;[13] but two initial considerations are required. First, it is necessary to note the importance of politico-military considerations in the study of defense management structures. In essence, this means taking account of all the management structures, civil or military, that are left to the central administration regarding civil defense, the organization of military forces, and defense economic requirements. These structures will be set to one side but should be noted, where relevant, as being part of the general problem of defense management. Second, as noted earlier in the context of politico-military considerations, there is a tendency for the two systems to reflect one another. If it is accepted that the main characteristic of the French political system is a tendency toward personalization and that the principal feature of the administrative system, whether military or civil, is a search for rationalization and efficiency, then it will be appreciated that a convergence of the two systems accentuates these characteristics. It is therefore appropriate to demonstrate that if the political organization of defense reflects the "presidentialization" of the French political system, the military and bureaucratic organizations reflect to an equal degree the characteristics of the administrative system.

In addressing the question of the organization of public authority in a wider context, it can be noted that, in accordance with the law, the general tendency toward the personalization of power that characterizes the Fifth Republic is clear with respect to defense. Although subtle nuances characterize certain details, in general terms it is possible to point to the assertion of presidential superiority to the detriment of the government and the prime minister, the increase in importance of the defense minister, and the reduction of the real function of Parliament.

As is often the case, constitutional provisions are ambiguous; they must therefore provide, once the central structures of defense have become established and, for the most part, accepted at a particular point in time, the unchallenged recognition of presidential authority such that the prime minister, as the head of government, takes on no more than secondary importance. The constitutional provisions that govern the French political system, in spite of adherence to the principles of parliamentary democracy, clearly provide for the preponderance of executive authority. They are a lot less clear when separating out the functions of the head of state and the government, particularly in defense matters. The military powers of the president are such that this title as head of the armed forces (according to Article 15 of the Constitution) is more than a mere formality and corresponds well with reality. As the guarantor of national independence and territorial integrity, and as the signatory of treaties (Article 5), the president of the Republic appoints the prime minister and members of the government (Article 8), presides over the Council of Ministers (Article 9), makes civil and military appointments, and signs decrees and ordinances (Article 13). He also acts as chairman over the various defense committees (Article 15), and, in the event of a serious crisis threatening the normal functioning of society, he can take any measure in the light of the circumstances to restore law and order (Article 16). Finally, he both negotiates and ratifies treaties.

In addition to his constitutional duties, the president exercises the power of appointment, is chairman of councils of state, and signs the legislation that he deems necessary. In times of crisis the president may hold and exercise exclusive civil and military power; under normal conditions, as a function of the powers conferred on him in Article 5 together with the political authority derived from his election by direct universal suffrage, the president has certain prerogatives in defense matters that are of immense scope in both theory and reality.

Any ambiguity in the president's power over matters of defense stems from the provisions within the Constitution regarding the role of the government in defense. It states that the government defines and directs the policy of the nation and is responsible for the armed forces (Article 20). The prime minister, who is responsible for national defense, stands in for the president, when necessary, as chairman of the various defense committees. Although the arrangements are very general, from a parliamentary perspective they identify the government and the prime minister as being the principal actors in defense matters.

This ambiguity is increased by the Ordinance of January 7, 1959, which defined the central organization of defense. By defining a concept of permanent and global defense, the statute both weakened the distinction between peacetime and war, and confirmed the legal supremacy of the prime minister for defense. It conferred on him not only the general management of defense but also its military management in the sense that he defines the objectives to be achieved, approves corresponding plans, and endorses the resource allocation to the services and the measures necessary to meet their requirements (Article 11 of the Ordinance of 1959). Under this provision, the prime minister draws up the general directions for defense negotiations, determines the preparation for and control over military operations, and coordinates the defense-related activities of other ministerial departments.

The Ordinance of 1959, on the other hand, accords relatively little significance to the president, other than his chairmanship of all the committees that decide on defense matters, including, for example, the Council of Ministers in which defense policy is defined, a National

Defense Committee in which general issues of defense management are decided, and a defense committee restricted to deciding on matters relating to military management. Herein lies a paradox, however: The prime minister presides, except when delegated, over no committee within which decisions are expected to be taken. Given his political subordination to the president, it is not easy to envisage his taking independent decisions under these arrangements. The ambiguity is not, therefore, what it formally appears to be insofar as actual practice has demonstrated, beyond any doubt, the president's supremacy over defense; it implies only the concurrence, or the compliance, of the prime minister.

The evolution of the central organization of defense has undergone two principal phases. In Michel Debré's government (1959–1962) the prime minister, as the responsible official for defense, was assisted by a minister for the armed forces. The title alone reflected his limited function. A similar disparity can be seen with respect to the advisory bodies: The prime minister was advised on matters concerning the armed services by a chief of staff (who became the chief of general staff) with responsibility only for the organization of the armed forces, their state of readiness, and interservice coordination. Without taking into account any presidential initiative, such a system involved numerous overlaps and reflected a readiness on Debré's part to assume total control over the management of defense under General de Gaulle's authority.

With the government of Georges Pompidou (1962–1968), the system was modified substantially on two fundamental points, by four decrees dated July 18, 1962. Politically, the prime minister who, constitutionally, had been the hub of the preceding arrangement, lost his constitutional powers over defense matters. The decisions that he had made personally within defense committees were transferred to those committees, thus making it easier for the president, who chaired and led them, to take his own decisions whenever necessary. Initially, the minister for the armed forces was given half the government's powers governing the use of the armed forces, conditional upon the approval of the defense committees, which in reality meant the president. Parallelling these changes, at the operational command level, the chief of staff of national defense and the chief of general staff were replaced by two new posts: the secretary general of national defense (SGDN) and the chief of staff of the armed services (EMA). The SGDN, situated at the right hand of the prime minister is, in fact, very close in status to the president as well, is primarily responsible for the coordination of different ministries in defense matters, and performs such duties as those of the secretariat to defense committees, coordination and execution of decisions, participation in negotiations involving defense, and the central control of information. With a mixed half-civilian and half-military staff and its own separate budget, the SGDN plays an important, though variable, role—depending on which party is in government.

The Etat-Major des Armées (EMA), with new and important powers, is the first deputy to the minister of the armed forces, and gained from the outset two important prerogatives over defense matters concerning the use and coordination of the armed services. These were less a matter of real decisionmaking power and more, ultimately, one of bolstering the institution in a constructive way.

Structurally, the system had almost reached a point of stability in two respects. The replacement of the minister for the armed forces by a minister of defense when Georges Pompidou became president of the Republic in 1969 confirmed the importance of the new post, and the appointment of Michel Debré, given his superior status of minister of state, emphasized again the functional significance of the post. On the other hand, the responsibility for control of the French Nuclear Strategic Force fell exclusively in 1964 to the president under the Decree of January 14, 1964.[14]

The changes introduced were the result of several factors: the end of the Algerian war, for one, and, for another, the replacement of Debré by Pompidou, a man considerably less interested in defense than his predecessor had been. The principal reason, however, was a structural one. Following the Algerian war, the French military underwent a thorough program of modernization. Furthermore, the steady progress of the Nuclear Strategic Force required a new deterrent strategy, which in turn pointed to the need for structural adjustment. The stabilization of presidential control over the management of defense policy was ensured by the fact that along with his constitutional authority as the head of state he controlled all the decisionmaking powers that were necessary to exercise real authority. In place of the traditional military cabinet to the president, which under the Parliamentary Republic was an office of assistants (aides de camp), a private office has been set up with a high-ranking officer as director, in addition to representatives of the three services and the Gendarmerie. The contacts between this private office and the service's own institutions (the SGDN and the Services Headquarters Staffs) both mark its importance and ease relations between the two sides.

Operationally, the president is exclusively in control of the nuclear forces and has direct access to a military command post in the Elysée Palace. As the Jupiter Command post, the palace is permanently connected via a secure communications network to the strategic forces operations center at Taverny (and, if necessary, to a second command post at Mont-Verdun in the Rhone) and, in like manner, to the armed forces operations center in the Defense Ministry. In secure and reliable conditions, the president can therefore exercise his function as commander-in-chief.

Decisionmaking power, even in the hands of only one person, cannot function without the management and support of senior civil servants and military officers. Management is exercised through a framework of government committees chaired by the president. At the top is the Council of Ministers, which decides on the general direction of policy in matters of defense; above all else, the president's chairmanship here is the most important. At a lower level, that of defense management, the Defense Council[15] comprises the president, the prime minister, the minister of defense, the principal ministries with defense interests, the chiefs of staff, the secretary general of national defense, the secretary general of the Presidency of the Republic, and the chief of the president's personal staff. The Defense Council is the principal locus of defense decisionmaking, and here again, presidential authority is paramount if only because the members are the president's closest associates. In short, the military management of defense is determined by the Defense Council alone; it is always chaired by the president but convened by the prime minister, who also decides the membership for each meeting. Consequently, all of the committees in which defense decisions of any importance are made fall under the immediate control of the president. The prime minister has, since 1962, been no more than a "second" to the president.

The aforementioned developments pertaining to "personalization" of defense decisionmaking, which have scarcely been in accordance with either the letter of the Constitution or the 1959 Ordinance, confirm that, in defense more than elsewhere, the idea of executive dualism is rigid and archaic. Supreme power is difficult to share, and the notion of a distinction between the power of arbitration as exercised by the president and the power of decision as exercised by the prime minister, even if it existed at the start of the Fifth Republic, does not correspond with the facts. The prime minister is little more than a collaborator with the president, a mediator close to parliamentary requests, and thus a sort of civil chief of staff.

The prime minister can exercise real control over defense management only through delegation from the president (as foreseen in Article 21 of the Constitution). Experience, however, has shown that successive presidents have preferred to exercise personal control over the armed forces as their head; even the interim president, who according to Article 7 is the president of the Senate, has been known to fully exercise these functions. This was the case in 1969 when General de Gaulle resigned; moreover, in 1974, when Georges Pompidou died, President Alain Poher emphatically insisted on being responsible, should the situation arise, for all major defense decisions, especially those concerning nuclear matters. Under these circumstances, the prime minister's role is inevitably limited relative both to that of the president and to the technical function performed by the minister of defense, who often acts as the authoritative spokesman of the head of state on defense.

The elevation of the minister of defense is indicated in legal terms by his formal powers, in administrative terms by the expansion of the Defense Ministry's central machinery, and in political terms by the personality of the incumbent. According to Article 16 of the 1959 Ordinance, the Decree of July 18, 1962, strengthened the role of the minister of defense. By the terms of Article 16 of the 1959 Ordinance, he was made responsible for "the execution of military policy and, in particular, the organisation, readiness, and mobilisation of the armed services. . . . He conducts international negotiations where defence interests are affected, directs military missions abroad and military representatives serving with alliance staffs." With the responsibility for the means of defense, the minister contributes to the formulation of strategic plans and makes sure they are implemented.

To achieve this, he has under his immediate authority on the military side the chief of staff of the armed forces, who is his closest adviser, and on the technical side, the deputy general for armaments (DGA), who is responsible for all technical aspects of defense; administratively and financially, he has the secretary general for administration. With the assistance of these three principal subordinates, he controls all aspects of the defense structure and, in particular, the means at their disposal.

The choice of minister of defense has invariably reflected the importance of the position. This was the case with Michel Debré under President Pompidou, and without a doubt the appointment of Charles Hernu, the current incumbent, is highly significant. He had long been very close to President Mitterrand, had concentrated on defense long before he joined the government, and was well respected in military circles.[16] As minister he plays a major role in the preparation of policy, both political and military, not merely by dint of his office but also on account of his personality. Thus at the ministerial level, as at the presidential level, responsibility for defense has become increasingly personalized. This trend tends to bypass Parliament, relatively speaking, as the principal collective policymaking institution.

The Fifth Republic is characterized by the constraints that have been imposed on Parliament. On the one hand, legislation is exclusively the domain of Parliament as defined in Article 34 of the Constitution, but on the other, even if control over the government is reserved for Parliament and the National Assembly can impose sanctions (Articles 49 and 50), it has lost much of its influence over policy. This is now determined by the government, under presidential authority (Article 20). This "cantonnement" of Parliament, as a matter of principle, applies *a fortiori* to defense.

According to Article 34, the law determines the general principles underlying the organization of national defense. Thus the Ordinance of 1959, although the government objected to it with reference to Article 92 when the institutions of defense were first established, can only be amended by law. The law also lays down the rules governing the fundamental safeguards granted to servicemen (e.g., military regulations were laid down by the Law of July 13, 1972, and later amended by the Law of October 30, 1975) and the obligations imposed by national defense on citizens themselves and their belongings (e.g., the regulations governing military service were laid down in the Law of June 10, 1971, and amended by the Law of July 8, 1983). Parliament must also pass laws ratifying international treaties (Article 53) and confirming a declaration of war (Article 35). On this last requirement, it should be noted that "it is essentially a case of a carry-over from past Constitutions and an assertion of a matter of principle."[17] The events leading to war at any given time do not easily conform to the established principles of international law. Legislative action by Parliament in defense matters is restricted only to organizational matters and cannot affect policy.

The situation is perceptibly different in budgetary matters. The annual defense vote is, in effect, defense policy translated into financial terms, and it is in this area that Parliament is of greatest significance. The budget is prepared by the minister of defense. Parliament cannot alter the budget without the agreement of the government because its members do not have the competence to incur expenditure (Article 40). Therefore, it can only approve or discuss the budget with the aim of extracting concessions from the government. Nevertheless, public debate initiated by the Defense and Finance committees are occasions for a general discussion of defense policy: They are never lacking in interest, even if the committees themselves are mainly conduits of the Ministry of Defense for the dissemination of technical details and lack adequate opportunity to conduct studies in order to match the experts.

The regular practice of passing laws setting down military programs that define the means and ends of defense allows for wider debate, even if it is possible on these occasions only to make points regarding the content of the legislation in accordance with formal parliamentary practice. Article 44 allows the government to limit the length of debates, decide which aspects of the law should be voted on, and, when committed to the text of the military program, prevent a direct vote. In this event, the text will be taken as agreed if the government is not otherwise defeated on a vote of censure (Article 49, line 3). By the same token, the government can, if in conflict with the Senate, give the casting vote to the National Assembly (Article 45). This happened early on in the Fifth Republic, when the bill concerning the military program that laid down the basis of the French nuclear forces had been rejected by the Senate and was then adopted by the National Assembly only after a motion of censure had been defeated. It can be concluded, therefore, that the most important commitment regarding the defense of France has not been passed by Parliament, but has come about only from the Assembly's lack of requisite authority on the subject to defeat the government.

With regard to issues of parliamentary control,[18] the Senate and Assembly committees can continually pursue problems within their competence by dint of their right of censure and access to information. Even so, they have only limited powers of investigation, and these are dependent upon government cooperation. For example, it has recently been specified that, contrary to earlier practice, the committees may not question responsible military officers on their duties without the authorization of the minister. The policy of the government is that *it* should be the only contact with Parliament and that it wishes to avoid American practices. The questions that members of Parliament can table may also be seen as an instrument of control, especially if they are followed by a short debate. The number and promptness of government replies has improved, particularly those in response to questions on current events, but the general practice of question time has not been important, especially where defense is concerned. Finally, it must be recalled that the Constitution has prevented further challenges to the government after a vote has been taken, which leaves any parliamentary group with the option of a motion of censure if it wishes to initiate a general debate on defense policy. The procedures designed to prevent this from happening frequently are very strict: A censure motion must be signed by ten deputies and, if it is defeated, which is normally the case with a stable government majority, the signatories may not table another in the same session. The opposition may table only three motions of censure during each session.

It is not possible to gauge the effectiveness of parliamentary control over defense policy because it continually comes up against the principle of military secrecy or, at least, against the discretion that is exercised over all matters of military concern. Given all these limitations on Parliament, the tendency is for the executive to gain political dominance in the central organization of defense. This again reflects the "presidentialization" of the political system and applies equally at the administrative and military organizational levels.

Despite a marked tendency toward centralization and the bureaucratic inertia characteristic of many administrative structures, France has undertaken an examination of its own administrative efficiency. Although such an examination is more difficult at the executive level, the search for efficiency has achieved some success at central coordination, including, it would appear, the central organization of defense. There are some exceptions, however. In any event, emphasis can be given to the search for a structural rationalization within the administration and a clear trend toward personalization within the structure of military authority.

The formulation of political decisions and their execution by the military have been helped by the existence of a complex but effective coordinating body made up of the SGDN on the one hand, and the central staffs of the Ministry of Defense on the other. Reorganized under the Decree of January 25, 1978, the SGDN's office can be said to have become the hub of the defense organization. Under the direction of an administrative officer, who is in direct contact with both the president and the prime minister, its principal role is to prepare the agendas for defense committees and to carry out their decisions. The SGDN's entire task is to ensure constant coordination, which constitutes the guarantee of a coherent national defense effort. The task is threefold. The first responsibility involves the establishment of an interministerial response to military, civil, and economic matters. To this end, the SGDN must coordinate the preparation and implementation of defense decisions pertaining to the various ministries. Civil defense is an example, particularly with regard to the protection of the population and security measures in general. Within each ministry, a senior defense official is in touch with the SGDN; the section dealing with defense matters is responsible for providing the means of command and essential contact with the government and circulates government information. The same procedure also applies to maritime and aeronautical issues, problems of sovereignty, and the protection of defense interests.

The second responsibility concerns the central control of information and the monitoring of international negotiations. In the former case, the SGDN provides the secretariat for the Interministerial Committee of Information (CIR), which is chaired by the prime minister, the Standing Committee on Information (CPR), and the Committee on Information Broadcasting (CMRR). It is at the meetings of these various bodies that information—either open or secret—supplied by the Ministry of Interior (Department of Internal Security and Department of Public Information) and the Ministry of Defense (Department of External Security, previously the Office of Foreign Information and Counter-Espionage) is gathered and collated. Two sections within the SGDN are responsible for this centralization of information and intelligence: a Department of Information and General Studies (DREG), which analyzes open information, and the Standing Situational Analysis Group (GPES), which constantly monitors strategic developments, questions of military cooperation, and, notably, relations with NATO.

A third significant responsibility concerns scientific and technical coordination. This is achieved by convening the Committee on Scientific Developments in Defense (CADS), and by increasing general awareness of security problems associated with defense research and the security of classified intelligence data. On a more general level, the SGDN is responsible for encouraging defense studies and military and strategic research (e.g., through the Institute of Advanced National Defense Studies [IHEDN] and the Commission on the Study and Teaching of Defense [MEED]). A document presscutting information service in combination with a central data bank guarantees the storage and processing of all relevant defense information.

Given these three areas of interministerial coordination in defense, the SGDN, with less than 700 staff members and a modest budget of F17 million in 1984, is a vital element in the defense management structure. Well adapted to the task and exceptionally dynamic, the SGDN has brought to the overall system a sense of rationality and a remarkable degree of effectiveness.

The personal importance of the minister of defense, supported by a secretary of state, has already been noted. It should be pointed out, however, that the Ministry is so structured as to provide a central support to the overall defense network. The Ministry's organization is structured around four principal functions: a technical support function centered on the Ministerial Delegation for Armaments (DMA), which is responsible for research and production of equipment; an administrative function provided through the office of the secretary general for administration, which is responsible for all administrative, financial, and social services; a control function delegated in an administrative context to the armed forces' inspectorate and, militarily, to the separate inspectorates of the three services, the Gendarmerie, the Home Defense Force, and the Health Service; and an intelligence and security function provided by affiliated departments, in particular the Directorate of Protection and Military Security (formerly the SDECE).

The bodies responsible for these separate functions are coordinated by the defense minister's civil and military office, to which is attached a particularly interesting planning agency—the Planning and Strategic Studies Group (GROUPES), formerly the Center for Forecasting and Evaluation (CPE). On instruction from the defense minister himself, the agency analyzes long-term strategic problems, technological developments, scientific advances, economic forecasts, and demographic and human changes, through either in-house or commissioned studies.

In order to link the politicians who decide on policy with the armed forces who carry it out, a military staff system is necessary. In the French case, this arrangement is characterized organizationally by a hierarchical and personalized structure and structurally by the management-control functions exercised by the General Headquarters Staff and the formulation-execution function under the charge of the headquarters staffs of the three armed services.

From an organizational perspective, the armed forces' headquarters (EMA) is undoubtedly the principal military body, above the headquarters staffs of the army (EMAT), the navy (EMM), and the air force (EMAA), as well as that of the Gendarmerie Nationale, a force that has increasingly come to resemble a fourth armed service. At the center of the EMA is a chief of staff (CEMA), who acts as an authentic commander-in-chief.

The amendment to the law by the Decree of February 8, 1982, stresses this hierarchical concentration and personalizing trend. Militarily speaking, other associated bodies perform only an advisory and consultative role. This applies to the Chiefs of Staff Committee, which is chaired by the minister of defense and comprises the CEMA and the three service chiefs of staff. The committee's principal function is to advise on the deployment of forces, the planning and allocation of resources, and any other issue raised by the minister. The service chiefs can be convened by the CEMA for consultation. Even so, the top committees of the three services are chaired by the minister and include the CEMA, *ex officio*. They also have only a consultative role and, again, act only at the discretion of the minister. The only exception concerns the appointment of general officers, in those instances when their consultation is obligatory.

All military decisionmaking powers reside, therefore, with certain responsible individuals, namely the service chiefs of staff. In considering the division of responsibility, it is necessary to differentiate clearly between the CEMA and the other service chiefs. The responsibilities of the CEMA can be seen from three standpoints. First, with respect to defense policy and strategy, the CEMA is the permanent military adviser

Figure 3.2   France: Ministry of Defense Central Administration

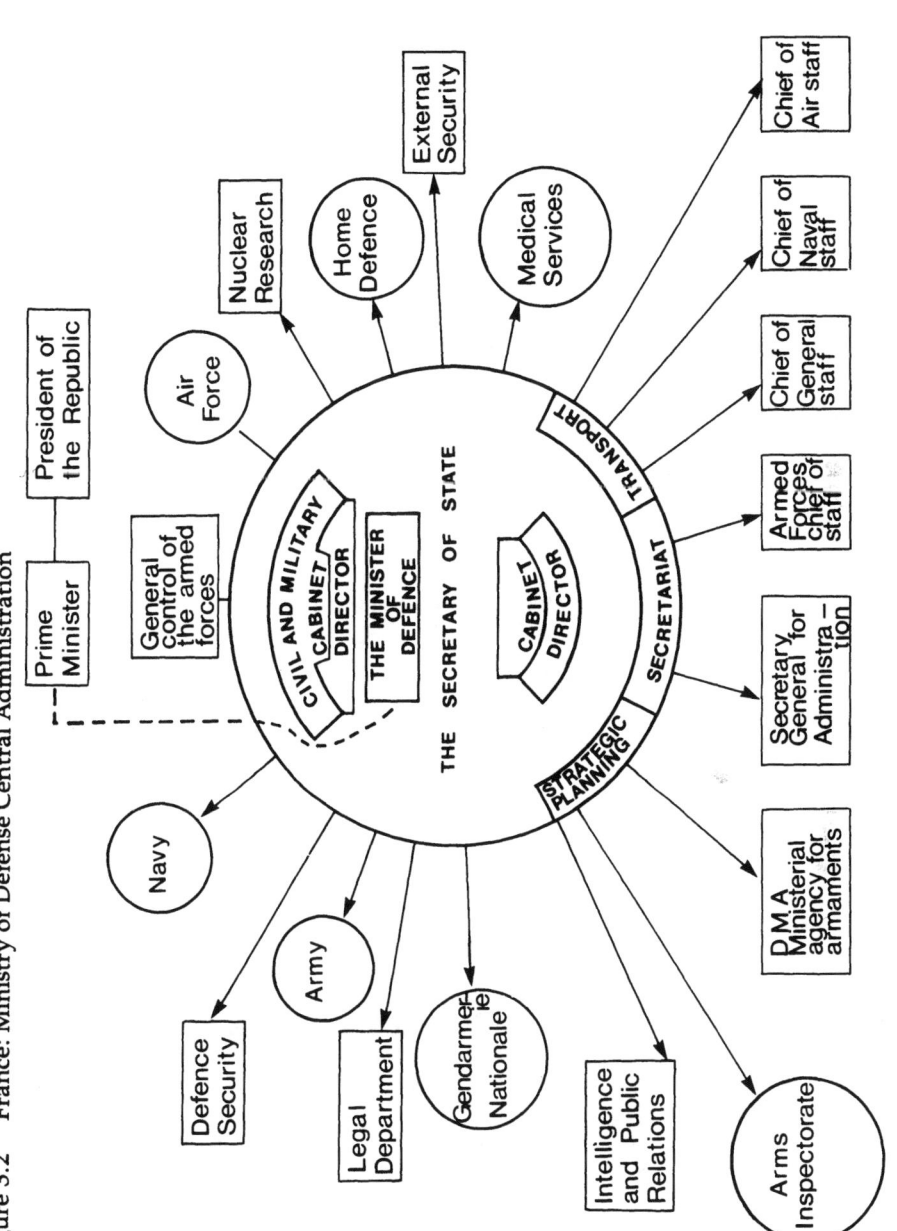

Source: Ministry of Defense, Paris, 1983.

to the minister. Regarding decisions based on policy and government directives, he has to analyze the threat, summarize the external developments, draw up appropriate plans of action, and recommend the composition and deployment of forces and equipment. He is responsible for the management of research as well as the use of military intelligence, and is charged, in the minister's name, with the handling of relations with foreign and allied forces and with international negotiations regarding the use of military forces.

Second, from an administrative and financial perspective, the CEMA has to coordinate the allocation of defense resources and, with the service chiefs and the heads of the technical services (especially the Délégué Général pour l'Armament [DGA]), draw up the planning and preparation of men and equipment. Even if the CEMA collaborates with ministerial departments in the preparation of the defense budget, the service chiefs submit their respective budgetary estimates directly to the minister and the CEMA prepares only those estimates of immediate concern to him. Third, with regard to personnel, the CEMA recommends the appointment of force commanders and is consulted on the appointment and suitability of general officers. And last, it is the CEMA who initiates all investigations and inquiries conducted by the Armed Forces Control Agency.

The powers of the CEMA are particularly important where the use of the military forces is concerned. The CEMA is primarily responsible for their state of readiness and their ability to achieve their assigned tasks. He exercises a permanent right of inspection and controls interservice higher military education and training. But it is at the level of operational command that his authority is most apparent. In the name of the president and the government, the CEMA exercises total command over military operations at all times. The force commanders are accountable to him, and the service chiefs act as his deputies. This system of supreme command operates even outside a crisis situation, although it did not apply before the 1982 Decree. As the supreme military commander the CEMA is available to take over operational control at a moment's notice, should the need arise. In the event of an acute crisis, it has always been envisaged that he would be appointed by presidential decree to the post of general chief of staff of the armed services (CEMGA). Insofar as Article 14 of the Decree of February 8, 1982, does not distinguish between the two titles (CEMA and CEMGA) with respect to overall command of wartime operations, the question as to why there are the two titles might reasonably be asked. General Jeannou Lacaze, the current CEMA, has provided an explanation: "The CEMA can be made the CEMGA (formerly known as Commander in Chief) by government decree. This is the first significant step directed at a potential aggressor: it indicates the government's view that a crisis situation is deteriorating and that extensive operations are envisaged." Confirming the permanent nature of his high position, however, he added, "during a limited crisis in peace-time, for example, Kolwesi or Chad, the CEMA is also responsible for the deployment of forces and for directing joint operations in the field."[19]

The CEMA has an elaborate organization at his disposal. His headquarters staff is made up of six divisions, three operational (nuclear, operational, and international) and three support (organization, planning/programming/budget, and communications/electronics/intelligence). Several combined service agencies are attached, such as the directorates of medical, fuel, and chaplaincy services. He is assisted by three deputies, one a major-general and two deputy chiefs of staff. Under their direction is the Centre d'Exploitation du Renseignement Militaire and the operations center, known as the Centre Opérationnel des Armées, which is continually manned according to circumstances by a flexible headquarters staff. This center is in constant contact with the force commanders, the territorial defense districts, French military representatives abroad, and allied commanders-in-chief. Military units on instant standby, such as the Rapid Action Force (FAR) and the proposed nuclear tactical unit, are of great significance and are or will be under the direct command of the CEMA, who is not required to consult with the service headquarters staffs before ordering them into action.

The main functions of the service chiefs are, on the one hand, to draw up guidelines for the employment, composition, and training of their respective forces, and, on the other, to specify their service requirements within the framework of the defense program and budget. They are also responsible for service personnel (except for general officers, who come directly under the Defense Ministry). Their tasks are therefore those of planning and administration. Operationally they have no autonomy, and they act as the CEMA's deputies. Their role is to ensure the availability and efficiency of operational units and to have them ready at the disposal of force commanders. Only in a time of crisis are they likely to exercise operational responsibility, and then only on the CEMA's orders. Nevertheless, the services' headquarters staffs should not be undervalued: Although they are not operational bodies, these staffs have the essential responsibilities for drawing up contingency plans and taking the necessary measures to gather together the relevant elements and define their uses before they are put to the CEMA.

Defense planning and preparation are dependent on the necessary provision of both men and materiel. It is by virtue of this fact that the service chiefs of staff can be seen as spokesmen for their respective services vis-à-vis the political authorities, in terms of their needs and legitimate interests.[20]

Far from undertaking a review of the merits of all the elements and connections of the system, which would be difficult to do in so short a space, or introducing concrete examples for which the underlying assumptions would have to be drawn out, my intention at this point is to evaluate the system's most notable features—namely, the personalization of the authorities and the rationalization of its structures and methods with respect to matters of control and efficiency. From this perspective, one can say that whereas the efficiency of the system seems satisfactory, matters of control appear more limited.

When they have been put to the test in delicate situations, such as the recent interventions in Chad and Lebanon, and in a less than favorable domestic political climate, the structural principles of the French system, whether in the making of defense decisions or in the relationship between the political and the military, have not appeared dysfunctional. Nonetheless, some problems can be identified.

First, from a political point of view, in matters of defense the concentration of power in the person of the president of the Republic is clearly a very positive element. Putting to one side the French commitment to a nuclear deterrent, where the personality of the president is a condition of an effective deterrence policy, the existence of a single supreme decisionmaker undeniably facilitates the speed of reaction and the coherence of decisions regarding defense as a whole. But the nature of the president's authority is a prerequisite for these outcomes. It is not only the personal authority drawn from his own character (although this is obviously an important consideration in military matters, where the stakes are always dramatized) but, above all else, his political authority that matters. Even if his direct election by universal suffrage confers authority on the president from the outset, he must nonetheless retain the agreement of the government and the approval of the parliamentary majority if he is to exercise this authority without constraint or limitation. In effect, the hybrid character of the French system—half-parliamentary, past-presidential—cannot function effectively without the agreement of the presidential and parliamentary majorities. This is so because the government, in addition to being appointed by the president and dependent on him, such that their good relations are essential, is also answerable to the National Assembly. This understanding between the majorities has been managed so far, but a breakdown is possible, particularly when an election occurs during a president's term of office. Such a rupture would undoubtedly undermine the real authority of the president and, with it, the effectiveness of the defense system, for it would produce the potential for tension between the president and the government with its new majority.

With regard to the techniques of decisionmaking and execution, the introduction of flexible coordinating structures such as the SGDN and the use of rationalized methods and analytical techniques of decision-making have been conducive to efficiency. Yet there are many risks that limit their effectiveness. First, there is the technocratic risk whereby those agencies that prepare and identify issues for decision will become constrained by the demand for rationality, in what are essentially political decisions. An emphasis on data processing could heighten this risk. However, we have seen that computerization, to date, has been developed to a greater extent in peripheral areas, such as weapons systems, than at the center, where, because it provides data only for situation evaluation, it leaves the decisionmaker relatively unconstrained.

Second, there is a double risk of a bureaucratic nature: On the one hand, the security, intelligence, and analysis agencies have been somewhat reduced and now come under the SGDN, the president's private office, and the General Staff Headquarters. Thus the possibility of interference, enervation, duplication, or, indeed, conflict could arise, especially between the permanent Situation Evaluation Group under the SGDN, the Army Operational Center under the EMA, and the president's close advisers. A more centralized structure permanently devoted to crisis management might be preferable, but then the bureaucratic risk would change only in character and reproduce the defects of a typically French tradition of hypertrophic centralization with its clumsy and sluggish responsiveness. The maintenance of a number of more flexible structures seems definitely preferable, so long as the coordination described earlier functions effectively.

The other bureaucratic danger is a more general and more classic one, deriving from the centralization of military management within the Ministry of Defense. In spite of a reasonably flexible functional structure, which clearly distinguishes administration (Secrétariat Général pour l'Administration), technology (Délégation Militaire pour l'Armament), and the military (military headquarters staffs) on a horizontal plane, from the areas of preparation/decision, execution and control on the vertical plane, the core of the Defense Ministry, lacking homogeneity as a result of separate civil and military staffs, is a ponderous machine.

Figure 3.3, though simplified, provides an adequate outline of the chain of military command.

This model does reveal some potential difficulties, however. The first, already mentioned, is the subordination of the chief of staff to three distinct political authorities: the president, the prime minister, and the minister of defense. Complete agreement among the three should preclude problems: The president should issue the strategic orders, the minister of defense should be able to implement them at the level immediately below, and, for the most part, the prime minister should remain in the background. Alternatively, in the event of conflict among the political authorities, the CEMA could find himself in a very delicate situation.

From a technical point of view, regarding the relations between the responsible military authorities, two difficulties relating to decisionmaking authority could arise: One might proceed from the fact that the president's special adviser and the CEMA have, respectively, control and coordination of both the nuclear and the conventional forces. This particular problem is unlikely to arise in the case of the nuclear forces, in which the operating procedures under the control of the president are detailed to such an extent as to preclude any interference. Conversely, the avoidance of this kind of problem for the conventional forces depends on perfect coordination between the president's staff and the CEMA. The second difficulty could result from a conflict between the CEMA and the service chiefs over the use of the armed forces. Theoretically, the principle is quite clear—the CEMA directly commands the forces and the service

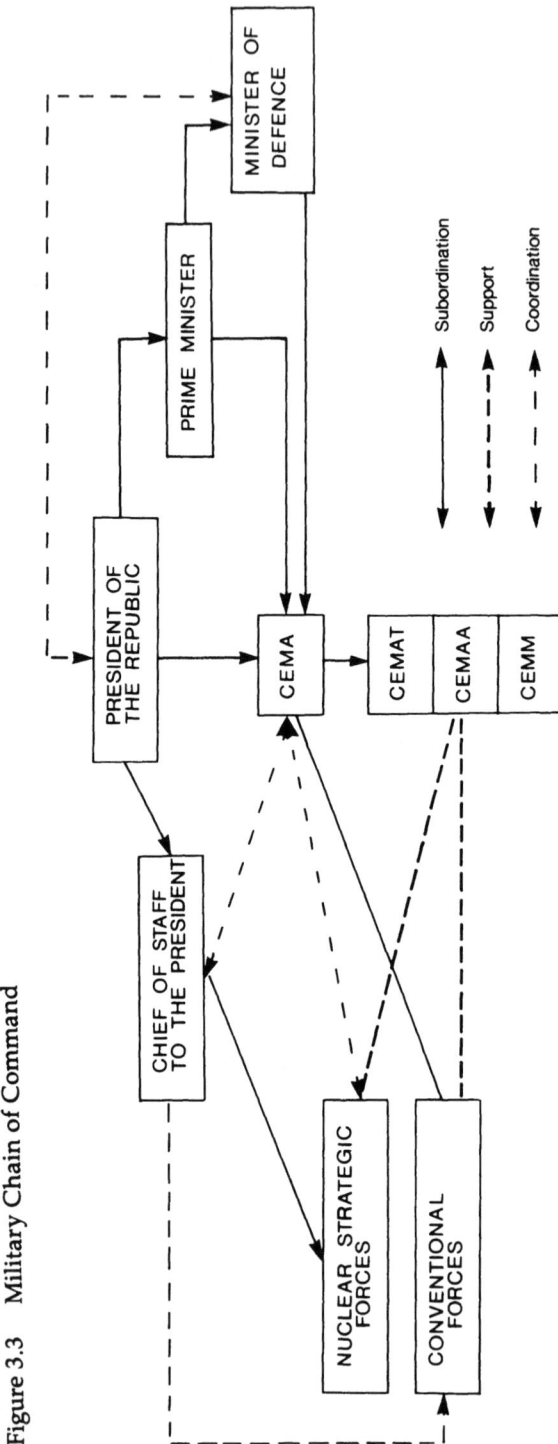

Figure 3.3   Military Chain of Command

chiefs provide support. In practice, however, complications occur as a result of interservice rivalries. That is, during a crisis, the service chiefs themselves would receive operational commands that they would have to coordinate with the CEMA headquarters.

Overall, then, the central organization of defense in France would appear to be an effective one. Moreover, it is a logical one, given the reservations just outlined, insofar as the embodiment of an equally political and military authority in one man and the rationalization of structures and methods are specifically designed to achieve effectiveness. On the other hand, the same objectives could well be achieved through a greater reduction in central control.

It would take a very detailed study to demonstrate in any depth the central controls over defense. Accordingly, only two phenomena characteristic of the French system, yet of more general significance as well, will be outlined in brief.

Within the French political system, parliamentary control of presidential and government defense policies, though not totally absent, must inevitably be limited: The technicalities of defense decisions, the constraints of speed and secrecy, and the inaccessibility of most military institutions to parliamentary influence lead ineluctably to reduced control. What controls there are usually consist of the approval of executive proposals on the one hand, and of the endeavor, *ex post facto*, to obtain the minimum essential information on their implementation and outcome on the other. Since this phenomenon seems to occur even in, say, the British system, where Parliament has retained a more important role, it is hardly surprising that it should be so marked in a presidential system like that of the Fifth Republic.

Civil-military relations in France are less straightforward. It cannot be maintained that the French military system is not under political control; indeed, the opposite has just been demonstrated at the organizational level, such that the military authority of the chief of staff (EMA) is clearly subordinate to the president's political authority. Moreover, the political change introduced in 1981 neither altered the subordination of the armed forces to governmental authority nor provoked any particular crisis. Although there may be some discontent in certain military quarters (a discontent that should not be overestimated), the only significant incident has been the resignation of the army chief of staff in 1983.

More significant still is the character of this political control. On the one hand, beyond a simple juridical subordination, which would not be enough to guarantee political control of the military, there is control within the military system itself, which, in a way, does guarantee it. This control is multilayered, comprising juridical elements, such as military hierarchy and discipline; sociological elements, such as the professionalization of the military (although this, of course, could have the contrary effect of enhancing the political resources of the military);

and ethical elements, derived from the specific values of the military system.

On the other hand, this control is in some respects a two-way process. Although their subordination may be ensured, the members of the military nonetheless exert significant pressure upon their political masters. In general terms, and particularly in the French case, the military system uses all its structural and functional resources to influence the political system. This is especially true for the framing of defense policy and the allocation of the necessary budgetary resources. Since 1981, the French military has been guaranteed that the essentials in matters of defense policy, such as those of organization and status, will be maintained and continued regardless of change elsewhere. The price of this guarantee has been the military's complete acceptance of policy changes and of certain potentially wounding symbolic decisions.

The acceptance of political change combined with the continued pursuit of military continuity can be said to characterize political control in French civil-military relations—as is true in many other major liberal states. A minimum control can therefore be regarded as having been established, thus pointing to an instructive similarity in the positions of the president and the armed forces. Just as the president, though not answerable to Parliament, is nonetheless permanently under the scrutiny of the electorate, so the armed forces, though strongly elitist, are both dependent upon their image in the eyes of the national community and concerned to achieve that ever-difficult balance between tradition and progress. As General Lacaze, the armed forces' chief of staff (CEMA), concluded in the interview cited earlier, "If the armed forces appear a rather conservative community it is because by their very nature they need to cling to fundamental values, to feel firm ground under their feet. But the forces are, in very large measure, a reflection of the Nation. They have shown in recent years that they have been able to adapt to the evolution of society and that they have not been hostile to change."[21]

Notes

1. L. Sfez, "La Decision n'existe pas," Le Monde Dimanche (May 23, 1982), p. ix. See also L. Sfez, "Critique de la décision," in A. Colin, Cahiers de la Fondation Nationale des Sciences Politiques (Paris, 1973), 368pp.

2. On this theme, see particularly Morris Janowitz, "The Emergent Military," in C. C. Moskos (ed.), Public Opinion and the Military Establishment (Beverly Hills, Calif.: Sage, 1971), pp. 255–270; D. R. Segal, "Convergence, Isomorphism and Interdependence at the Civil Military Interface," Journal of Political and Military Sociology 2 (1974), pp. 157–172; S. P. Huntington, The Soldier and the State (New York: Vintage Books, 1964), especially pp. 80ff.

3. Le Monde (November 8, 1983), p. 7.

4. See J. P. Marichy, "Le problème des relations civilo-militaires aux Etats-Unis: Pour une nouvelle approche méthodologique," in L. Mandeville (ed.), Le système militaire des Etats Unis (Paris: Editions J. P. Delarge, 1976), pp. 282–310.

5. D. Chantebout, *"L'organisation Générale de la Défense Nationale en France depuis la fin de la Seconde Guerre Mondiale"* (Paris: Paris Publishing House, 1967), pp. 76ff.

6. S. Bindel, *"La Recherche de Défense,"* *Défense Nationale* (October 1983), pp. 121–135.

7. Contre-Admiral Yves Morel, "Fédération des systèmes informatiques de Commandement," in *Défense*, no. 29 (June 1983); Numéro spécial "Informatique et Défense," pp. 9–11; J. Miheleno, "Evolution technologique et Stratégie Militaire," *Défense Nationale* (January 1984), pp. 169–172.

8. Armée de l'Air: Système de Traitement et de Representation des Informations de Défense Aérienne (STRIDA); Marine: Système de Commandement de la Marine (SYCOM) et Sous-Système d'Exploitation Navale de l'Information Tactique (SENIT); Armée de Terre: Système Automatise de Commandement et de Renseignement de l'Arvant (SACRA).

9. On the general level of decision theory, see Sfez, "La Decision," above for a remarkable treatment.

10. Lieutenant-Colonel A. Thieblemont, "L'opinion sur l'Armée et la Défense en 1983," *Armées d'Aujourd'hui*, no. 87 (January/February 1984), pp. 12–16, and no. 88 (March 1984), pp. 8–11.

11. Thus an agreement has been signed between the minister of defense and the minister of national education to develop the beginnings of this spirit of defense, despite, or because of, the fairly widespread antimilitarist sentiments of the signatories.

12. Marichy, "Le problème des relations," pp. 303ff.

13. The general bibliography on this theme is quite small. B. Chantebout's work (cited in note 5) needs updating. Michael L. Martin's book, *Warriors to Managers: The French Military Establishment Since 1945* (Chapel Hill: University of North Carolina Press, 1981), does not include the developments of the central organizations, any more than does the collective edited work by J. P. Marichy, "Le système militaire français," in J. P. Marichy (ed.), *Annales de l'Université des Sciences Sociales de Toulouse* (Toulouse, 1977), 245pp. One might refer to a recent small popular work, Hubert Haenel, *La Défense Nationale* (Paris: P.U.T. Que sais-je?, 1982), p. 128, and to official publications.

14. The arguments that followed the publication of his text can provide confirmation, if it were needed, of presidential supremacy. On the one hand, defense decisions may be taken by the president by decree, although one might argue that a law was necessary since it is a fundamental principle, under Article 34 of the Constitution, that defense is a matter for this law. In this way, the president, aware of his exclusive role in defense matters, gains control of the supreme weapon. On the other hand, this decree, which concerned only the Aerial Strategic Forces (the only ones in existence in 1964), has not been modified with the development of the Naval Strategic Forces and the tactical nuclear weapons of the three services. One could deduce from this that responsibility for a nuclear launch is in some way part of the presidential prerogative, without which there would be a need for more elaborate specification.

15. Note that the Ordinance of 1959 speaks of the *Committee* of Defense, but it is traditional to use *Council* (from which comes the systematic use of the term *Consul*) in referring to the meetings presided over by the head of state. In the same way, it must be noted that the Superior Defense Council provided for by Article 8 of the ordinance for "the study of defence problems" has never met, the Council of Defense having absorbed all its functions.

16. See Charles Hernu, *Soldat Citoyen: Essai sur la défense et la securité de la France* (Paris: Flammarion, 1975), and, by the same author, "Ce n'est plus la discipline mais la conviction qui fait la force principale des armées" and "Les structures representatives de participation dans l'Armée Française" (in collaboration with J. Marceau), in Marichy "Le système militaire français," pp. 39–46, 129–154.

17. See P. Dabezies' commentary on Article 35 in F. Luchaire and G. Conac (eds.), *La Constitution de la Republique Française,* Tome II (Paris: Economica, 1979), pp. 506–508.

18. On this problem, see S. Cohen, "Le controle parlementaire de la politique de Défense Nationale et de l'Institution Militaire en France et aux Etats-Unis," in Mandeville, *Le système militaire des Etats-Unis,* pp. 152–235.

19. *L'Express* (March 26, 1982), p. 76.

20. On this point see the report by L. Mandeville and A. Sorbara, "Le métier des armes et le problème de la representation collective des intérêts des militaires," *Politica Militaire* 4, no. 12 (April-May, 1982), pp. 47–54.

21. *L'Express* (March 26, 1982), p. 73.

4

Central Organizations of Defense in the Federal Republic of Germany

Wilfried Freiherr von Bredow

Background

The debate on security and defense in the Federal Republic of Germany is characterized by a pattern of hills and valleys of public interest. Recently, this interest has been steadily growing. Unfortunately, public debates on the necessity and the possibilities of keeping the fragile peace in Central Europe are too often fed with illusions. There are "positive" illusions—one needs *only* to demonstrate one's good intentions in order to obtain international security. There are also "negative" illusions—in order to guarantee international peace one needs *only* to overcome this or that enemy of international order, this or that group of people with economic, or political, or simply paranoid interests in further armament and even war.

Both highly ideologized perceptions (which fall into the category of the "only-perceptions") fall short of the complexities of the international system. There is not the slightest evidence for the assumption that peace and international security are just around the corner and could easily be won, provided the one and only obstacle (a governmental system, a socioeconomic class, the spirit of male chauvinism, or something of the sort) could be removed. Instead, a sober analysis of the international system comes to a quite different conclusion: "The international order is notoriously lacking in mechanisms of peaceful change, notoriously dependent on war as the agent of just change. The society of states, always divided about the rules and institutions necessary to sustain order, is more divided still about the requirements of justice."[1] But if it is correct to define war, in the tradition of Clausewitz, as a continuation of political interaction with other instruments, and if therefore politics in the current international system still has to be aware of the sudden emergence of war, then the armed forces of a nation do not lose their salient importance for the status and the power of that nation in the international system. Evidently, the concept of national security has been enlarged during the past few decades by nonmilitary components. For highly industrialized nations the most important of these is the economic aspect of security, which depends partly on a functioning world economy. This does not mean, however, that the military aspect of security can be neglected. The context of nuclear deterrence has made the responses of the leading antagonistic powers and their respective allies to the challenge of providing national security in an unstable international environment even more complicated.

The Federal Republic of Germany is especially affected by this complexity. After the total breakdown of the National Socialist regime in 1945, Germany was divided into several parts. Its reunification seemed to require a matter of some years; and initially at least there was the unification of the four zones of occupation. But the developing East-West conflict into the form of a cold war caused this prospect to fade away. The border between the "two camps," the "Iron curtain," ran and still runs through Germany, separating, since 1949, two states—the Federal Republic of Germany in the west and the German Democratic Republic in the east. Each state is politically, economically, and, since 1955, militarily integrated in one of the antagonistic cold war alliances. The alliances confront each other at the border with large armed forces and sophisticated military equipment.

Because of this peculiar situation, any attempt to draw a picture of West Germany's central organization of defense should start with a short review of the foundation of its armed forces, the Bundeswehr. When the plans for the rearmament of West Germany (plans whose initiative originated mostly in the United States) came into being, concrete political constraints had to be observed in order to make it clear once and for all—to the Germans as well as to the victims of National Socialist warfare—that the new German armed forces were substantially different from the former twentieth-century armed forces, the Kaiserliches Heer, the Reichswehr, and the Wehrmacht. The original conception of the Bundeswehr, therefore, contained numerous elements that made it a new type of military organization, at least in the context of German military history and traditions.

A short look at the foundation of the Bundeswehr will be the first part of this chapter. A second and rather brief section will present the current shape of the Bundeswehr, and a third, the financial framework of the armed forces. The next part will introduce the structure of West Germany's military organization and the main features of its legal base. The constitutionally determined tasks of the Bundeswehr and their translation into military terms will follow. The problem of civil defense is dealt with before we finally look more deeply into the decisionmaking structures of West Germany's security policy.[2]

The Foundation of the Bundeswehr

In many political documents of the post-1945 period, Prussian-German militarism was denounced as one of the main factors responsible for National Socialism. Antimilitarism was to be one of the objectives of reeducation, and the anti-Hitler coalition agreed at the Potsdam Conference in July and August 1945 on the comprehensive demilitarization of Germany. Many Germans also adopted this attitude toward the military and became postwar pacifists.

The international system, however, did not allow the Germans a farewell to arms. The East-West conflict overshadowed the visions of a cooperative "One World," and from the spring of 1947, at the latest, the rift between the United States and the USSR became the dominant pattern of world politics. For a variety of reasons, military planners in both Washington and Moscow began to think about a military contribution from "their" respective Germany. The Federal Republic of Germany (FRG) was founded in 1949, but the Armed Forces of the FRG did not exist until 1955. This remarkable fact expresses in a symbolic way the primacy of the political over the military.

During the first years of the new republic, a vigorous public debate took place, at the national and the international levels, about the possibility, necessity, danger, and character of a West German contribution to Western defense. Initially the opponents of German rearmament seemed to prevail.

Fears of a revival of traditional German militarism (or what was considered to be this militarism) spread not only among the victims of National Socialist expansion, but also among West German citizens. Though it may seem an oversimplification, it is reasonable to assume that for a long time after 1945, the Germans in the FRG were paralyzed by the political, military, and human failure of their nation in the previous decade. Many of them preferred to think that politics and current affairs should not be of any concern to them, and that the future of Germany should be placed on the periphery of world affairs. They were not then aware of the fact that the cold war between East and West had placed them, once again, right in the center of the most bitter of current international conflicts; but even those who did not indulge in a fatalistic-quiescent attitude toward politics were often very skeptical about the compatibility of the two main objectives of West Germany's foreign and defense policy. They felt that *integration* into the Western Alliance, combined with *rearmament* as one of its principal means, would not open the road to *reunification*, as argued by the government; instead, it would close it firmly for a long time. The policy of integration into the West, and especially of military integration into a West European Defense Community (later, NATO), was therefore also questioned from a purely German nationalist point of view.

Mainly because of international developments and a surprisingly successful administration in other fields, especially the economic field, the foreign policy of Chancellor Konrad Adenauer overcame all sorts of opposition to his security policy. By the end of 1955, when the first soliders of the Bundeswehr took their oath in the barracks of Andernach, one of the major controversies of the Republic seems to have disappeared from the agenda.[3]

The influence of the Zeitgeist, however, as well as the long public debate about the old Wehrmacht and the new Bundeswehr, the legal construction of these new armed forces, and their Gestalt posture can hardly be overemphasized. For the first time in Prussian-German history since the middle of the seventeenth century, the political community was creating and shaping the armed forces—an uncommon, yet rather productive, development.

More than anything else, two fundamental decisions made the Bundeswehr a new type of German armed force. First, the international situation in the early 1950s did not allow national German armed forces to be set up in the traditional way. After the failure of the European Defense Community in 1954, the West German Forces were integrated into NATO. More or less all troops were assigned to NATO, leaving practically no discretion for a purely national military policy. Not only did the West Germans accept this arrangement, but they also developed a special orientation toward the alliance and a special NATO-mindedness. The overall national problem of the confrontation of two German armed forces in Central Europe is mostly masked by this orientation.

Second, the political and military planners of the Bundeswehr agreed on the principle of strong civilian control over the armed forces, which were to be firmly integrated into the democratic structures of the society. A group of reform-oriented men (soldiers and civilians) developed the institutional and ideological framework for this integration. Concepts like the "citizen in uniform" or "the armed forces for democracy" and the comprehensive approach of the principle of *innere Fuhrung* were not always immediately understood and had to be modified several times. They could, however, help mitigate the incompatibility between modern democratic society and the armed forces that has so often been described by social scientists since Auguste Comte and Herbert Spencer.[4]

The Armed Forces

The present (1984) strength of the Bundeswehr is 495,000 soldiers and 180,000 civilian employees.[5] Of these, 257,000 soldiers belong to the category of long-term volunteers (professional soldiers and limited career personnel with between three and fifteen years of active service). The government intends to increase the number of these volunteers from 258,000 in 1984 to 266,000 in 1986.[6] The army, with 334,000 soldiers (peacetime strength), accounts for the bulk of the armed forces. It has at its disposal eleven divisions together with thirty-six brigades of A-1 status (highest readiness and availability status of NATO forces) and

Figure 4.1   Defense Expenditure of the Federal Republic of Germany, 1970–1981

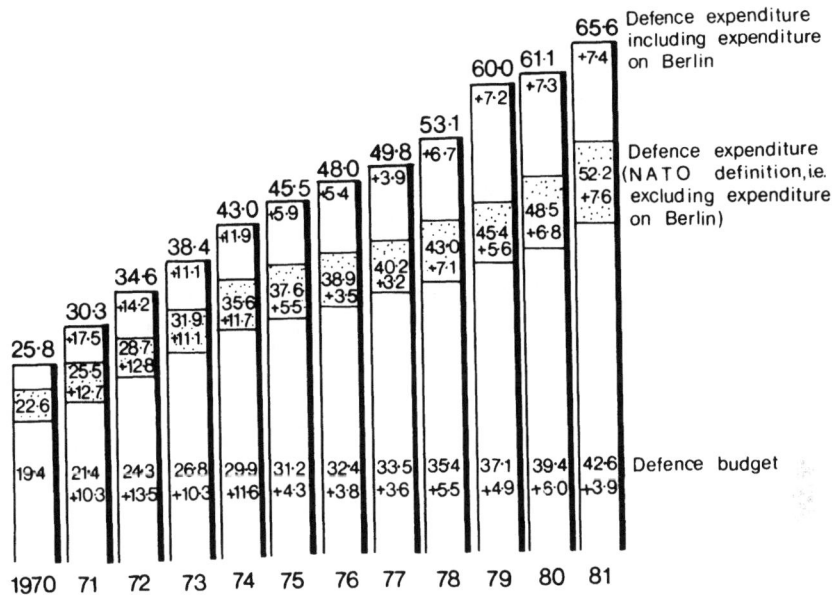

Source: The Role of the Federal Republic of Germany in NATO (Bonn: Ministry of Defense, 1982).

six civil defense brigades. The most recent reform of the army structure (Heeresstruktur 4) outlined the following distribution: seventeen armored brigades, sixteen infantry brigades (one of them a nonmechanized mountain brigade), and three airborne brigades. There are also units at the division and corps levels, whose armored and artillery capacities have been considerably increased during the past few years.

The air force has 110,540 servicemen and the navy, 38,059. The territorial army has been neglected for a long time, but it is now emerging as a comparatively strong reserve force. Recent publications of the Federal Ministry of Defense mention approximately 450,000 soldiers in the territorial army and 850,000 reservists (including those of the territorial army) altogether.[7]

The Financial Framework

The first decade of the Bundeswehr, 1955–1965, can be regarded as its construction period. Since then its size has hardly altered, but this is not to say that the permanent process of modernizing weapons and equipment should be underestimated.

"Security costs money" is the introductory phrase of that part in the 1979 West German Defense White Paper which deals with financial questions. Defense costs a good deal of money, indeed. In 1983 the defense budget was considerably more than double the size of the 1965 budget. As in all Western countries, the share of the armed forces in public spending has been decreasing over the years, but this does not indicate a reduced defense commitment on the part of the population. Rather, it is a consequence of the steady expansion of the public sector in modern industrial economies.

One of the pernicious problems associated with the defense budget of West Germany is the growing weight of operational costs (i.e., pay, administration, and training) compared with investments (i.e., military weapons and equipment). Two difficulties in particular have resulted. First, the high percentage of operational costs is reducing the flexibility of the defense budget; and second, the dramatic increases in defense research and development costs make it more and more difficult to meet the different requirements of the services. Experts have calculated an increase of 100 percent in the system costs of airplanes and missiles over the past fifteen years (without accounting for inflation). This, plus an average annual 4 percent increase in prices, is heavily influencing the costs of new systems—a factor of 3.6 from one generation to the next. These problems will have a strong impact on defense planning in West Germany over the next several years.

The Constitutional Role of the Armed Forces

The constitutional role of the armed forces is concerned with the most important regulations regarding the construction and maintenance of armed forces, their structures, their position within the political system, and their relationship with civilian society. Some of these regulations had already been formulated during the formative period of the Federal German Republic and have been integrated into the Constitution (Grundgesetz). But these are only a few. The bulk of those parts of the Constitution concerning the armed forces have had to be included in the Grundgesetz as a supplement. The more important features of the Constitution with regard to the armed forces are listed and then discussed:

1. Article 1, section 3, determines the Bundeswehr as part of the Executive; therefore, its personnel are subject to the basic rights, which are inalienable.
2. Article 4, section 3, deals with the rights of conscientious objectors.
3. Article 9, section 3, forbids the use of the Bundeswehr within the territory of the Federal Republic of Germany against organized strikes.
4. Article 12(a) regulates conscription and liability for service in case of a state of emergency.

5. Article 17(a) authorizes the restriction of some basic rights during the period of conscription or alternative service for conscientious objectors and during states of emergency.

It seems to be of special importance that, during the foundation period of the Bundeswehr, nearly all political forces supported the principle that armed forces should not be subject to anticivilian tendencies. All servicemen in the Bundeswehr—officers, NCOs, conscripts, professionals, reservists—were to have equal political rights and should consider themselves "citizens in uniform" (Staatsburger in Uniform). This idea is part of a concept termed *innere Fuhrung*. There is no exact English translation for this term,[8] which comprises a number of moral, ideological, and legal components. Since 1955 there has been a lively discussion within the Bundeswehr and among the public about the viability of this concept. Generally, two groups can be distinguished: the reform group, on the one hand, and the traditionalists, on the other. This divided opinion is, of course, an oversimplification, but not totally unjustified.

It is somewhat complicated to describe the principles of the *innere Fuhrung* concept. They are probably inexplicable unless the specific situation of Germany after the total collapse of the National Socialist regime and the defeat of the German Wehrmacht at the end of World War II are taken into consideration, in conjunction with the political atmosphere that prevailed during the following decade after this defeat during which (West) Germany had no armed forces. The political reconstruction of Germany was deeply influenced by the idea that the Germans should learn from the political mistakes of the Weimar republic. The existence of armed forces without a deep-rooted loyalty to the democratic regime was widely regarded as one of these mistakes. So it is that the Constitution, and many of the institutions created in the new Federal Republic, demonstrate the intention to establish a genuine democracy, without the Weimar's flaws. Much of this intention was still alive when the discussion about a new West German Armed Force started, and hence those who were to serve in the Bundeswehr had to identify themselves closely with the norms and values of a democratic society. They were to be politically conscious and responsible soldiers of the democracy. The concept of *innere Fuhrung* was elaborated, therefore, in order to create a framework for military life in the barracks that would conform with this supreme goal.

A definition from the early 1960s describes *innere Fuhrung* as

the duty of every military superior to educate soldiers who are capable and determined to defend freedom and the rights of the German people in a hot and a cold war against every aggressor. Innere Fuhrung is based on the values of the Constitution, acknowledges the political situation, transfers trustworthy military virtues and experiences of the past into our modern time and takes into consideration the consequences of modern military technology.[9]

The problem with this concept of *innere Fuhrung* is its scope: It is, so to speak, too much at once. For example, it is an "ideal model" of the modern soldier, who is challenged by ideological propaganda and by sophisticated technology; it is also a collection of norms to guarantee the integration of the military into civilian structures; and it is last, but not least, a leadership doctrine and a precept for military education, which, if taken seriously, has considerable consequences for the structure and ordering of daily military life.

The main arguments against the *innere Fuhrung* concept are twofold. First, from a conservative standpoint, *innere Fuhrung* neglects traditional features of the military. It thus betrays the quasi-eternal true dimensions of the profession of arms in that it does not give adequate emphasis to the traditional values of the "fighter" and overestimates the managerial aspect of military service. And second, from a more technocratic point of view, *innere Fuhrung* is too abstract, overgeneralized, and "rational"; consequently, it is difficult to translate into practical, everyday terms.

Obviously, many of the ideas and proposals of the reform group have not been put into practice. "Progressive" critics of the Bundeswehr have, from time to time (and sometimes with good reason), regretted the "conservative backlash" within the armed forces. It should be noted, however, that the main principles and dynamics of *innere Fuhrung* (together with the continual discussion about it) have nonetheless become a genuine part of the self-perception of the Bundeswehr; they have also been useful in tackling internal problems and problems with civilian society.[10]

Innere Fuhrung grew out of post–National Socialist German history. It would be wrong to consider it as a model for other armed forces. It cannot simply be exported to other countries with other historical experiences and political cultures. But the necessity of restructuring from scratch a huge and efficient military organization was also a unique and great opportunity to use a number of insights afforded by modern social and organizational sciences. This mixture of moderate and "purified" German military tradition and modern scientific knowledge makes the introduction of the *innere Fuhrung* concept a fascinating social experience.[11]

As Gunter Wapuski and Dieter Wolf have pointed out, "The armed forces and their civilian administration are fully integrated into the Executive. There is no separation between the political and military leadership of the armed forces (a separation which characterized the Reichswehr)."[12] According to Article 65(a) of the Constitution, the federal minister of defense bears the political responsibility for the armed forces, but he has also the necessary military authority to supervise education, training, and equipment. This authority is called "Befehls und Kommandogewalt" (supreme military and organizational authority). In cases of a state of emergency, the Befehls und Kommandogewalt will be transferred to the chancellor (Article 115[b]).

The new institutional structure of the military leadership of the Bundeswehr is, like so many other features in this context, based on negative experiences in German history. The Federal Ministry of Defense is the supreme agency for all the armed forces and their administration. There is no General Staff. The highest representatives of the services are immediate subordinates of the defense minister. The inspector general functions as the highest military adviser to the minister and as the most senior representative of the armed forces; he is not, however, the supreme military commander.

The relatively undistinguished status of the inspector general is regarded as unsatisfactory by the armed forces, and from time to time discussions about changes have taken place. In 1966, the inspector general of the armed forces, General Heinz Trettner, tried to raise the competence of this position by proposing to make the inspector general a deputy of the federal minister and thus give him a share in the power of command. These proposals have not been realized; at the time, General Heinz Trettner resigned, and his successor, General Ulrich de Maiziere, once again (and successfully) stressed the more diplomatic aspects of this position.[13] Most of the military units of the Bundeswehr are, in peacetime, already assigned to NATO, so they are only partly subject to national command. In all questions concerning training and equipment, armament, organization, logistics, dislocation, and leadership of the troops, NATO's recommendations are binding. NATO's Supreme Allied Commander (Europe) (SACEUR) has the right of inspection. In cases of a state of emergency the operational leadership of these units is transferred to SACEUR. The units are not, however, subject to NATO where discipline is concerned.

The Bundeswehr was, from the beginning, conceived as a service of conscripts. The decision that it should be so was incorporated into the Constitution. It would appear that the dominant reason for this decision was political and not military (they do not contradict each other). The first federal president, the popular Theodor Heuss, called conscription, in an often-quoted phrase, the "legitimate child of democracy." As Count Wolf von Baudissin has put it, "The more pluralistic the base from which soldiers are recruited, that is, the broader the political and social status of soldiers, the less likely is the probability of domestic misuse of this instrument of power."[14]

In spite of this generally accepted principle, the proportion of professional soldiers and long-term volunteers in the ranks of the Bundeswehr is growing, especially in the navy and the air force. Technological and economic reasons, but also demographic constraints in the near future, may generate a further decrease in the proportion of draftees. Conscription is, however, not really a controversial issue in the Federal Republic of Germany, and no serious political group is demanding its abolition. On the contrary, there is some consideration given to the idea to extend

Figure 4.2 Federal Republic of Germany: Sections in the Ministry of Defense

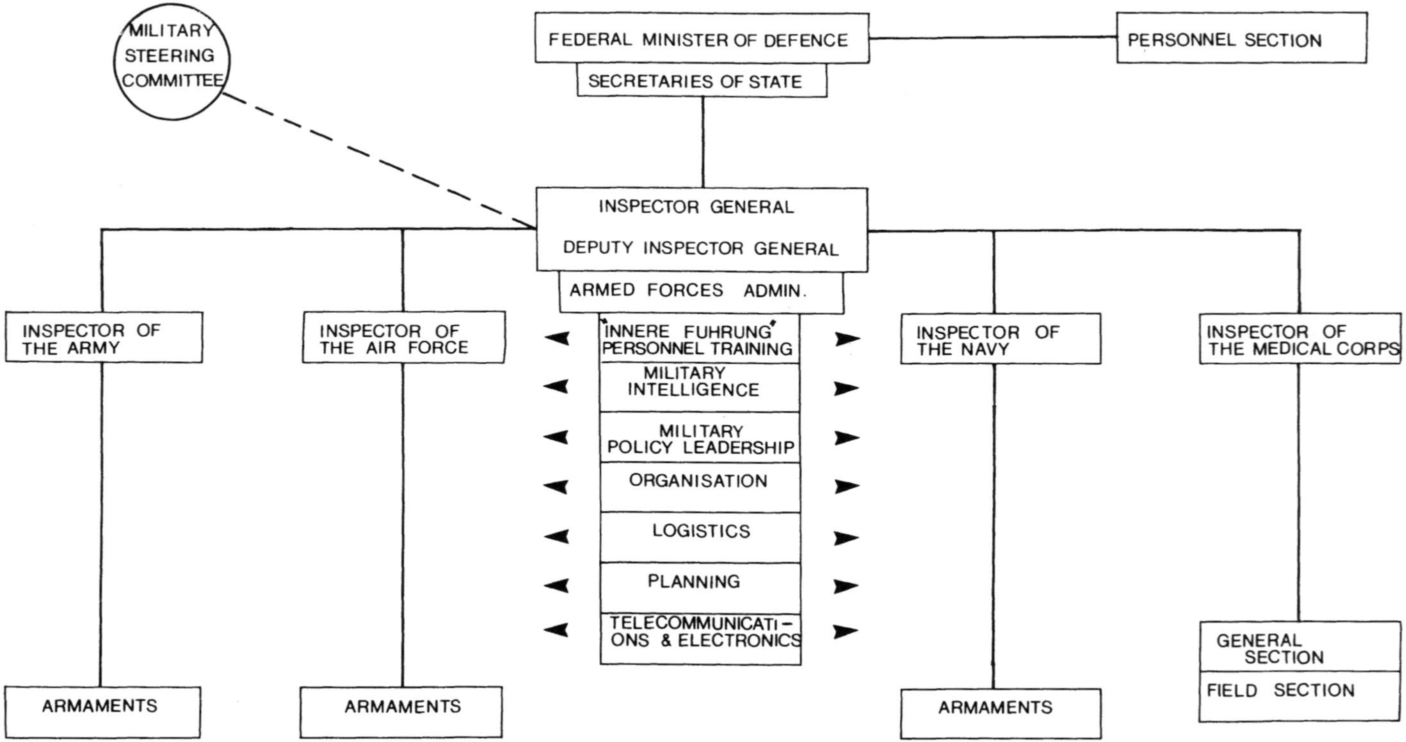

Source: G. Vollmer, *Die Streitkräfte* (1978), p. 90

Figure 4.3   The West German Armed Forces

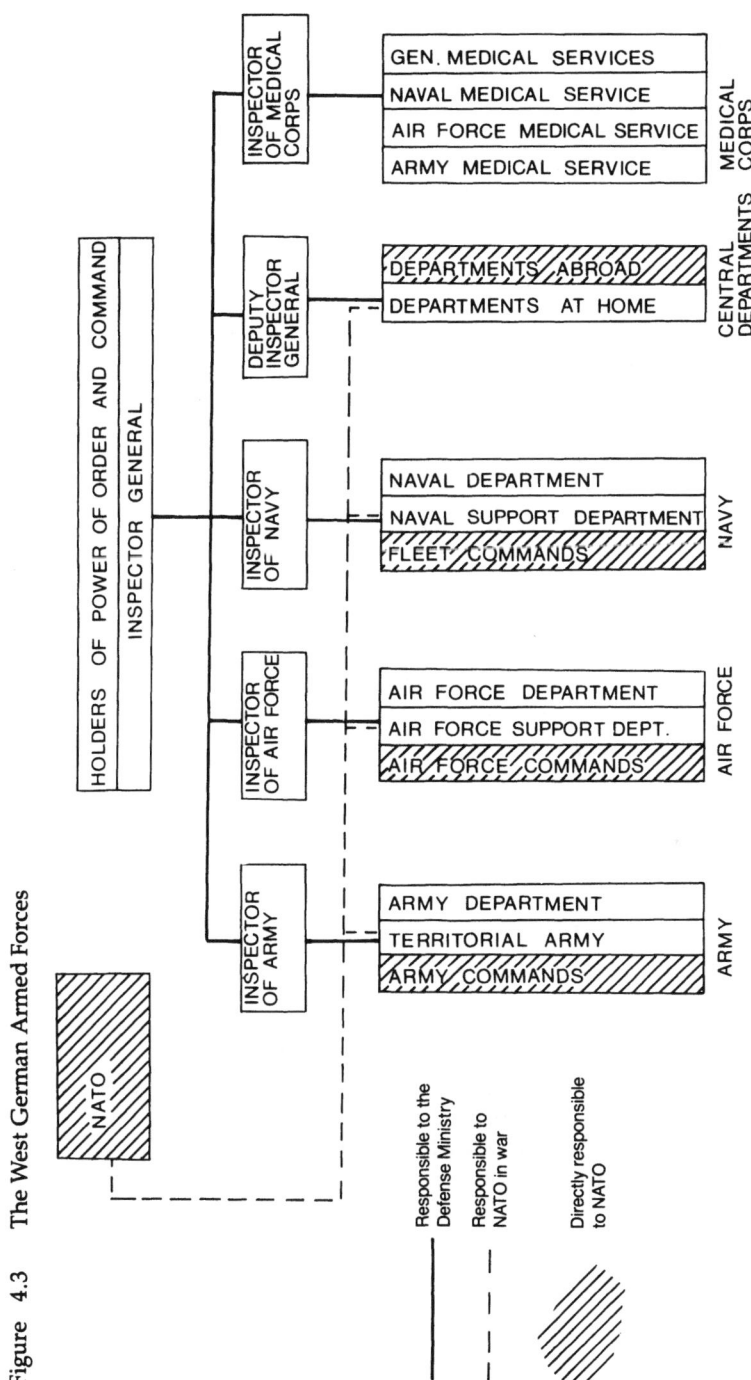

Source: G. Vollmer, *Die Streitkräfte* (1978), p. 92.

Table 4.1
Development of Numbers of Applications for Conscientious Objection

Year	Number
1956–1958	2447
1960	5439
1967	5963
1968	11952
1970	19362
1972	33792
1975	32565
1978	39698
1981	58090
1983 (Jan–June)	46241

Source: A Krolls, *Kriegsdienstverweigerung. Das unbequeme Grundrecht* (Frankfurt, 1980), p. 45; *Antimilitarismus-information*, No. 6 (1982) and No. 1 (1983).

conscription to young women, but it is an idea that is extremely unlikely to be realized. Conversely, the constitutional right to conscientious objection and its exercise by large numbers of young men have had a considerable impact on military planning.

Paradoxically, the right to conscientious objection was put into the Constitution in 1949 when no German armed forces existed. The "Fathers of the Constitution" wanted to erect a barrier against anticipated steps to force Germans to serve in foreign armed forces. After 1955—and as Table 4.1 suggests, especially since the end of the 1960s—conscientious objection has become an openly debated political topic and, in a certain way, an indicator of the degree of defense motivation within civilian society.

Because of the large numbers of accepted conscientious objectors, it is not easy to find occupations or jobs in civilian society in which they can serve their alternative service. The armed forces are concerned by the phenomenon of conscientious objection in at least two ways. First, they are losing many potential high-school draftees (as conscientious objection is a matter of concern mainly for better-educated, middle-class people); and, second, those who apply for conscientious objection while already doing their military service are a bureaucratic nuisance and have a bad effect on morale at the platoon and company levels.

A strong legislative control of the Bundeswehr is secured through the special arrangement of the Defense Committee of the Bundestag. This committee can meet between election periods and can (and frequently did) declare itself an investigatory committee with special investigatory competence.[15] With the exception of the early years of the Bundeswehr and some issues of particular public interest during the following decades, the Bundestag and the Defense Committee have mostly abstained from interfering deeply in military affairs, partly because such interference did not seem to be necessary, and partly because the members of Parliament have had to rely on information from the military bureaucracy.

One constitutional innovation in German Public Law is the institution of the parliamentary defense commissioner (Wehrbeauftragter), a kind of ombudsman. The Wehrbeauftragter functions as an auxiliary organ of the Bundestag in order to guarantee the rights of the individual soldiers (who always have the right to contact his office) and to supervise the implementation of the *innere Fuhrung* concept. He has to report annually to the Bundestag. At first, this institution (which is described in Article 45[b] of the Constitution) was regarded with some skepticism by the officer corps, but it is now widely accepted. The commissioners have dealt with a broad range of problems and thus contributed to the organizational efficiency of the armed forces. The annual reports make interesting reading because they shed light on various internal difficulties of the Bundeswehr. In some cases, the commissioner has influenced the policy of the Ministry of Defense, mainly in areas such as housing problems and social policy, but also in matters of discipline. After some "useful" clashes in the early sixties,[16] the collaboration between the commissioner and the armed forces improved considerably.

Constitutionally Defined Functions of the Bundeswehr

The armed forces of the Federal German Republic are a means for defense (Article 87, section 1). Article 26, section 1 strictly forbids aggression and all preparations for it. Defense, *stricto sensu*, is the fundamental function of the Bundeswehr; all other functions are simply devolved from it. The 1975/76 White Paper describes these functions in the following way:

The defence function means, primarily, deterrence. The Armed Forces, together with allied troops, are to deter any aggressor from using military force, or from threatening with military force. This demands high morale, efficiency, and combat readiness. In time of political tension, or in a crisis, the Armed Forces increase their defence readiness according to the situation and the orders of the political leadership, thus protecting the political manoeuvrability of the government. In cases of a state of emergency, it is the duty of the Armed Forces to repulse, together with allied troops, the aggressor as near to the border as possible, and to regain lost territory. If the aggressor is in a very much superior position, his aggression must be delayed until either the political leadership can stop the military conflict by political means or a further step in defence escalation has been decided on. Territorial troops under national orders protect the operational freedom of NATO-troops.[17]

In the light of NATO's current military strategic principles, the Bundeswehr secures, through deterrence, the establishment and maintenance of peace. The transfer from the normal legal order into a state of emergency is regulated by several articles of the Constitution. They comprise the emergency laws and are now incorporated, following a bitter parliamentary and extraparliamentary debate in the late 1960s, into the Constitution. In a crisis situation, before the official announcement of the state of tension (Spannungsfall, as defined in Article 80, section 1), some of the regulations for emergency may be practiced, but only following a formal decree of the federal government and with the special consent of the Bundestag. It is the Bundestag that confirms the beginning of a state of tension and finally of a state of emergency (Verteidigungsfall). With respect to the latter, Article 115, section 1 determines "the confirmation that the federal territory is under military attack, or that such an attack is due in the near future (state of emergency), is made by the Bundestag with the consent of the Bundesrat." This escalation underlines the character of the Bundeswehr as a political instrument under close political surveillance.

However, the problematic aspects of deterrence as a means of defense, and its degree of compatibility with a defense strategy, if deterrence fails, had hardly been discussed in West Germany until only recently when a partly competent, but for the most part rather emotional, public debate emerged.[18] This debate has continued throughout 1984.

The Military Missions of the Bundeswehr

The military missions of the Bundeswehr are derived from its political missions and are formulated according to the current strategic doctrine. For West Germans, the principle of forward defense is, understandably, of special interest. "Forward defence requires the capability and intention of NATO to respond without delay and with efficiency. The reaction of NATO must prevent a long period of fighting on the territory of the Federal Republic. Such combat would finally destroy the substance of all the values we are defending."[19] The army, with its combat units, must be ready at any time to respond to a surprise attack. Most of those parts of the army that depend on mobilization have to be operational within three days. The three German army corps have positioned their battle sector between the sectors of allied troops. This "stratification" is an expression of alliance solidarity and a political signal to the potential aggressor that it would be attacking not only West Germany, but the alliance itself.

The forces of air defense and air space surveillance are attached to NATO in peacetime. The German Air Force has been given the mission to lead the combat against hostile air forces in such a way as to ensure that the armed forces assigned to NATO and German territory are protected against air attack.

Finally, the navy of the Bundeswehr—a comparatively small service—has the task of protecting the territory of the Federal German Republic against attacks from the sea along its coastline. Furthermore, it has to contribute to the protection of access to the Baltic Sea and the North Sea. The strategic objectives of NATO are to blockade the Atlantic Ocean–Baltic Sea connection and to deny the naval forces of the Warsaw Pact access to control over it.

Following the discussions about the rearmament of West Germany, during which, for a certain time, a national military strategy was put forward as an alternative to Adenauer's course of Western integration, a general consensus about defense requirements for the Federal Republic emerged according to which the country could be adequately protected only if it were a member of the Western Alliance. The geostrategic position of the country, its lack of territorial depth, its limited military capacities, and its interests in a functioning Western economic system made it quite impossible to conceive a national military strategy that would both be internally consistent and could protect the Federal Republic against violence or the threat of violence. This general consensus still exists today, but it is challenged from both extremes of the political spectrum.

The Use of the Armed Forces in Domestic Affairs

"The use of the Bundeswehr against parts of the West German population would always be a sign of the failure of West Germany's political leadership."[20] This sweeping (but certainly correct) statement does not, of course, refer to the activities of the Bundeswehr in cases of natural catastrophe. In the last decade, a handful of such events occurred in which the armed forces have proved very effective and, in the process, gained a kind of nonmilitary popularity in the regions concerned. Furthermore, the task of protecting various civilian facilities in cases of a state of tension or emergency, and the task of traffic control, belong to a set of "normal" military duties of the armed forces. The earlier quotation refers to the cases mentioned in Article 87, section 4 of the Constitution. "In order to prevent an imminent danger to the existence, or to the liberal-democratic basic order, of the Federal Republic or of one of its states the Federal Government may," in accordance with a strictly regulated set of procedures, "use the Bundeswehr as support forces to the State Police and the Bundesgrenzschutz. This use is aimed at protecting civilian targets and to fight organized and armed rebels. The use of the Bundeswehr is to be terminated if one of the two parliamentary bodies requires its termination."

Today, given the considerable stability of the political institutions in the Federal Republic of Germany, nobody seems fanciful enough to design a realistic scenario with regard to the emergence of a situation

Figure 4.4   Common Defense

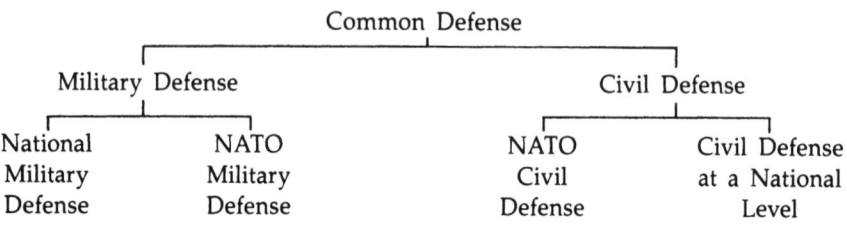

for which Article 87, section 4 could be applicable. When the spirit of the constitutional regulations are translated into a concrete decision-making process, a controlled escalation is evident and follows with four stages of which the first step in the prevention of the danger in question is a matter for the federal states and their police forces. At the second stage, a state under pressure, according to Article 91, section 1, must ask other states and the federal government for support. Then and only then, when all previous measures have proved ineffective, the federal government is given as a third step the authority to use the armed forces. The fourth and last stage is then dominated by the Bundeswehr and, to a lesser degree, by the Bundesgrenzschutz. The forces of the Bundesgrenzschutz have developed during the last fifteen years into a kind of federal police force. Many legal commentaries on the constitutional regulations governing emergencies underline the necessity for restricted action with respect to the use of military forces in domestic situations, as described in Article 87, section 4.

Civil Defense as Part of Common Defense

A modern war in industrialized countries inevitably involves the civilian population in the fighting much more deeply than any "classical war" ever did. Modern industrial societies are particularly vulnerable because of the complexities of their infrastructure and their extreme divisions of labor. Even minor damage may have widespread and devastating consequences.

The Federal Republic of Germany is generally assumed to have only a very limited capacity to prevent any of the damage that a military conflict would bring. Therefore, civil defense plays—at least theoretically—an important part in the framework of common defense. It is, however, a part that can barely be observed, and one that is not dramatically emphasized by those responsible for West Germany's security policy. There is, in spite of this, a clear definition of the tasks of civil defense and an outline of its organizational provisions in the event of war in Central Europe.

Figure 4.5   Tasks of Civil Defense at the National Level

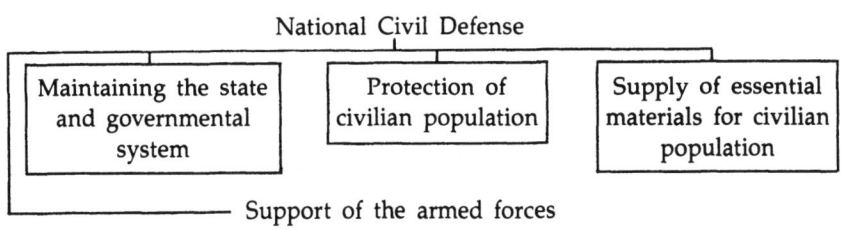

NATO civil defense means, among other things, consultation on and coordination of civil defense, participation in the planning of crisis management, Germany's national contribution to the setting up and activation of civilian war agencies responsible to NATO, and activation of bi- and multilateral agreements on civil defense.

The tasks of civil defense at the national level are outlined in Figure 4.5.

Maintenance of the state and governmental systems involves the following considerations: matters of principle and leadership, overall appraisal of the situation, civilian contingency and early warning plans, psychological defense, training of executive personnel, exercises and analyses, and overall budgetary matters.

The security of the civilian population involves contingency plans, self-preservation, shelters, warning and alarm systems, health services, residence regulations, and the protection of the national heritage. Finally, the supply of essential materials encompasses personnel management, call-up of essential workers, social security, the economic infrastructure, and property. In a general sense, these support functions are designed to ensure the operational freedom and effectiveness of the armed forces.[21]

The highest organ with which to coordinate common defense in the Federal Republic of Germany is the Federal Security Council, a committee of federal ministers with the chancellor as its chairman. The Ministry of the Interior is responsible for the coordination of civil defense measures as part of the common defense. Some special problems of civil defense, however, are consigned to other ministries or to special agencies at the federal or state level.

The legal basis of civil defense is impressively elaborate but not very clearly arranged. A most important part of this legal foundation is, once again, the seventeenth supplement to the Constitution of June 24, 1968: the so-called Emergency Constitution. Nonetheless, the Federal Republic of Germany does not spend much money on civil defense, which commands only a small fraction of the total defense budget. A general evaluation of civil defense in the Federal Republic leads to the conclusion that it has not yet found its proper, or commensurate, place within the overall framework of the common defense.

National and International Aspects
of Defense Organization

In this survey, primarily the normative-constitutional aspect of West German central defense organizations has been considered. This is certainly an important aspect, but a more comprehensive study would include a functional approach—not so much because of a supposed contradiction between normative theory and the actual process of everyday decisions, but because of the relevance of organizational routines in "normal times." It is, for example, a frequent observation in the literature of political science regarding the political system of the Federal German Republic that the Bundestag and the Defense Committee only marginally influence the elaboration and control of West German security policy.[22] In comparison with the executive agencies, a rather small group of MPs, defense journalists, and scientists with a professional interest in security matters has more influence, in general, than the formal institutions of civilian control.

The planning of defense policies and force goals today involves a process that operates at both the national and international levels. The international level seems to be of greater importance for the Federal German Republic. Decisions about the planning of the German Armed Forces and strategic concepts in the Federal German Republic are, of course, centered in the Ministry of Defense, but they are also closely related to the military and political institutions of NATO. Within the Defense Ministry the planning of the size, structure, and composition of the Bundeswehr is accomplished primarily by the following sections: the General Administration of the Armed Forces, the individual administration of the three services, the Finance Department, and the Armaments Department.

Basic data for internal alliance planning consist of military assessments, economic appreciations, a political analysis of the following five-year period, force proposals from major NATO commanders, and the force goals of NATO members whose realization is incorporated in an annual Defense Planning Questionnaire. NATO's Defense Planning Committee has overall responsibility for these activities. In the Federal Republic of Germany, these international connections are perceived not as an interference in internal affairs, but as welcome guarantees for the multinationality of West German defense goals.

By way of conclusion, it can thus be noted that what was initially predominantly regarded as a means of controlling the West German defense contribution to the Western alliance has today developed into an opportune international structuring of West Germany's defense organization.

Notes

1. Hedley Bull, *The Anarchical Society: A Study of Order in World Politics* (London: Macmillan, 1977), p. 189.

2. I am indebted to Mr. Tjark Roessler of the Federal Ministry of Defense for his valuable remarks and suggestions. But it should be noted that this survey does not reflect his, or the Ministry's, positions on the questions raised in it.

3. A very instructive book on the diplomatic wrestling about West German rearmament is Robert McGeehan, *The German Rearmament Question: American Diplomacy and European Defense After World War II* (Urbana: University of Illinois Press, 1971).

4. See Militargeschichtliches Forschungsamt (ed.), *Verteidigung im Bundnis, Planung, Aufbau und Bewahrung der Bundeswehr 1950–1972* (Munich: Bernard and Graefe, 1975).

5. The figures in this chapter come mainly from *White Paper 1979, The Security of the Federal Republic of Germany and the Development of the Bundeswehr* (Bonn, 1979); and Gunter Vollmer, *Die Streitkrafte* (Regensburg: Walhalla and Praetoria, 1978). Recent figures, when published, were considered.

6. See Gwyn Harries-Jenkins, Jurgen Kuhlmann, and Tjarck Roessler, "The Limits of Conscription: The German Case," in G. Harries-Jenkins (ed.), *Armed Forces and the Welfare Societies: Challenges in the 1980s* (London: Macmillan, 1982), pp. 96–123.

7. Federal Ministry of Defense, *The Role of the Federal Republic of Germany in NATO* (Bonn, 1982), p. 2 of Annex.

8. *Innere Fuhrung* is translated as "moral leadership" by Gordon A. Craig in the chapter entitled "Soldiers" in his lucid book, *The Germans* (New York: New American Library, 1983), p. 245.

9. The author of this definition is the former Inspector General Ulrich de Maiziere. In West Germany, discussion about the *innere Fuhrung* concept has produced a huge number of studies about it. A useful survey from a moderate, reform-oriented, former general is the book by Carl-Gero von Ilsemann, *Die Bundeswehr in der Demokratie: Zeit der Inneren Fuhrung* (Hamburg: R. V. Decker's Verlag G. Schenck, 1971).

10. See Note 8.

11. The best-known officer of the reform group in the Dienststelle Blank and the Ministry of Defense was Wolf Count von Baudissin. He was undoubtedly the intellectual head of this group. Cf. his books: *Soldat fur den Frieden: Entwurfe fur eine zeitgemasse Bundeswehr* (Munich: Piper, 1969); *Nie Wieder Sieg! Programmatische Schriften 1951–1981* (Munich: Piper, 1982).

12. Gunter Walpuski and Dieter O. A. Wolf, *Einfuhrung in die Sicherheitspolitik* (Munich: Oldenbourg, 1979), p. 184.

13. A comprehensive (but not exactly breathtaking) study on the constitutional aspects of the problems of Befehls-und-Kommandogewalt is Klaus Hornung, *Staat und Armee: Studien zur Befehls-und Kommandogewalt und zum politisch-militarischen Verhaltnis in der Bundesrepublik Deutschland* (Mainz: v. Hase & Koehler, 1975).

14. Wolf Count von Baudissin, "Armed Forces and Society in the Federal Republic of Germany," in *The Development of the Military Profession in International Perspective: Report of the Military-Sociological Congress at the Hague* (May 1982), p. 25.

15. See Hans-Joachim Berg, *Der Verteidigungsausschuss des Deutschen Bundestages: Kontrollorgan zwischen Macht und Ohnmacht* (Munich: Bernard and Graefe, 1982).

16. See Wilfired v. Bredow, *Der Primat militarischen Denkens* (Cologne: Sammlung Junge Wissenschaft, 1969); Wolfgang R. Vogt, *Militar und Demokratie: Funktionen und Konflikte der Institution des Wehrbeauftragten* (Hamburg: R. V. Decker's Verlag G. Schenck, 1972).

17. *White Paper 1975/76*, "The Security of the Federal Republic of Germany and the Development of the Bundeswehr (Bonn, 1976), p. 86.

18. Some useful studies are, among others: Horst Afheldt, *Verteidigung und Frieden: Politik mit militarischen Mitteln* (Munich: Hanser, 1976); K. Peter Stratmann, *NATO-Strategie in der Krise? Miliarische Optionen von NATO und Warschauer Pakt in Mitteleuropa* (Baden-Baden: Nomos, 1981); Franz Uhle-Wettler, *Gefechtsfeld Mitteleuropa* (Munich: Bernard and Graefe, 1980).

19. *White Paper 1975/76*, p. 87.

20. Knut Ipsen, "Der Einsatz der Bundeswehr zur Verteidigung, im Spannungs- und Verteidigungsfall sowie im inernen bewaffneten Konflikt," in K. D. Schwarz (ed.), *Sicherheitspolitik: Analysen zur politischen und militarischen Sicherheit* (Bad Honnef: Osang, 1977, 2d printing), p. 435.

21. *White Paper on Civil Defence* (Bonn, 1972), pp. 20, 21. See also the *Brochure Zivilschutz heute* (Bonn, 1980, 2d printing).

22. Helga Haftendorn, "Management der Sicherheitspolitik: Ein Beitrag zum Entscheidungsprozess der Bundesrepublik Deutschland," in: Schwarz, *Sicherheitspolitik*, pp. 339–384.

5

Central Organizations of Defence in Great Britain

Martin Edmonds

The development of the central organization for defence in Great Britain since the end of World War II was characterized in 1971 by Professor Michael Howard, arguably the country's foremost exponent of the subject, as a reflection of the dialectic between two contrasting conceptions, or models. On the one hand were the advocates of the "Hankey" model, who argued the case for separate and independent departments of government responsible for each of the three armed services; on the other were supporters of the "Mountbatten" school, who looked to a single Ministry of Defence with functional responsibility, a single chief of Defence Staff with functional responsibilities across the board for operational matters, and *in toto*, "a system of total central-isation."[1] At that time, eight years after the most radical reorganization of the Central Organisation of Defence since the war,[2] the judgment was that Britain had "reached a position midway between the two models" and the question was reasonably posed whether, given the circumstances, both military and political, the right balance had been reached.

Although the consensus among those who considered this question at the time was that further centralization and functionalism would be a retrograde step, as a clear distinction had to be respected between military concerns and priorities (and among the three services) and the Ministry of Defence as a civilian organization, "the process of unification and of developing a defence-wide approach" continued, albeit at a gradual pace. In view of the various developments and piecemeal reorganizations that took place between 1963 and 1983, the Conservative government resolved to thoroughly review the Central Organisation of Defence and "to make proposals for its further evolution to meet the challenge of today's circumstances."[3] In March 1984 the secretary of state for defence (SSD) circulated a consultative document that invited comment on new proposals for a system of management information modeled on practices already in operation in other government ministries; this was followed in July 1984 by the publication of a White Paper outlining, inter alia, proposed changes to the central organization for defence. In essence the White Paper not merely reaffirmed the development toward the Mountbatten model of functional centralization that had taken place after 1963 but took the trend a significant stage further by reducing yet again the standing of the three services. This change was effected by subordinating the three service chiefs of staff to a chief of defence staff (CDS), who would act as the government's principal military adviser.[4]

The July 1984 White Paper generated a roar of protest from the service chiefs of staff, who exercised their traditional right to approach the prime minister directly. In part their objection was to the apparently precipitate and secretive way that the proposals had been announced, without, they felt, adequate prior discussion and consultation with the parties most immediately affected—principally themselves. But more significantly, they were tendering what would appear to be the final line of resistance to the reduction in service influence over the content and direction of defence policy to that of a second line of advice. To understand and appreciate the depth of resistance to the reorganization and the issues surrounding it, it is helpful to go back to the period immediately following the military defeat of Germany and Japan when the seeds of the central issues concerning the central organization in Britain were first sown.

The lessons of World War II were several and varied, but arguably the most important was that future conventional wars would be fought by means of combined operations by the three services; thus the central organization for defence should take this fact firmly into consideration.[5] The organization proposed in the government's 1946 White Paper on the Central Organisation for Defence, however, did not depart radically from what already existed or go as far as many would have wished. Indeed, the Attlee government almost took pride in the fact that "the proposals [did] not involve any drastic break with the past and were rather designed to carry a stage further the process of steady evolution through which [the] central organisation for defence has developed during the past forty years."[6] In fact the reorganization largely institutionalized the machinery that had been set up under Winston Churchill's wartime leadership, in which he combined the executive offices of both the prime minister and (although it was undefined) the minister of defence. The War Cabinet contained two defence committees, one for operations and one for supply, with a common secretariat, and through Churchill's dual role a unified defence policy was achieved. However, the three service chiefs of staff were separately responsible for the operational conduct of their respective services and each was a member of the Defence Committee (Operations), which directed military policy. Although a Chiefs of Staff Committee existed (as it had since 1942) and a Joint Planning Committee and Joint Intelligence Committee had been established, "everything else was done within the separate Service Ministries themselves."[7]

The 1946 reorganization regarded the idea of a combined General Staff as being inferior to the Chiefs of Staff Committee and Joint Staff system because, on the strength of the German experience with the OKW (Obercommando der Wehrmacht), "the cleavage between planning and execution could set up dangerous antagonisms."[8] Likewise, the idea of a single Defence Ministry as a logical development of the service cooperation established during the war and "as a means of giving full play to scientific development in weapons" was rejected as a step that, although envisaged at a later stage, could not and should not be taken then. The basis of this judgment was that it was "a cardinal principle of the British organisation that it should be the men responsible in the Service Departments for carrying out the approved policy who are brought together in the central machine to formulate it."[9] Since the prime minister presided over the Defence Committee of the Cabinet, and, ex-officio, chaired meetings of the Chiefs of Staff Committee, an independent chairman of the Chiefs of Staff Committee was not considered necessary to ensure political control over defence.

The 1946 Central Organisation for Defence clearly laid down the basic principles underlying British postwar defence management, principles that have continually been challenged and debated, and constantly modified since then. They were principles with which some fundamentally disagreed from the outset. An early critic was Field Marshal Lord Montgomery, who argued that the coordination between the services and the relationship with central political leadership that had worked well in war would break down in peacetime as partisan service interests assumed higher priority.[10] In 1948 his view was confirmed when it appeared that "each Service [had] developed within itself a system which provides for specialisation where it is wanted and yet ensures overall unity in direction. But the fact remains that we have not achieved for the three Services in combination a system which is comparable to that which each Service has evolved for itself. . . . We need a unified defence policy."[11] Sharing this view, Air Vice-Marshal E. J. Kingston-McCloughry argued later that too much attention was paid to the traditions and inhibitions of the services "at the expense of the concept that they are three elements of a single force."[12]

Prime Minister Clement Attlee, a prewar critic of duplication and waste caused by the lack of central control over the three services, was nonetheless conservative in his outlook regarding postwar structural reform; provided that the reorganization of defence achieved the immediate aim of economy, decisions regarding the degree of autonomy of the services were to be dictated by considerations of pragmatism and moderation.[13] The result, based on the recommendations of an advisory group led by Churchill's chief of staff, General Lord Ismay, was the creation of a new Ministry of Defence headed by a minister whose function was "the apportionment of available resources between the three Services in accordance with the strategic policy laid down by the Defence Committee; framing general policy to govern research and development and the correlation of production of programmes; and settling questions of general administration on which a common policy for the three Services was desirable." Although these functions were detailed in the White Paper and the ensuing Ministry of Defence Act that took effect in January 1947, the overall impression made by the new organization was that the defence minister could exercise only very limited authority. The prime minister was the ultimate person responsible for policy and the chiefs of staff for its execution. Further, the chiefs of staff were to present, "directly and personally," advice on the technical aspects of strategy and plans to the Defence Committee and the Cabinet, thus bypassing the minister of defence. The execution of policy was explicitly left with the service ministries, which remained untouched in the reorganization and retained their traditional responsibility to Parliament for their appropriated expenditures. The minister of defence, heading a small ministerial department, would therefore account to Parliament only on matters common to the three services, such as research, development, production, central administration, joint intelligence, combined operations, home security, and, with the Chiefs of Staff Committee, strategic planning.[14]

The stress placed on the 1946 Central Defence Organisation was more on what the minister of defence could not do than what he could;[15] the future of the new Ministry of Defence as a coordinating body, rather than as a link in the chain of responsibility between the service chiefs and the Defence Committee, therefore depended on the personalities of those appointed to serve as defence minister. With this somewhat loose—and, some would argue, fragmented—arrangement in which responsibility for the direction and execution of defence was never clearly defined, Britain's defence decisionmakers faced the new challenges of the postwar world.[16]

By the mid-1950s it had become clear that the new central defence structure was not up to the challenge, partly because of the nature of the changed circumstances and partly because of the inherent weaknesses in the system. With regard to the former, the problems associated with the development, production, and control over nuclear weapons, the rapid increases in the costs and technical complexity of new weapons, Britain's involvement in the Western Alliance, the Korean rearmament program, the retreat from Empire, and the ever-increasing pressures to effect overall economies in defence while improving military efficiency and reducing waste and duplication not only exposed inherent organizational weaknesses but raised questions as to where, and at what level, responsibility lay for the planning and execution of defence policy.

The inherent weaknesses of the central defence system exposed by these factors were that the service chiefs were the only ones with independent briefs; conversely, both the chairman of the Chiefs of Staff Committee (first appointed in 1955) and the minister of defence lacked any clear definition of their responsibilities, and the Joint Service Staffs had a dual allegiance—to their Services, on the one hand, and to the

Ministry of Defence, on the other, with the former taking priority.[17] Pressure for further reorganization toward centralization of control steadily increased and led, in 1955, first to the appointment of a chairman of the Chiefs of Staff Committee, who was to link the chiefs of staff more closely with the minister of defence; second, a new Defence Committee of the Cabinet, with a wider defence brief; and, third, a strengthening of the power of the defence minister by increasing the size of his department and expanding his function to include responsibility for the composition and balance of the armed forces—"a responsibility which implied certain powers of initiative."[18]

Two factors weighed heavily against an acceleration of the centralization of defence at the time. The first was the steady increase in the powers of the services and the service ministries, which had carried the responsibilities for all the changes after 1945 from demobilization to long-term weapons programs. The second was the sheer political strength of the services, in terms of both their relationship with Parliament and their own professionalism, traditions, and public standing. Any pressure for greater interservice cooperation in the planning and execution of combined operations, as indeed were being taught in the service academies, was quickly recast in terms of total integration into a single "defence force" and "mud-coloured uniforms," with all the prejudice and resistance that such interpretations implied. Belief systems are hard to break down, and the belief in the uniqueness of separate service problems, requirements, and solutions, to say nothing of centuries of military and naval—almost "tribal"—traditions, should not be underestimated.

One principle of parliamentary democracy is that "no one should exercise power without authority and [this] is a rule of life which applies with even more force to military affairs than civilian."[19] In the mid-1950s this principle came under scrutiny with respect to operational control of the Suez invasion in 1956. The ad hoc arrangements whereby the prime minister, Sir Anthony Eden, assumed responsibility through his minister of defence and the chairman of the Chiefs of Staff Committee for the operation as a whole, with direct links to the commander-in-chief on the spot, not only bypassed the service ministries, but also provided the foundation for the reorganization of central defence outlined in the Central Organisation of Defence White Paper of July 1958.[20] A second factor hastened the reorganization: The new prime minister, Harold Macmillan, had earlier served as minister of defence and during his time in office had made abundantly clear his frustration at being impotent relative to the service ministries. It was therefore no surprise that, along with his minister of defence, Duncan Sandys, he pressed through organizational reforms. Initially, this was achieved through Sandys's force of personality, backed by the prime minister's authority, as had been provided for in the 1946 White Paper, but this time it was followed with institutional reform.

It was widely expected that the Macmillan/Sandys reforms would reduce the service ministers to the level of ministers of state and that the Ministry of Supply would disappear, but neither happened. Of any organizational significance was the creation of a chief of defence staff, with his own personal staff, who would serve the defence minister as his chief of staff, as well as a redefinition of the defence minister's brief making him responsible for, as opposed to coordinator of, "the formulations and applications of a unified policy relating to the Armed Forces as a whole and their requirements."[21]

Pragmatism, however, dictated what could structurally be achieved; the recasting of Britain's defence policy announced in the 1957 "Defence: Outline of Future Policy" White Paper was as much as the system could wear. Even so, the full weight of service and parliamentary opposition was brought to bear, including the familiar specters of the integration— and emasculation—of the services and of a defence minister "supremo." Nevertheless, the authority of the defence minister had been established in the 1957 White Paper, which, in the teeth of service opposition, had ended conscription, substantially reduced the size of the army, curtailed the future airplane projects of the air force, and redefined the role of the navy to that of an antisubmarine force. With the political emphasis on effecting necessary economies while balancing future commitments with capabilities, no further institutional reorganization was thought to be necessary, provided that the advice given to the minister was unbiased and that his authority was unchallenged.

The furor caused by the 1957 Defence White Paper continued well into the 1960s as the three services separately, and sometimes collectively, lobbied to get a number of policy decisions affecting them reversed. It was an unsettled period both within the Ministry of Defence and the separate service ministries, but one that served to highlight the central issue regarding defence policy: who ultimately exercised control. With further pressure for economy, and as the National Service finally wound down in 1961, it was inevitable that a closer look would be taken at possible areas for further service integration. In 1960, for example, the Commons Select Committee on Estimates recommended on grounds of economy that the forces' medical services should be merged, but this was strenuously—and successfully—opposed by the services as being impractical on operational grounds.[22]

The distinction between policy control over such matters as the "shape, organisation, and disposition of the Armed Forces, their equipment and supply (including research and development) and their pay and conditions of service," on the one hand, and operational control over the services, on the other, was, however, never fully resolved. Nor was it likely to be while the services retained their own ministers and received separate appropriations. As one observer noted, "the Defence Ministry has been superimposed upon the Services, and has not grown organically out of them."[23] To make matters worse, there was an increasing awareness that in the wake of the radical changes to Britain's defence posture, "the machine has not wanted the right things at the right time. It has done badly on both ends and means. . . . The only way to remedy this is to exercise a clear choice between options in a full knowledge of the facts, [but] the whole organisation of defence . . . makes this virtually impossible."[24]

Impetus for change can come from within or outside an organization, or it may be a combination of both. During the period leading up to the reorganization of Britain's central organization of defence in 1963, the main driving force undoubtedly came from within, and for the most part from the chief of defence staff (CDS), Lord Mountbatten. He was acutely aware of two central problems within the defence system. The first was that the minister of defence could only try and coordinate the activities of the services and their ministries and did not control them, and that his capacity to do so successfully depended on force of personality; the second was that he, as the CDS, and the department's chief scientific adviser, Sir Solly Zuckerman, were having to operate in virtual isolation from the services. He resolved, therefore, to take the initiative to rectify these weaknesses by proposing that the central organization of defence should be radically restructured. This, from his perspective, entailed strengthening the Ministry of Defence at the expense of the service ministries, and was an objective that would require all his inside knowledge of both the services and Whitehall and the fullest use of his own tactical skills to accomplish.[25] With a long service career behind him in the navy, Mountbatten well understood the strength of the opposition to his envisaged reforms, which included the abolition of both the service ministries and the service chiefs of staff.[26] However, he never disguised his objectives, and went on record at an early stage opposing the development of strong service ministries "since defence problems are interlocking and needed central direction from the top."[27]

Ultimately, the task of restructuring the central organization of defence rested with the minister of defence at the time, Peter Thorneycroft, who took office in 1962. Once persuaded, presumably by Mountbatten's authority and arguments, of the urgent need for reform, Thorneycroft invited two retired generals, Lord Ismay and Sir Ian Jacob, to advise him on any changes, and to "put into perspective some of the objections about the central control of defence and the more prevalent fallacies about it."[28] The choice of advisers was indicative of Thorneycroft's "evolutionary" approach, although Jacob had earlier, in 1956, indicated that he favored the integration of the services at the highest level under a single defence minister.

Within weeks, rather than months, the Jacob-Ismay Report was complete. On March 4, 1963, Thorneycroft announced to the Commons "one of the most important constitutional changes" in the postwar era.[29] At the end of his statement the consensus was that a working compromise had been found whereby the interests of greater central control over defence had been met while avoiding the more revolutionary and politically sensitive ideas contained in the Mountbatten blueprint. In essence, the services' opposition had been blunted by their being unable to claim that their individual character and identity had been jeopardized, even if in the process they were to lose some of their separate prestige and influence.

The details of the restructured central organization for defence were contained in a White Paper dated July 1963. The principles upon which the new structure was based stipulated that (1) control over defence policy required greater knowledge . . . than could be secured with four separate departments responsible to separate ministers; (2) the secretary of state for defence (SSD) should have complete control over both defence policy and the administration of the three services; (3) the services should preserve their separate identities, despite increasing interdependence; (4) the Ministry of Defence should be organized on a defence rather than a single-service basis; (5) policy and management could not be isolated from each other; and (6) the new organization should be flexible.[30] In line with these principles, the Ministry of Defence, now to be headed by a secretary of state, would be responsible for "all questions of policy and administration which concern the fighting Services as the instruments of an integrated strategy." Overall strategic policy, with defence seen in the context of other government priorities, was to be the responsibility of a Cabinet Defence and Overseas Policy Committee (DOPC), to be chaired by the prime minister with the chiefs of staff and the CDS "in attendance." The traditional right of the chiefs of staff to have direct access to the prime minister was, nonetheless, preserved.

The most radical change, which was to have constitutional implications, was the demise of the separate ministries for the armed services—the Admiralty, the War Office, and the Air Ministry—each of whose statutory powers was to be subsumed within a single Ministry of Defence under a secretary of state. Disappearing with them were the separate service councils (although in the navy's case, this was to cause some terminological difficulties that only Mountbatten's royal connections were able to resolve).[31] In their place, three ministers of state for defence and three parliamentary under-secretaries were to be appointed with responsibilities to be defined by the SSD.

At the top of the new structure, a Defence Council was established to "exercise the powers of command and administrative control previously exercised by the Board of Admiralty and by the Army and Air Councils." With the SSD as chairman, it was to comprise the three ministers of state, the CDS, the three chiefs of staff, the chief scientific adviser (CSA), and the permanent under-secretary (PUS). Whereas the Defence Council was to deal with major defence policy issues, defence management was delegated to the army, navy, and air force boards of the Defence Council, each to be chaired by the SSD or, by delegation, one of the ministers of state. Within the Ministry itself, the principal advisers to the SSD were to be the CDS, the CSA, and the PUS, each with his respective staff.

On the military side, the Chiefs of Staff Committee remained untouched. It was to continue to be chaired by the CDS and was "collectively responsible to the Government for professional advice on strategy and military operations, and on the military implications of defence policy." Through the CDS, the service chiefs were to be responsible for military operations. Finally, the service staffs, with the existing joint service staffs, were to form the basis of a Defence Headquarters Staff. Responsible to the CDS, this Defence Staff was to have the "corporate duty to find the best defence solutions to the problems with which they are faced." This was to be accomplished through four new organizations: a Defence Operations Executive (DOE), a Defence Signals Staff (DSS), a Defence Intelligence Staff (DIS), and a Defence Operations Requirements Staff (DORS). All four were to work alongside the existing Joint Planning and Joint Warfare Staffs in the same building.[32]

Perhaps the most symbolic change was the colocation of the more senior service staffs within a single building, vacated for the purpose by the Board of Trade. Although the services retained their old buildings, at least the top political, administrative, and service personnel were under one roof. However, colocation and functional distribution of responsibility does not necessarily lead to greater cooperation, understanding, or integration. It did not happen when the U.S. Armed Services went into the Pentagon, custom built for the purpose, and there was no reason to suppose why, in Britain, with longer-established service traditions, it should happen overnight.

One aspect of defence reorganization that received less attention at the time was the supply side, but it was one that was increasingly to become a focus of concern. As pressures for economy and efficiency mounted, so also did the unit costs and complexity of weapons and weapons systems specified by the three services. In the competition for scarce resources, modern weapons became not only the symbols of interservice rivalry and, ultimately, of their prestige, but also that area in which the services assumed a prerogative. This was most evident during the period following the 1957 Defence White Paper when several major weapons development programs were canceled, and again after the 1962 Nassau Agreement, which determined that it was the navy that was to assume the mantle of the country's independent deterrent force in the early 1970s with the U.S. Polaris system as the successor to the air force's "V" bomber strike force.

Until 1959, the responsibility for supplying the service departments— although the Admiralty operated somewhat differently and independently from the others—rested with the Ministry of Supply (MOS). Within the MOS, separate controllers operated with virtual autonomy to meet the requirements of the army and the air force. In 1959, the MOS was reorganized and its army-related responsibilities were transferred to the Ministry of Defence. Its air force–related activities, however, were passed to a new Ministry of Aviation, which also assumed a responsibility for the civil side of aviation. The general feeling was that the MOS had

had only a marginal, and for the most part neutral, influence on defence policy. The RAF disagreed, believing the MOS to be a barrier to its interests. After 1959, however, the reorganization effectively meant that the three services each had its own procurement agency. The challenge, therefore, was to ensure the appropriate level of funding for their requirements from the total resources available to the MOD.[33] Somewhat unexpectedly, the 1963 reorganization made little attempt to incorporate the Ministry of Aviation into the MOD. Such a move, it was claimed, would generate "a heavy additional load." Instead, it was thought adequate to colocate Ministry of Aviation personnel with responsibility for managing defence programs within the Ministry of Defence building itself, space permitting.[34]

The 1963 reorganization was not without its critics. The more perceptive among them anticipated that an insufficient effort had been made to curb the tendency of the services to pursue their separate interests, especially in acquiring new weapons, and that the CDS and the chiefs of staff, as executors of policy and advisers on policy right up to Cabinet level, still did not have the checks to prevent or limit their influence on the content and direction of stragetic and defence policy. The *Economist* at the time was pessimistic; "there seems to be far too much genuflection in the White Paper to the old tripartite Service order. . . . The whole scheme could too easily degenerate into a system for perpetuating . . . the old compromises on small matters of administration and securing unification only in some high policy decisions where unification could sometimes be most idiosyncratic."[35] A more penetrating criticism was made by Alastair Buchan, director of the Institute for Strategic Studies in London, who noted that the weak link in the capacity of the SSD to direct his department was the relatively junior role assigned to the person in charge of budgetary control. Without strong financial control, Buchan felt, central assessment and control of competing (service) claims and ideas on resources, weapons, roles, and strategies over time would be difficult, if not impossible.[36] Ultimately, the success of the Mountbatten-Thorneycroft reforms depended on those involved, but, as a *Times* editorial noted, "the Whitehall revolution has its Robespierre [i.e., Mountbatten]: it will be interesting to see how many Dantons emerge from the Service Ministries."[37]

When presenting his case before the Commons, Thorneycroft noted that the previous system had not given the SSD adequate control over defence spending, and that an integrated defence policy was hard to formulate because of "the natural tendency of three proud and great Services to consider problems of national defence from separate, individual points of view."[38] However, the strength of the services' lobby proved too much for the original provisions of the Defence (Transfer of Functions) Bill. Following both the debate in the House[39] and, assuredly, the arguments put to him by the service chiefs, Thorneycroft agreed after some struggle[40] to a compromise with the opponents of a unified defence structure: Instead of having three ministers of state for defence with functional responsibilities, there were to be three full ministers, one for each of the services, "as they would be dealing with high officers and important aspects of policy."[41] Although these service ministers would not be members of the DOPC, the increase in their status would ensure easier access to it and thereby increase service influence at the highest defence and strategy policymaking levels.

The answer to the question as to whether or not the SSD and his central defence decisionmaking staffs could exercise greater control over policy, defence spending, and service management was soon to be found when the Labour party under Harold Wilson formed the government in 1964, and Dennis Healey was appointed head of the Ministry of Defence. The Labour party was committed to reducing the burden of defence spending, and Healey was charged with the task of reviewing Britain's defence commitments with a view to reducing the overall defence burden on the national economy. Included in his review was a commitment to rationalize the organizational structure of defence along functional lines. Early reorganization along these lines included the apportionment of the responsibility for Britain's relations with the NATO, CENTO, and SEATO military alliances to the three defence ministers and, in line with the recommendations of the Nye Committee on War Office reorganization, the merger of the four army arms directors under a single director for army equipment policy.[42] These were followed both by the appointment of a committee to investigate ways of rationalizing "the control and employment of aircraft for all three Services to the greatest possible extent," the recommendations of which were implemented in 1965, and by a functional reorganization of Defence Intelligence.[43] Even at this early stage the decision was taken to close down the Ministry of Aviation and bring the procurement of military aircraft into the Ministry of Defence, although the responsibility for research and development to meet service and MOD specifications was to be assumed by a new Ministry of Technology.[44]

Throughout this transition period, the SSD was at pains to emphasize that functional reorganization would not affect the existing identities of the three services. The 1964–1965 defence review, which focused mainly on policy, service roles, equipment, and long-term costings with a view to achieving significant economies, was put to the test where the balance of influence and power lay, especially with respect to the cancellation of several major Service equipment programs. Although the services lost most of these equipment battles, they did score two significant victories. A MOD committee established to inquire into the structure of the Ministry of Defence—namely, the Geraghty Committee—had recommended the abolition of the service ministers, but this was argued out. The second of the services' successes was its defeat of the government's attempt to integrate the three service headquarters organizations on purely practical grounds. This failure, however, served only to point the way to further integration of the services along functional lines, step by step, according to the dictates of the overall defence budget, the need for economy, and changes in the defence environment. The introduction of piecemeal integration along functional lines is what in fact happened. Whatever his preference Healey—though a confirmed functionalist—deferred any major structural reform and adopted a purely pragmatic approach. He was evidently not prepared to repeat the experience of 1965 when, as a consequence of major cuts to the navy's shipbuilding program, the minister for the navy, Christopher Mayhew, and his chief of naval staff resigned, causing considerable disruption in the process.

It has been suggested that Healey's strong personality, coupled with a detailed knowledge of defence matters, enabled him to dominate his colleagues and obviate the need for central structural reform "because he could manage the machine without it."[45] The trend toward functional reorganization, albeit a piecemeal process, nevertheless continued unabated and enjoyed the backing of Healey himself, especially given that it furthered his objective of exercising better financial control and improving the long-term costings of defence options. In January 1967, the three service ministers were reduced in status to that of undersecretary of state, and in their place two functional ministers, one for Administration and one for Equipment, were established.[46] It is generally believed that their change in status had been one of the recommendations of the Geraghty Committee. However, these two functional ministers, with their respective staffs, barely impinged on the powers of the service chiefs. Superimposed, as they were, over the existing three-service structure within the ministry, the new ministerial posts did little more than expand a functional ministerial structure to direct and control three nonfunctionalized services.

Functionalism and functional costings became the catchwords from 1967 onward. An early interest was directed to the command structure of the three services, and by 1968 the existing army and navy geographical commands were reorganized along functional lines. The RAF's bomber and fighter commands were merged into one Strike Reconnaissance and Defence Command to reflect the "teeth," as opposed to the "tail," elements of the service.[47] By means of these structural changes, economies in manpower and administrative costs were expected to be achieved. By 1968, it could therefore be concluded (even though there had been no significant reorganization at the center, which incorporated the services), that the locus of influence had shifted from the services and the chiefs of staff to the SSD, mainly because he, alone, ultimately had the authority to allocate—and withhold—funding at a time when it was becoming increasingly tight. Indeed, the SSD and his civilian advisers were perceived to have become so powerful that many felt there should be some check on him. For this, they looked to the chiefs of staff, speaking from their respective positions of responsibility for the implementation of defence policy decisions.

Although the three services each continued to have separate budgets and votes, each had a (second) PUS accountable for how they spent their appropriations, and the extent to which functional reorganization would have the desired effect remained limited. It was therefore inevitable that the next organizational change, announced in February 1968, would change the system of budgeting and accounting from a triservice one to a single defence budget, each with a second PUS for administration and for equipment serving as the accounting officers, and would combine the separate service planning staffs into a single central defence planning staff. Arguably, this was the most significant change of all, yet Healey took time off to reassure the chiefs of staff that this development still represented only the integration of the Defence Civil Service Staffs, and that there was "no question of a single Armed Service, and certainly not in his lifetime."[48]

Healey had been at the helm of the Ministry of Defence during six years of extreme economic stringency when he introduced his eighth White Paper in 1970. In it he felt sufficiently confident to claim that Britain's military capability was unsurpassed in Western Europe, but he acknowledged that his final job was to streamline the central organization of defence. From the loose-knit federal structure he had inherited in 1964, he had made significant progress in strengthening central control over defence policy and management, but his ultimate objective was to lower the policy-related level of authority to the equivalent of that of an assistant secretary while ensuring that the services themselves retained their individual identities. With this in mind, he proposed that a minister for the armed forces should replace those for administration and equipment, and should be supported with three functionally related parliamentary under-secretaries. With this one move, the services faced the potential demotion of their political representative two rungs down the decisionmaking ladder; to compensate for loss of influence, the CDS was to gain in authority by assuming a military responsibility for defence policy, plans, operational requirements, intelligence, and signals.[49] As it happened, a change of government determined that the services were to retain their separate parliamentary under-secretaries, which led some observers to conclude that the "tide of functionalism" had been stemmed.[50]

Developments independent of the Ministry of Defence, however, vitiated the halt in the functional trend. Military equipment was inexorably increasing in cost and complexity, and it raised immense problems for industry to deliver on time, to specification, and at the right price. Budgetary pressures dictated that a closer look should be taken at the structural arrangements for defence procurement with the intention of improving efficiency all around. With three services and two government departments involved (the Department of Technology having given way on military aircraft research and development to the Ministry of Aviation Supply), the control process was getting out of hand. Furthermore, the decisionmaking machinery for weapons procurement at the center was becoming complex, involving three committees—the Defence Research Committee, the Defence Operations Requirements Committee, and the Weapons Development Committee.

After a lengthy investigation by an advisory group headed by Derek Rayner, the recommendation was made for a new Procurement Agency to be established as part of the central Ministry of Defence structure. To assist the transition, a minister of state for defence procurement was appointed in 1971. In 1972, the Procurement Executive was established with a chief executive at its head, answerable to the SSD, and with controllers under him responsible for Land, Sea, and Air Systems; Research and Development; Guided Weapons; Policy; Finance; and Sales.[51] The service chiefs of staff would, however, be responsible for specifying their respective requirements, which would be scrutinized by the relevant defence procurement-related committees.

Following the incorporation of the Procurement Executive in 1972, relatively little alteration was made to the central organization of defence for the next ten years, except that the minister for defence procurement was dropped in 1972. Toward the end of the decade, however, economic pressures, especially those related to procurement costs, meant that a review was in order. The outcome was that, in June 1981, the previous structure consisting of one minister of state responsible for the armed forces and three single-service parliamentary under-secretaries was altered to from one consisting of two ministers of state, one for the armed forces, and one for defence procurement, each with a parliamentary under-secretary. The change was justified on the functional grounds that it strengthened both ministerial support for the SSD and the political direction available to the department.[52]

In other respects, the central structure remained untouched, except that the standing of the CDS was upgraded in the relative sense that advice from the chiefs of staff to the SSD and the Defence Council was downgraded.[53] In reality, this decision, precipitated perhaps by the tendency of the parliamentary under-secretary for the navy to put his service's interests before the government's priorities, formally broke the link between the services and the government with the effect that the chiefs of staffs no longer had political representatives within the Ministry or channels to the Cabinet that were independent of the SSD.[54]

Thus by 1981, one might have thought that the functional restructuring of the Ministry of Defence was complete and compatible with, at least, the principle—or the political expedience—of retaining the separate identities of the three services. This was not in fact the case. Prime Minister Thatcher, concerned both with cutting the level of public spending and with improving the efficiency and productivity of government departments, looked closely at the Ministry of Defence—one of the largest spending departments—as an area in which efficiencies could be found, despite her own commitment to raise servicemen's pay and increase defence spending along the lines set by NATO. Her brief to her defence secretary, Francis Pym, was to find savings where possible; but rather than meet her requirements, Pym tended to see the services' viewpoint. She replaced him with John Nott, a man more in her own mold, who embarked on a close scrutiny of service spending in relation to Britain's overall commitments. To help achieve these economies, a new post was created, that of director-general of management audit, with John Mayne, a management expert, the first incumbent. As if to enhance her endeavors to tighten up the Ministry of Defence, Thatcher appointed her own principal private secretary, Clive Whitmore, to be the new PUS in July 1982. Any progress that had been made in these directions was brought to a standstill by the Falklands conflict, at the end of which Nott tendered his resignation. The choice of his replacement, Michael Heseltine, was indicative of the prime minister's continuing determination to see efficiency increased, given that he had come from the Environment Ministry where he had been noted for introducing management systems that had brought significant savings.[55]

One change that Nott introduced was the further elevation of the CDS within the Ministry of Defence hierarchy. Not only was the CDS to be clearly superior to his Chiefs of Staff Committee colleagues, but he was also to have a deputy of rank and status equivalent to that of the service chiefs.[56] No longer could the CDS act as merely the "spokesman" for the Chiefs of Staff Committee; his was clearly a "center" appointment with the responsibility to chair the Appointments Committee consisting of all the top Service Officers and to act as head of all the central defence staffs, assisted by his deputy.[57]

However, the task of completing the efficiency reforms fell to Heseltine. One of his first moves was to introduce the system he had employed in his previous job—the Management Information for Ministers System (MINIS). The MINIS was designed "to provide an overall picture of all the functions of the Department and to allow them to exercise their management of these functions positively, rather than reactively."[58] Clive Whitmore and John Mayne were charged with the task of applying the system to the Ministry of Defence. The result was incorporated in the White Paper on the Central Organisation for Defence, published in July 1984. The White Paper itself reflects the aggregate of changes that had taken place within the Ministry since 1963, together with the innovations aimed at increased efficiency consequent upon Heseltine's arrival and the return to power of Thatcher in mid–1983.

Understandably, in the light of almost forty years of Defence Ministry experience, the individuality and uniqueness of the armed services were guaranteed. "The government is determined to uphold the leadership, loyalties and traditions which are essential to the morale of the individual Services and their fighting capacity," the White Paper intoned.[59] However, the objective was to seek out the best possible value in defence terms, which, interpreted, meant increased fighting effectiveness, a minimum of bureaucracy, clear lines of accountability, and the fight on an integrated basis "covering both our own forces and those of our Allies."[60]

Regarding the higher echelons within the Ministry, no change was introduced that had not been incorporated or anticipated in 1981, with the one significant exception of the formal positioning of the CDS within the overall structure of the department. The SSD would continue to be responsible for the coordination of policy and administrative matters affecting the services. Defence policy would remain the charge of the Cabinet DOPC, chaired by the prime minister. Under the SSD, the Defence Council would continue to exercise command and control over defence matters as defined in the 1964 Defence (Transfer of Functions) Act, but it would have the additional participation of the vice-chief of defence staff (VCDS) on account of his day-to-day responsibility for the running of the Central Defence Staffs. The three Service Boards would continue in existence, each chaired by the minister of defence for the armed forces, who in turn, with the minister of defence (procurement), would be responsible for a whole array of defence functional categories.

The most radical change, however, concerned the responsibilities heaped upon the CDS and the PUS serving as the SSD's principal military and civilian advisers. The CDS chairs the Chiefs of Staff Committee, as before, but tenders independent military advice on strategy, forward policy, resource allocation, commitments, and operations; he also plans, directs, and conducts all military operations, and directs the work of the Central Defence Staff. His appointment will be at the discretion of the SSD and the prime minister and will not, as in the past, rotate on a "buggins turn" basis among the three service chiefs. Under the VCDS the Defence Staff's role is "the corporate duty of finding the best solution to problems of the day, whether of an operational nature, strategic planning, defence policy, or equipment priorities."[61] The Defence Staff, which absorbed the functions of the previous Central Military Staffs, is grouped under four sections: strategy and policy, programs and personnel, systems, and commitments—each headed by a deputy chief of defence staff (DCDS), who is a serving officer of three-star rank, with the exception of the first section, which calls for a civilian posting at the deputy secretary level. The Defence Intelligence Staff remains separate but is accountable to both the CDS and the PUS.

The PUS, as head of the department and principal accounting officer, is responsible for the organization within the Ministry, long-term financing and budgetary control, and advice on the political and parliamentary aspects of the department's work. Under him a second PUS is responsible for an Office of Management and Budget (OMB). This office represents a new departure, in that it is designed to exercise close scrutiny over resource allocation and expenditure. The OMB encompasses four areas, each headed by a deputy secretary, covering Resources and Programmes, Finance, Administration, and Civilian Management. The aim is to achieve strong central control over the Ministry's corporate planning, including such issues as service rationalization and standardization. No radical change was envisaged for the Office of the Scientific Adviser, or for the Defence Procurement Executive, other than to streamline their respective organizations.

All these alterations have left relatively little policymaking authority to the service chiefs. Each remains the professional head of his service and is responsible for its fighting effectiveness, including matters of morale, management, discipline, and efficiency. However, each is also expected to tender advice through the CDS to the SSD, although, somewhat paradoxically, the traditional right of the service chiefs to make representations to the prime minister directly has been retained. Management of each of the services is the responsibility of a Service Executive Committee, acting as a subcommittee of the service boards and in accordance with centrally determined policy directives. The Service Executive Committees have direct access to the Central Defence Staffs to ensure "the necessary linkage" between policymaking and the day-to-day management exercised by the various service commanders-in-chief.[62] Since all these changes constitute internal departmental adjustments, no constitutional or statutory enactments have been necessary (see Figure 5.1).

Whether or not the 1984 organizational adjustments will succeed in effecting the efficiency, cuts in overheads, improved financial control, and sharpened lines of accountability remains to be seen. What it is unlikely to do is to put to rest once and for all the dichotomy between the roles and responsibilities of the services and the chiefs of staff as policy advisers and as managers and executors of policy decisions. Certainly, the chiefs of staff have been subordinated to the CDS and his Central Defence Staffs, and since 1981 have lost their political champions and representatives; they are not happy with either development, and made direct representation to the prime minister to that effect when the reorganization plans were made known. Significantly, perhaps, this move got them nowhere; their action would, however, suggest that those serving on the Defence Staffs will be unlikely for some time to be able to divorce themselves from their service experience and background when considering the nation's defence problems.[63]

In a perceptive response to the 1984 reorganization proposals, Field Marshal Lord Carver, a one-time CDS, observed that it is a fallacy to divorce policy from management. The services, he argued, perceived as their principal "function" to fight on land, sea, or in the air, and that defining defence "functions" for administrative, political, or financial convenience could well have the opposite effect of what was intended, especially if it is done by people with neither service experience nor real knowledge of, or stake in, the issue.[64] If the reorganization is intended to put an end to interservice rivalry over scarce resources or for particular roles, because budgetary control is taken out of their hands, the services' long experience of fighting the battles of Whitehall would suggest that—short of going the whole way and creating a single defence force with the "mud-coloured uniforms" that everyone professes they want to avoid—there are many more battles still to come.

One of the strongest supporters of service interests is public and parliamentary opinion, which helps to explain why no government has yet had the temerity to force through the total integration of the armed services. This is not to suggest that defence policy and the structure of defence figure high on the list of public concerns—the question of cruise

Figure 5.1   The Higher Organization of the Ministry of Defence (1984)

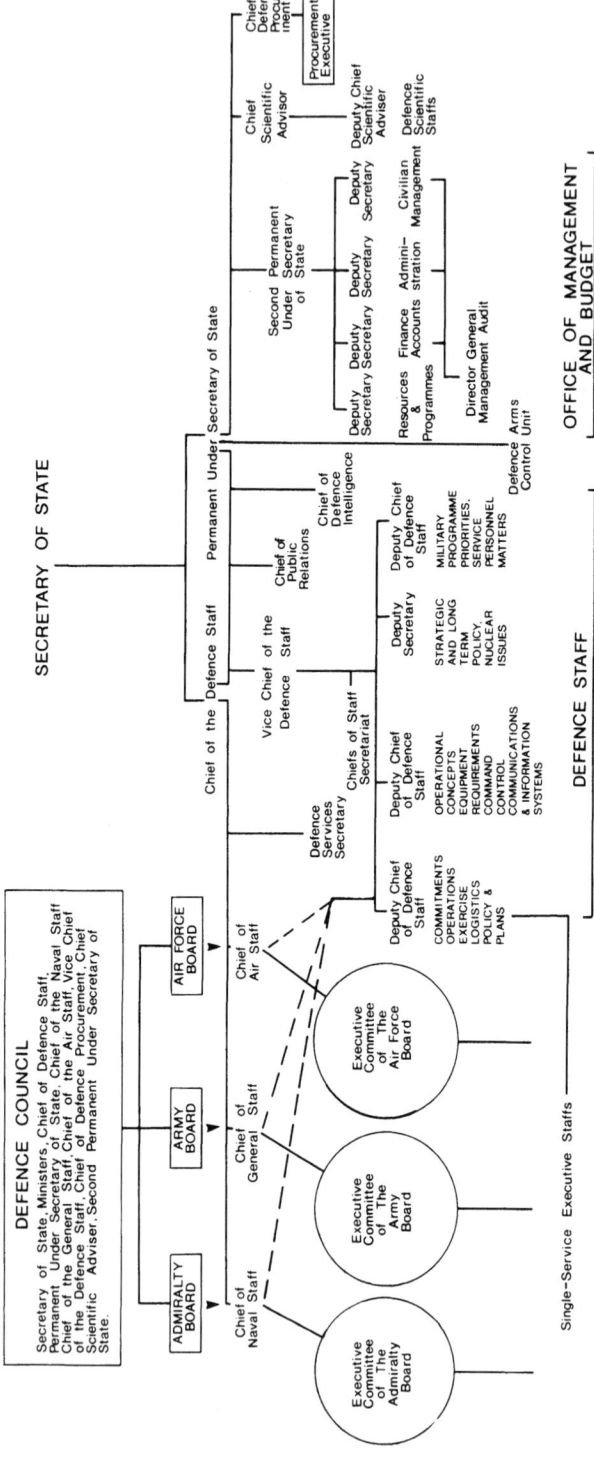

Source: Central Organisation for Defence, Cmnd 9315 (London: Her Majesty's Stationery Office, July 1984).

missiles and arms control notwithstanding—or that administrative wrangling within the Ministry of Defence captures the public imagination. Rather, the reality is that the services enjoy a latent public sympathy, and when government policies impinge on the traditions, associations, and morale of the services or specific units within them, they are met with instant protest. The attempts to restructure the British infantry in the 1960s provoked enormous public protest, and the decommissioning of ships still generates considerable public nostalgia. The services are very adept at nurturing this sentiment, for very practical as well as prudent reasons, and they generally maintain a very close link with the public. In this respect, the British public, as the Falklands dispute revealed very clearly, is both conservative and surprisingly emotional, and any attempt at service integration is likely to be political dynamite.

In this context, public opinon and Parliament constitute a negative influence on defence policy: There are some things, even if they are ostensibly in the interests of economy, efficiency, or rationalization, that simply cannot be done. In terms of positive influence affecting defence policy and management, however, neither Parliament nor public opinion can be considered to have a very impressive record.

Lack of information has been one explanation for Parliament's record, although significant improvements have occurred in the amount and quality of information available since the introduction of functional costings in the late 1960s. Nevertheless, no matter how comprehensive the available information on defence may be, it is always *ex post facto* and Parliament can do little other than react to policy, rather than acting as an input to policy formulation. A second consideration is that defence has not been a popular field in which MPs hope to make their reputations, nor is it a policy area that, until recently, has figured prominently in party election manifestos. The change was brought about by the open dispute over the modification of the intermediate-range nuclear missiles to be stationed in Britain under a NATO agreement and the wider issue of the British independent nuclear deterrent (Trident), the concern for arms control measures within Europe.

Constitutionally, Parliament controls the armed forces. This situation has come about after centuries of gradual erosion of absolute power: Whereas once the authority to raise armies and wage war was held by the Crown, the Monarch is now merely the titular head of the armed forces. All officers in the services hold the Queen's Commission, which, symbolically at least, signals the political independence of the armed forces from the government of the day. The existence of the British Armed Forces, however, dates back in constitutional terms to the 1688 Bill of Rights. It was this statute which determined that the maintenance of a standing army in time of peace, unless it had the consent of Parliament, was against the law. The effect of the act was to require Parliament to give constant approval to Britain for having armed forces in peacetime, a consent achieved initially by annual acts of Parliament that renewed the statutes governing the armed services. Since 1955, this annual renewal was put on a quinquennial basis, but annual continuing Orders in Council were required to be passed by both Houses of Parliament. In 1981, the Armed Forces Act removed the need for separate acts for each of the three services and brought the three in line with one another, although the annual continuation order still applies.[65] The Defence (Transfer of Functions) Act of 1964 established the Ministry of Defence, with the Defence Council as a Department of State.

If Parliament is responsible for the constitutional existence of the armed services, its annual consent is implicit in the annual appropriations acts, the statement on defence estimates before the House of Commons, and the activities of the Commons Public Accounts Committee and its specialized Defence Committee. In 1979, the latter took the place of the old Estimates Committee (the subcommittee on defence and foreign policy), with the significant difference that its almost permanent membership and professional advisers have substantially increased the specialist knowledge on defence matters available to Parliament. Questions, both written and oral, put to the prime minister and to the SSD, as well as to defence spokesmen in the House of Lords, give a regular opportunity for MPs and their lordships to raise defence matters, as does the annual defence debate and, when the situation warrants, emergency debates.

The Falklands conflict of 1982 afforded many instrumental lessons, both for the government and for the armed services and focused on the performance of weapons systems, the relations between the forces and the media, and the problems of logistics, tactics, and strategy in a theater of war several thousands of miles from home. Less attention was given, however, to the problems of control of the forces engaged in the war, the chain of command, and the various lines of responsibility. One reason, perhaps, was that these problems were at the time reasonably clearly defined, although this was a function more of good judgment— a feature that had always been emphasized in earlier discussions of central defence reorganization—than of clearly established structure. The defence committee of the Cabinet—a war committee—under the prime minister exercised political direction, with Admiral Sir John Fieldhouse, commander-in-chief, Fleet, responsible for the operational conduct of the war. To a marked degree, Thatcher left the military to get on with the operation with a minimum of interference, once it had become established that a diplomatic solution—the Belgrano incident notwithstanding—was not possible. Subordinate to Fieldhouse were Rear-Admiral Sandy Woodward and Brigadier Julian Moore, who were responsible for naval and land operations, respectively. Since the services were left with a relatively free hand operationally, it has to be concluded that the degree of rivalry that existed between the three services, to the extent that the air force had to be involved with long-distance aerial bombardment of Port Stanley and coordination between the other two was not always as smooth as perhaps it should have been, is indicative still of the need for central planning and control. To meet this criticism, the CDS, assisted by his Defence Staff, has been made responsible for the conduct of military operations in wartime. Responsibility for the control and use of nuclear weapons remains the exclusive prerogative of the prime minister, however.

In conclusion, the central question regarding the central organization for defence in Britain has been, and remains, that of control over defence policy formulation, planning, and execution. In the past, too many lines of accountability were blurred, a situation that was exacerbated by separate service ministries, separate accounting officers, and separate political masters. The consequence was that service influence, collectively and separately, had been oriented more toward sectional and partial interests than toward overall defence and national interests, with the associated wastage of time, effort, resources, and policy relevance. Economy and finance more than organizational logic served as the catalyst to change, with emphasis given primarily to functional approaches and their associated costings.

The history of the British central organization for defence has witnessed the strengthening of control at the center, not simply by politicians and civilian advisers but by a central military (i.e., defence) staff. The SSD today exercises considerable control from the center and presides over a large, specialized, and integrated central defence staff, as well as an Office of Management and Budget, to ensure constantly that value for money is being achieved over all defence functions. This is a far cry from the 1946 conception, although the central question remains unresolved as long as the separate services are perceived to be operationally more effective than a single defence force. Given centralization, functional approaches, close financial control, and so on, are the British Armed Forces necessarily likely to be better equipped, better trained, better prepared, and more committed to defend Britain's interests than they had been before these structural changes were made? Clearly, Michael Heseltine thinks so; but as with past attempts at reorganization, the final outcome will depend on the degree of commitment by all concerned, civilian and military alike, to want to make it work. Where, indeed, are today's Dantons?

Notes

1. "Does the Present Central Organisation of Defence Meet the Requirements of the 1970s?" A discussion held at the Royal United Services Institution (RUSI), January 13, 1971, M. Howard, chairman (London: RUSI Report, 1971), p. 1.

2. *The Central Organisation of Defence*, Cmnd. 2097 (London: Her Majesty's Stationery Office [hereafter referred to as HMSO], July 1963).

3. *The Central Organisation for Defence*, Cmnd. 9315 (London: HMSO, July 1984).

4. Ibid., pp. 2–3.

5. *Central Organisation for Defence*, Cmd. 6923 (London: HMSO, October 1946), p. 2.

6. Ibid., p. 2.

7. Michael Howard, *The Central Organisation for Defence* (London: RUSI, April 1970), p. 6.

8. *Central Organisation for Defence,* Cmd. 6923, p. 5.

9. Ibid., p. 5.

10. Lt. Gen. H. G. Martin, "Three Services, One Command," *Daily Telegraph* (February 28, 1958).

11. Cited in the *Guardian* (March 5, 1963).

12. Cited in R. Goold-Adams, "The Organisation of Defence," *Royal United Services Institution Journal* (May 1960), p. 186.

13. F. Johnson, *Defence by Ministry* (London: Duckworth, 1980), pp. 12–18.

14. *Central Organisation for Defence,* Cmd. 6923, pp. 8–10.

15. Howard, *Central Organisation for Defence,* p. 7.

16. J. Barents, *Notes on a Visit to Britain Regarding the Central Organisation for Defence* (NATO Fellowship, April 1959), p. 1.

17. Institute for Strategic Studies (ISS), *Internal Memorandum on the Ministry of Defence* (1958), p. 7.

18. Howard, *Central Organisation for Defence,* p. 9.

19. Goold-Adams, "Organisation of Defence," p. 189.

20. *Central Organisation for Defence,* Cmnd. 476 (London: HMSO, July 1958).

21. Ibid., p. 1.

22. *Times* (August 5, 1960).

23. I.L.M. McGeoch, "The Political Control of the Armed Forces," *RUSI Journal* (May 1961), p. 218.

24. Leonard Beaton, "The Split Personality," *Guardian* (November 23, 1960).

25. To see how he went about this task, that is, by reorganizing service overseas commands *before* introducing integrated commands at home, see Johnson, *Defence by Ministry,* pp. 68–102.

26. Howard, *Central Organisation for Defence,* p. 15.

27. L. Beaton, "Service Rivalry Bad for Defence," *Guardian* (September 22, 1961).

28. *Times* (January 12, 1963).

29. *Times* (March 5, 1963).

30. *Central Organisation for Defence,* Cmnd. 2097 (London: HMSO, July 1963), pp. 1–2.

31. Howard, *Central Organisation for Defence,* p. 19.

32. *Central Organisation for Defence,* Cmnd. 2097, pp. 2–6.

33. W. Snyder, *The Politics of British Defence Policy* (Columbus: Ohio State University Press, 1964), pp. 141–147.

34. *Central Organisation for Defence,* Cmnd. 2097, p. 12.

35. *Economist* (July 20, 1963), p. 328.

36. A. Buchan, "Manning Britain's Defence," *Observer* (July 21, 1963).

37. *Times* (April 25, 1963).

38. *Hansard,* House of Commons (July 31, 1963), p. 467.

39. *Hansard,* House of Commons Defence (Transfer of Functions) Bill, Second Reading (November 21, 1963), cols. 1195–1317.

40. Peter Thorneycroft, "Defence Reforms that Could Check Service Rivalries," *Times* (June 23, 1966).

41. *Times* (December 6, 1963).

42. *Times* (November 24, 1964).

43. *Ministry of Defence Press Release* (London: Ministry of Defence, January 8, 1965).

44. *Observer* (February 7, 1965).

45. *Hansard*, House of Commons, Defence [Rationalisation of Service Functions] (July 21, 1965), cols. 1576–1577.

46. *Times* (December 12, 1966).

47. *Ministry of Defence Press Release* (March 1, 1967).

48. *Times* (February 23, 1968).

49. *Daily Telegraph* (February 20, 1970).

50. "Does the Present Central Organisation of Defence Meet the Requirements of the 1970's?" p. 2.

51. *Government Organisation for Defence Procurement and Civil Aerospace (Rayner Report)*, Cmnd. 4641 (London: HMSO, April 1971), p. 13.

52. House of Commons Defence Committee, 2d Report, *MOD Organisation and Procurement*, vol. II, Session 1981-2, HC 22-II (June 16, 1982), pp. 15–16, 501–502.

53. *Statement on Defence Estimates, 1962*, Cmnd. 8529.1 (London: HMSO, 1962), p. 36.

54. *Times* (May 30, 1981).

55. *Times* (October 6, 1982).

56. *Times* (February 12, 1982); *Times* (October 13, 1982).

57. *Statement on Defence Estimates, 1982*, vol. I, Cmnd. 8529-I (London: HMSO, June 18, 1982), p. 36.

58. *Statement on Defence Estimates, 1983*, vol. I, Cmnd. 8951-I (London: HMSO, 1983), p. 29.

59. *Central Organisation for Defence*, Cmnd. 9315 (London: HMSO, July 1984), p. 1.

60. Ibid., p. 1.

61. Ibid., p. 4.

62. Ibid., passim. See also M. Heseltine, *"MINIS and the Development of the Central Organisation for Defence: A Consultation Document"* (London: Ministry of Defence, March 1984).

63. Martin Edmonds, "Armed Forces and the National Security System: The Meaning and Basis of Compliance," in University Services Study Group (USSG), *A European Reconnaissance* (Edinburgh: Edinburgh University, 1971).

64. Lord Carver, letter in the *Times* (March 22, 1984).

65. Peter Rowe, "The Soldier, the British Army and the Law," in Martin Edmonds (ed.), *British Military Systems* (Centre d'Etudes et des Recherches sur l'Armée, Toulouse University Press, forthcoming).

6
The Italian Central Organization of Defense

Virgilio Ilari

History of the Italian High Command (1908-1947)

According to Article 5 of the 1848 Italian Kingdom's Statute, the king had "the command of all the land and sea forces" and was thus able to declare war without parliamentary approval. The ministers of war and navy, who were chosen from among the general officers, were directly responsible to the Parliament, and parliamentary control of military policy was limited to the discussion of military budgets and bills under Article 33. However, the king had to choose a certain number of senators from among the senior generals and admirals; moreover, many officers returned members to the Chamber of Deputies.

In 1907-1909, for the first time, a civilian, Senator Severino Casana, was appointed minister of war, and for this reason, in 1908, the chiefs of the Royal Army and Navy staffs came directly under the control of the king; they were responsible for technical matters in the preparation for war, whereas the ministers of war and navy were responsible for their own departments and directly answerable to the Parliament. During the period 1915-1918 the king officially held the office of Supreme Command of the Royal Army and Navy. However, the respective chiefs of staff were effectively in command on the grounds set forth in the clause "by Our order," which was contained in the Royal Agenda of May 23, 1915. They transmitted their instructions to their respective ministers in matters that fell within their own spheres of responsibility. Then, in 1920, for a second time, a civilian, Ivanoe Bonomi, was appointed minister of war, and in 1921 both chiefs of staff were made directly responsible to their respective ministers. The Army Council, a newly appointed board, was directed by its vice-chairman, Field Marshal Armando Diaz. It should be noted that Diaz had replaced General Luigi Cadorna as army chief of staff and from 1922 to 1923 served as minister of war in the first Mussolini cabinet.

Translated by Sandra Talansky, University of Macerata.

After the 1925 Mussolini coup d'etat, the high command was placed in the hands of the premier. Mussolini, with the exception of the period 1929–1934, assumed the duties of the Ministries of War, Navy, and Air Force (which was created in 1923). Mussolini also became the chairman of the Supreme Defense Board created in 1923, which included the ministers of war, navy, air force, foreign affairs, home affairs, colonies, communications, finance, and national economy. The vice-chairmanship was given to the chief of general staff, Marshal Pietro Badoglio, who held the title from 1925 until 1940. However, the extensive powers of interservice coordination of this position were greatly reduced in 1927, when the duties were changed to being a mere "military adviser" to the premier, and the vice-chairman was authorized to relate to the other army, navy, and air force chiefs of staff only "through their respective ministers." In the years of Mussolini's premiership, this coordination took place through the miliary undersecretaries placed at the head of the three service departments.

This method of communication caused rivalry and hostility between the chiefs of staff and their respective undersecretaries, particularly in the army and air force. These undersecretaries were both general officers and politicians who, in fact, exerted ministerial powers without having to answer to any superior political authority other than Mussolini. On June 11, 1940, the king appointed Benito Mussolini, who had been "first marshal of the empire" since 1936, as "commander of the troops operating on all fronts." The Supreme Headquarters (Comando Supremo), through which Mussolini exerted his command, was at that time under the direction of Field Marshal Badoglio. A new Undersecretariat for War Production (Fabbriguerra) was formed in May 1940; in February 1943 it was expanded into a new ministry, but it was abolished in January 1944.

In June 1941 the powers and responsibilities of the chief of general staff were greatly increased. It became his duty to propose "the highlights of the war plan" to the premier and, after approval, to dispatch the respective directives to the chiefs of the armed forces' staffs. The chief of general staff also had the "high management and coordination of military preparation," with surveillance and control powers over each of the armed forces; coordination among the army, navy, and air force intelligence services; and coordination of the requests for equipment and armaments ordered by each armed force, after these had been examined, first by the Arms and Munitions Technical High Committee. Orders were subsequently send to the Undersecretariat for War Production.

After the military coup d'etat of July 25, 1943, the king regained supreme command of the armed forces and exercised power first through the chief of general staff, General Vittorio Ambrosio, and then, from November 1943 to February 1945, Marshal Giovanni Messe. The chiefs of the navy and air force staffs were appointed ministers of their corresponding departments.

In May 1945, after the liberation of northern Italy, the new democratic authorities attempted to reduce the military powers of the king and to increase those of the new premier, Feruccio Parri. In so doing they were introducing a system of high command similar to that of 1927. For example, the chief of general staff, General Claudio Trezzani, was reduced to the status of "military adviser" to the premier and authorized, with the other chiefs of staff, to direct his activities "through their respective ministers." Furthermore, a new Committee of Defense replaced at the cabinet level the former Supreme Defense Board, which was abolished in October 1944. This new committee was presided over by the premier, who was assisted by the chief of general staff, and consisted of the ministers of the three military departments and those of foreign affairs and the Treasury.

In 1944 the ministers of war and air force became civilians; Admiral Raffaele De Courten was the only service chief of staff to become a minister as well, from 1943 until 1946. However, in 1945–1947 real responsibility for military policy was given to the chief of army staff, General Raffaele Cadorna, son of the chief of staff during World War I. In 1944–1945, Cadorna had been commander of the Corps of Liberty's Volunteers and had served in the integrated headquarters for all the partisan groups of northern Italy. The undersecretaries, as civilian politicians who had previously acted in their ministries on behalf of their own political parties, correspondingly lost most of their power and influence. The ministers, who were generally members of political parties different from those of their undersecretaries, delegated some powers and responsibilities to them, but as they were not members of the Cabinet, the undersecretaries had neither direct duties nor political power.

The Constitutional Organization
of National Defense (1948)

According to the Republican Constitution, in force since January 1, 1948, Italy "disavows every war meant to infringe the liberty of other nations, and for the settlement of international quarrels," and consents, subject to the same conditions as other nations, to limit its sovereignty to foster a peaceful and just international system (Article 11). However, the defense of one's own country is considered a citizen's "sacred duty." Military service is compulsory, according to the provisions of the law, provided it is without damage to the political rights and job security of the conscripts. Military regulations must conform to the Republic's democratic principles (Article 52).

The Italian Parliament is competent to debate a "state of war" and to give the government the necessary powers (Article 78); it also ratifies by law all major international treaties (Article 80). In accordance with Article 87, paragraph 9, the president of the Republic has "the command of the Armed Forces and the Chairmanship of the Supreme Defence Council, as constituted by law, and can declare a state of war deliberated by the Chambers." Debate concerning the limits and contents of the presidential command of the armed forces became a classic "Doktorfrage" of Italian studies of constitutional law, but it has not resulted in any significant changes in common political practices.

In fact, presidential command has always been regarded as only a formality given to the president in order to ensure the necessary political neutrality of the armed forces. During the Gronchi presidency (1956–1961), which was charged with "presidentialism," some attempt was made to demonstrate that the Constitution had given the president an "actual" command of the armed forces, but the prevailing opinion is that an "actual" command could not be given to an office such as that of the presidency of the Republic, which itself was devoid of political responsibility to Parliament.

On July 28, 1950, the Supreme Defense Council, as defined by the Constitution, was passed into law (Law No. 524). Chaired by the president of the Republic, the council includes the premier as vice-chairman, the ministers of defense, foreign affairs, home affairs, treasury, industry and trade, and the chief of defense staff. The minister of budget and economic programming was also included as a member of the council by Article 4, Law No. 48, which was passed on February 27, 1967. According to the judgment of the chairman, other ministers may be co-opted as well as *inter alia*: the chiefs of the army, navy, and air force staffs; senior military commanders; the chairmen of the National Research Council and Central Institute of Statistics and other advisory boards (including those of the Defense Department); representatives of the Resistance movements of 1943–1945; and experts in scientific, industrial, economic, and military matters.

The Supreme Defense Council was set to meet twice a year with the assistance of a permanent secretariat. Although it was formed to discuss all matters of national defense and military policy, the council was deprived of any real direction or control because the president of the Republic, as chairman, had no direct political responsibility to Parliament. Professor Predieri, a retired officer and a specialist in the constitutional organization of national defense, has stated that defense and military policies are delegated to the government under parliamentary control, according to Article 95 of the Constitution, whereas the Supreme Defense Council, within the boundaries of these policies, decides the directives binding both the president of the Republic, as the commander of the armed forces, and the cabinet.

From the beginning, however, experience has denied any importance to the council; in fact, even its twice-yearly obligatory meetings have currently been cut to only one session a year. Moreover, the council was convened in November 1983, for the first time since 1980, expressly to settle some political disagreements concerning the Italian participation in the Multilateral Force (MLF) peacekeeping operation in Lebanon.

The Government's Responsibility
for Defense and Military Policy

Some criticism has been addressed to the fact that the Italian Constitution lacks a defense board at the governmental level, a situation that had also existed in 1923–1944 and 1945–1947. Indeed, no explicit mention is made in Italian law of the duties and responsibilities of either the government or the minister of defense regarding national defense and military policy. The criticism is based on an interpretation of Article 95 of the Constitution, an article which gives the premier the general responsibility for the government's policy and the ministers a collective duty to decide upon the activities of the Cabinet and those of their respective departments.

According to the 1977 law (No. 801), the premier is the "national authority" for security—that is, for state secrecy and intelligence. In 1967, 1970, and 1977, four other interministerial committees, in some way connected with national defense and security policy, were created—namely, the committees for Economic Programming (CIPE), Industrial Mobilization (CISMI), Civil Protection (CIPC), and Intelligence and Security (CIIS). All continue to operate. Between 1954 and 1977 eleven technical commissions were appointed to support interministerial cooperation in matters of intelligence and security (CESIS, 1977); civil protection, civil defense, civilian emergency plans, evacuation and assistance to refugees (CIER); cultural goods protection, supply, and national traffic (CR, CRTN, COTIR, respectively); and national transport in case of war (CITN, COTIT).

An attempt to support the executive branch by establishing a Political-Strategic Committee was made between 1979 and 1981, when, during the NATO "Wintex-Cimex" headquarters exercise, the premier and some ministers met with the military authorities at the Inter-Services Operational Center (COPI). At present, however, the power and influence of these meetings are not recognized because they lack the necessary legal status.

In late 1983, Prime Minister Bettino Craxi also created another consultative board; this was the Cabinet Council, which included the leaders of the five government parties and the chief ministers, and which met to discuss national policy about the cruise missiles and Lebanon affairs. The Italian Constitution, however, makes no reference of any sort to a War Cabinet, Defense Overseas Policy Committee, Crisis Management Committee, or National Security Council.

The present Italian high-command structure exhibits two serious disadvantages: The first is a lack of experience in defense and military policy at the premier and Cabinet levels. This has led to a disconnectedness among foreign, defense, and national security policies, in spite of the usual interministerial "cooperation and exchange" and numerous diplomatic-military integrated boards, panels, and commissions such as the Atlantic Council (Italdelega), Military Committee (Italstaff), and International Secretariat (Italnato) of NATO, on which there are Italian representatives. The second disadvantage is the exclusion of any military authority from a decisionmaking or even advisory capacity at any level higher than that of the minister of defense. This is in spite of the chief of defense staff's membership in the Supreme Defense Council, and the inclusion of a premier's military adviser in the presidential secretariat. The position of military adviser, created in 1979 by the Cossiga Cabinet, was subsequently canceled in late 1982 by the Fanfani Cabinet. At present, only the president of the Republic has a "military adviser" (a sort of aide-de-camp) as well as an "adviser for security." Matters of defense policy regarding NATO, the Mediterranean area, and nuclear and disarmament affairs are delegated to the Italian Foreign Office, which is supported by a few military advisers seconded from the armed services, such as those who form the panel of military experts on disarmament issues.

Two examples serve to illustrate the relative impotence of the military in the formulation of defense policy. The first concerns one of the major decisions in postwar Italian defense policy—namely, the deployment of Jupiter missiles (1959). The decision was made in spite of contrary advice from the military authorities, who had recommended negotiations with the U.S. government in order to gain substantial military compensation to offset the additional risks associated with the missiles' deployment. The issue caused a conflict between the military authorities and the minister of defense, Giulio Andreotti, who was supported by the deputy chief of the air force staff, General Nino Pasti. The decision resulted in the resignations of the chiefs of defense and army staffs, Generals Giuseppe Mancinelli and Giorgio Liuzzi.[1]

The second example concerns the deployment of cruise missiles in Southern Italy. In her thesis on the Italian agreement to the deployment, Nina Gardner has stated that the decision was made for reasons of inter-party harmony. She argued that the then premier, Francesco Cossiga, and the Socialist party leader, Bettino Craxi, were not prepared to discuss the matter, and that Craxi referred the U.S. authorities to his private defense consultant, Stefano Silvestri of the International Affairs Institute. In Gardner's opinion, the chief role in this affair was played by Craxi, who chose the Atlanticist point of view in order to exclude the Communist party and the leftists in the Socialist party, thus winning U.S. support for his own candidacy for the Cabinet presidency. The military authorities were thus presented with a fait accompli and could not exercise even any influence or advice on the issue.

The Political Role of the Minister of Defense

The post of defense minister is an important one for coalition governments. Republicans held this position three times: in 1947–1948 by Cipriano Facchinetti, in 1948–1953 by Randolfo Pacciardi, and in

1983 by Giovanni Spadolini. From 1966 to 1968 the Ministry was headed by a unified Socialist, Roberto Tremelloni, and from 1970 to 1974 by a Social Democrat, Mario Tanassi, who was later to become involved, coincidentally, along with the chief of air force staff, General Diulio Sergio Fanali, in the Lockheed scandal. From April 4, 1980, until late 1983, the minister of defense has been a right-wing Socialist, Lelio Lagorio.

During all other periods, the post has been held by Christian Democrats. Eleven political leaders of this party alternated as head of the Ministry of Defense, starting in 1947 with Mario Cingolani, until 1980, with Adolfo Sarti. However, only five of the eleven held office for more than one year—namely, Paolo Emilio Taviani (1953–1958), Giulio Andreotti (1959–1966 and 1974), Luigi Gui (1968–1970), Arnaldo Forlani (1974–1976), and Attilio Ruffini (1977–1980). Gui was also implicated in the Lockheed affair but, unlike Tanassi, was acquitted. Vito Lattanzio (1976–1977) was forced to resign his office after Kappler, the German war criminal, escaped.

Because of the great potential political influence arising from its international, military-industrial, intelligence, and client connections and opportunities, the office of defense minister has proved very appealing. In fact, it was the object of a political struggle in 1970–1974 between Tanassi and Andreotti, both of whom wanted control of the power it afforded.

Conflicts between the ministers of defense and the military authorities have been the exception in the history of the Italian Republic. Randolfo Pacciardi, in his capacity as minister of defense, acted on behalf of the military. Giulio Andreotti swept away opposition from Generals Giorgio Liuizzi and Giuseppi Mancinelli, with the help of his military supporters Giuseppe Aloia, Aldo Remondino, Giraudo, and, above all, Giovanni De Lorenzo. Andreotti also created an Italian defense-industrial base and used his military-industrial contacts for political purposes, by taking advantage of his privileged access to military intelligence; moreover, by employing this access with the help of the military, he was able to impose psychological pressures on the politicians, particularly those of the Socialist party, during the period of the "opening to the Left" (1960–1966). In 1974 Andreotti won the approval of the Left, when he charged the director of defense intelligence, General Vito Miceli, with having aided and abetted those responsible in the 1970 rightist Borghese coup d'etat attempt. This, however, was a charge that was never proved.[2]

In 1981 the political parties, particularly those of the Left, lodged a protest against the public statements by the chief of defense staff, General Vittorio Santini, who had supported a raise in officers' pay. During parliamentary debate, Defense Minister Lelio Lagorio had supported the position of General Santini. Furthermore, he made an attempt to settle the issue over the constitutional limits within which military authorities would have the right to express opinions in public, even when such opinions differed from those of the defense minister.[3] However, even

ter General Santini continued to make public declarations concerning
increase in officers' pay and threatened resignation if Parliament did
t accede to his demands, the minister still felt obliged to reaffirm in
editorial (*L'Italia Internazionale*, November 1982) his view that, under
e existing constitutional system, the minister of defense was the only
ne responsible for military policy, and that all other military authorities
re subordinated to him.

arliamentary Control

Parliamentary control in defense and military policy suffers from
oth the lack of a clear distribution of political responsibility and the
ong antimilitarist and anti-Atlanticist tradition of the Left. The anti-
tlanticist policy was finally relinquished by the Socialists in 1961, and
nore gradually by the Communist party in the period 1973–1979. The
nore recent opposition of the Communists to the deployment of cruise
nissiles and its pacifist stance should not imply that the Communist
party has rejected Atlanticism. In fact, a motion calling for the withdrawal
of Italy from the Alliance, proposed by the Stalinist minority at the last
Communist party congress (1983) was rejected by a 95 percent majority.

Antimilitarism, though disavowed in the past by all of the political
parties, with the exception of the Radical party, maintains instead a
strong influence on the politics, ideology, and supporters of the left
wing of the Christian Democrats, Socialists, and Communists, and of
the leftist Independents. Since 1973 these political groups have given
up their old policies of the 1960s in order to appoint a parliamentary
commissioner to control and protect democracy inside the armed forces,
along the lines of the Swedish "ombudsman" model.

The defense committees of both chambers, provided for by parliamentary regulations, generally include a few members of Parliament
coming from the armed forces. In 1948 they were all Christian Democrats,
but in the recent past (1979–1983), the legislature included three Christian
Democrats from the armed forces: two admirals in the Senate and one
officer from the Carabinieri, Bruno Stegagnini, in the Chamber of
Deputies. There was also a military representative for the neo-Fascists,
Vito Miceli; the Socialists, Falco Accame; the Social Democrats, Magliane;
and the leftist independent parties, Nino Pasti.

In the present legislature (1984), there are only four representatives
from the active armed services: two Christian Democrats, one Social
Democrat, and one neo-Fascist. However, many civilian members of
Parliament, mostly from the Left, have had wide experience in defense
and military matters, and are supported by the specialized research
institutes of their parties. The Socialists have the Instituto pergli Studi
di Politica Internazionale (ISPI); the Communists, the Centro Studi di
Politica Internazionale (CESPI); the Radical Party, the Instituto di Ricerca
per il Disarmo lo Sviluppo e la Pace (IRDISP); the Leftist Independents,

the Archivo Disarmo; and the left wing of the Christian Democrats a
the Socialists, the Instituto per la Relazioni con i Paesi dell Afri
America Latina e Medio Oriente (IPALMO). There also exists an interpa
institute, the Instituto Studi e Ricerche Difesa (ISTRID), and many otl
private and university institutes with political connections.[4]

The defense committees are involved in the preliminary discussio
of every bill, budget, and political activity concerning the armed forc
and the ministry of defense. The less important bills, presented by t
government and requested by the minister of defense, are passed
the committees following a short, formal procedure consisting of e
amination and discussion. The committees also meet jointly with oth
parliamentary committees, such as the committees of constitution
affairs, foreign affairs, home affairs, industry, and budget.

The defense committees are able to request hearings from the minist
of defense and military authorities, and they have powers of inqui
and inspection. In September 1982, a conflict arose between the Chambe
of Deputies' defense committee and the minister of defense regardir
the limits and contents of these powers. The conflict was caused whe
the defense committee directed an inquiry into the security and reactiv
readiness of the armed forces after the Red Brigade made a terrori
attack on some barracks and military installations.

Other parliamentary committees of inquiry have been convened b
law on such matters as the unified intelligence services (SIFAR) affai
and the 1964 coup d'etat attempt (1967-1971), as well as in matter
regarding armaments and military procurements (1977-1983). In additior
a permanent parliamentary control committee on intelligence and securit
services has been provided for by the 1977 improved reform law.

The minister of defense or his proxy, an undersecretary, reports yearly
to the Parliament on such matters as the defense budget, military
discipline, and the completion of special armament programs. Defense
bills are usually concerned with matters of personnel and administration
and political discussion on defense and military policy are generally
occasioned by the budget and the financing of special bills.

The Ministry of Defense (1947–1965)

On February 4, 1947, by Decree No. 17, a new minister of defense
replaced the former ministers of war, navy, and air force. However, the
departments remained separate, each under the management of a new
general secretary, a general officer. According to Decree No. 306 (May
10, 1947), the general secretary replaced the former Cabinet office director.
Very little was changed in the prewar structure of the military departments, which retained their directorates (Direzioni Generali) and inspectorates as well as their technical and administrative advisory boards.

To effect coordination, a new Defense Cabinet Office (Gabinetto della
Difesa) was established, with legal, budget and administrative, and

military procurement branches, together with a new Budget Coordination Committee chaired by the minister of defense and composed of the general secretaries, the chiefs of staff, and those responsible for the budget and accounting offices. Some degree of armed services unification was introduced in 1948 through the substitution of a new chief of defense staff for the former chief of general staff. This substitution was followed in 1949 by the institution of the High Military Studies Center (CASM) and the unification of the armed forces intelligence services (SIFAR), and in 1951 by the unification of the former army, navy, and air force councils into a new interservice technical advisory board, the Armed Forces High Council.

The duties and powers of the chief of defense staff, determined by Decree No. 955 (April 21, 1948), were very different and more extensive than those of the chief of general staff as defined by the decrees of May 31, 1945. The chief of defense staff was placed directly under the minister of defense, and the army, navy, and air force chiefs of staff were placed under the direction of the chief of defense staff. Within these limits, the responsibilities of the chiefs of staff were (1) to coordinate the organization, the preparation, and employment of the armed forces, and the activities of the unified intelligence services (SIFAR); (2) to propose to the minister, with the necessary but not binding opinion of the concerned service chief of staff, the outlines for the service organization; (3) to trace out, "on the grounds of the minister's directive," the "outlines of the operational plans and general criteria" for the land and sea frontiers, sea traffic, and air defense; and (4) to give instructions for interservice training, combined maneuvers, and studies on interservice cooperation.

The armed forces' High Council (Consiglio Superiore delle Forze Armate) was conceived to counterbalance the influence of the chiefs of staff over the minister of defense. It was established in law on January 9, 1951 (as Law No. 167) and subsequently modified by Decree No. 1478 (November 18, 1965) and Law No. 1176 (March 8, 1968) (see Figure 6.1). As specified in the army, navy, and air force sections, the High Council is headed by a board of three general officers, one from each service of higher rank or seniority, who do not hold the position of minister, undersecretary of state, chief of staff, or general secretary. Each is chairman of his respective section. Each section includes a vice-chairman and the general or admiral holding the higher rank or seniority after the chairman; there are four ordinary members as well—namely, the appropriate chief of staff (normally represented by his deputy) and three officers or civil servants who serve, respectively, as military, technical, and administrative affairs reporters. The minister, undersecretaries of state, and the chief of Defense staff have the right to participate at the council meetings. The law also provides that officers and civil servants may be called in as extraordinary members or advisers.

The High Council holds both plenary and separate departmental sessions. It gives necessary, but not binding, advice to the minister of

Figure 6.1   The Italian Defense Ministry

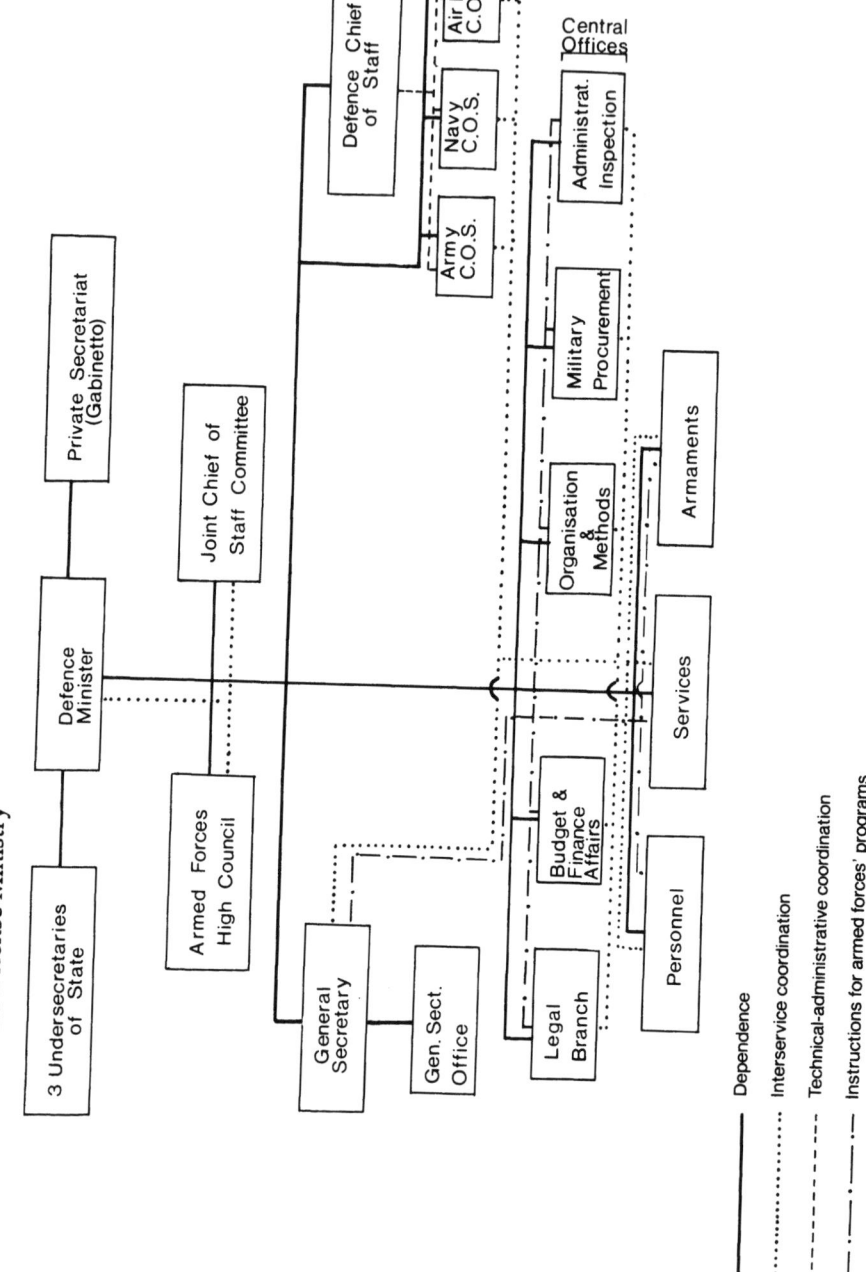

Dependence

.... Interservice coordination

--- --- Technical-administrative coordination

—·—·— Instructions for armed forces' programs

Source: Del Decrees, November 18, 1965, Nos. 1477–1478

defense on the main questions regarding the structure and combat-readiness of the armed forces, military discipline, recruiting, careers, pay, procurement, financial programs, and the military clauses in international treaties. Decisions are made by majority vote, and in case of parity the chairman's vote prevails.

The Council was intended to serve as an independent advisory board counterbalancing departmental interests with the chiefs of staffs' advice and activities. In fact, the limited independence of its chairman and vice-chairman has obviated its authority and actual importance.

The 1947–1951 "interservice" trend under the hegemony of the army (from whose ranks, during this time, the chief of Defense staff was selected) was stopped in the 1950s by the expedient of largely obsolete legislation governing the powers of the chiefs of army (1927), navy (1935), and air force (1926) staff.

The Reform of the Ministry of Defense (1965)

The reform of the Ministry of Defense and its staffs was deferred, awaiting the decisions concerning the proposed European Defense Community (EDC), whose formation had implied a complete reorganization. When the EDC proposals foundered, the need for reform was initiated at the same time as Christian Democrat, Giulio Andreotti, became minister of defense in 1959.

In 1959–1961 an Armed Forces Representative Commission (CORI) formulated concrete proposals for the reform of the Ministry of Defense. Then, on December 12, 1962, Parliament ordered the executive branch, under Law No. 1862, to promulgate legislative decrees concerning the reorganization of the Ministry of Defense, military staffs, and arsenals and factories, as well as the modification of legislation pertaining to national military service, civilian personnel, and military courts. The reform, based on delegated Decree Nos. 1477 and 1478 (both dated November 18, 1965), was put into effect in 1965–1966 (again, see Figure 6.1).

The legal, budgetary, administrative, and procurement branches of the former Gabinetto were expanded to form five central offices: legislation (Leggidife), budget (Bilandife), organization and management methods (Ormedife), procurement (Allesdife), and administrative inspections (Ispedife). Each of these offices had research, technical advisory, and coordination duties in support of the general directorates. The Gabinetto itself became the minister's private secretariat and concerned itself with the minister's political relations, relations with Parliament, ceremonies, press, information, and so on.

The thirty General Directorates (Direzioni Generali) were reduced to nineteen in 1965. Each was defined according to its functions instead of its relationship with the armed services. For example, eight are concerned with personnel matters: army officers (Personale Ufficiali), army NCOs and privates (Sottuffesercito), navy (Maripers), air force (Persaereo), employees (Difeimpiegati), workers (Difeoperai), pensions (Difepensioni), and welfare (Difeassist). One directorate is concerned with draft and mobilization (Levadife), and three more with engineering (Geniodife), medical (Difesan), and quartermaster (Commidife) services. There is one legal directorate (Contendife) and one for general services (Difeservizi). Finally, there are five general directorates concerned variously with R&D and procurement activities associated with ground (Terrarmimuni), naval (Navalcostarmi), and air (Costarmaereo) weapons and equipment, communications (Telecomdife), and motoring vehicles (Motordife). In July 1980, the minister of defense had a bill passed concerning the unification of the departments of Terrarmimuni, Motordife, and parts of Geniodife.

Each central office and general directorate contains a general director, one or two deputies, a senior office executive, some inspectors and advisers, and various subdivisions often grouped into inspection branches (e.g., the *Reparti*). These divisions were organized into two or more sections. Membership of the more important offices within the directorates were distributed proportionately between the army, navy, air force, and civil service.

In an effort to bring up to date the recruiting and training of civil servants, the Defense Civil Servants School, Civilscuoladife, was created. During the period 1968–1976 an official review, *L'Amministrazio ne della Difesa*, was published for the purpose of studying and reviewing the main problems of defense management, programming, and expenditures. In the late 1960s, and influenced by Robert McNamara's managerial ideology, studies were carried out to adapt the U.S. planning, programming, and budgeting system (PPBS) to Italian defense management and control. On the basis of this model, a theoretical Unified Functional Defense Structure (SFUD) was developed. In spite of its mention in the *Defence White Book* of 1977, the PPBS/SFUD was in fact abandoned due to the growing difficulty of interservice coordination and obsolete legislation.

According to Decree No. 1478 (1965), the army, navy, and air force general secretaries were to be replaced by a general secretary of defense, who, in turn, was to be a three-star general chosen on a rotational basis from the three services. The general secretary of defense became the minister's chief adviser on all technical-administrative matters. The duties of this office include the development of directives according to the general criteria approved by the minister of defense (1) to coordinate the major activities of the Central Offices and the General Directorates, (2) to inform the minister about administrative actions, and (3) to give information concerning the completion of technical-financial defense programs to the chief of defense staff. On November 24, 1978, a decree was passed making the general secretary of defense the Italian national armament director responsible for Italian involvement in NATO and Conference of National Armaments Directors (CNAD) activities.

The Office of the General Secretary of Defense, Segredifesa, is divided into four departments, or Reparti. The first coordinates regulations and personnel (OAP); the second coordinates administrative activities; the third manages and coordinates defense-industrial procurement in association with the central office of Allesdife; and the fourth oversees financial programming and, since 1978, coordinates the R&D activities formerly assigned to the Technical Scientific Council of Defense (CTSD). The first department is headed by an admiral, the fourth by an air force general, and the second and third by army generals.

Following the law passed in January 1982 concerning interservice administration, the powers of the general secretary of defense were greatly increased. It gave the chief of the second Reparto (administrative coordination) the power of intervention in administrative procurement procedures. Accordingly, Bilandife and the general directors were in fact placed under the offices of the Segredifesa and thus decreased the minister's authority.

The practicality of separating military procurement from that of administrative activities is currently (1984) under discussion within the government. Two possible changes have been suggested. One concerns separation of the office of the national armament director from that of the office of the general secretary; the other concerns the placement of two national directors, one for armament and one for administration, under the general secretary of defense. In this second case, the National Armament Directorate would absorb Allesdife and a part of Ormedife, as well as the third and fourth Reparti of the Segredifesa. The National Administration Directorate would then absorb the rest of the central offices and the Segredifesa.

The rationale for an Italian centralized organization of defense would imply that the nineteen general directorates should be placed under the direct control of national directors as well as of the general secretary, and would then be answerable to both the minister of defense and the general directors. In this way, the growing influence of the armed forces' chiefs of staff in the general directorates would be counterbalanced, thereby ensuring more effective interservice coordination.

The Structure of the Staffs Since 1965

The most sensitive point of the reform was that concerning the relationship between the chief of defense staff and the chiefs of army, navy, and air force staffs. The reform aimed at improving interservice coordination under more effective direction from the chief of defense staff; the move, however, evoked strong reactions from the chiefs of the armed forces staffs for several reasons. According to Decree No. 1477 (November 18, 1965), the responsibilities and duties of the chief of defense staff, while unchanged compared with those of 1948, became more explicit and his powers were increased. With the power of appointment of senior officers, except for three-star generals who must be appointed by the government, the chief of defense staff acquired powers of coordination with respect to technical-scientific activities, unified intelligence services, and operational planning and financial programming matters.

To perform these duties, a Defense Staff, the Difestat, was created, with five departments (Reparti): personnel, operations, plans and military policy, logistics, and budgeting and communications. The headships of the Reparti were held, respectively, by three army generals, a navy admiral, and a general of the air force.

Placed under the direction of the Defense Staff, among others, were the armed forces' intelligence service, SIFAR, and, following the reform in 1968, SID; the High Military Studies Center (CASM) and Interservice Staff Institute (ISMI); the Military Center for Civil Defence Studies; liaison offices and agencies of Italian representatives and delegates to international organizations and headquarters; the Defense Service Unit; and the Technical Scientific Council of Defense (CTSD), which had been formed in 1961 to coordinate and direct the armed forces' research and testing activities. In 1978 the CTSD was absorbed into the third and fourth Reparti of the Segredifesa, and following the 1977 reform of the intelligence services, the military intelligence (SISMI) and the State intelligence (SISDE) services were placed under the direction of the premier and the Interministerial Committee for Intelligence and Security (CIIS).

The chief of defense staff's directives to the other chiefs of staff and the general secretary were specifically required or approved by the minister of defense. These directives demanded prior consultation with the concerned military authorities, and, for the first time, they became a binding commitment on the military authorities.

Also for the first time, a law was passed that gave the same duties and powers to each of the army, navy, and air force chiefs of staff. In effect, they became the minister's "high advisers" in matters pertaining to their own spheres of responsibility, with the right to send him proposals concerning laws and regulations and to give instructions by means of a minister's proxy to the administrative offices of the Defense Ministry.

Since the abolition in 1965 of the army, navy, and air force general secretaries, who had previously held the same rank as their corresponding chiefs of staff, the reponsibilities and powers of the army (Statesercito), navy (Maristat), and air force (Stataereo) staffs were considerably clarified and expanded in the field of administration and logistics. Many administrative duties, formerly the responsibility of the general directorates, were transferred to the armed forces' staffs, which added, for this purpose, a newly formed Logistic Inspectorate (Ispelog).

A sixth department, including the previous Programming and Budget Office, was added to the other five Reparti of each armed force staff (i.e., personnel; intelligence, or SIOS; planning, training, and operations; services, infrastructures, movement, and transport; and general affairs). The staff's inner organization was determined by directives from its own chief. In this way, the general directorates concerned with military procurement and personnel, which separately represented each armed service, became, in fact, quasi-external agencies of the armed force staffs.

From a political point of view, the 1962–1966 period of reform decreased the influence of the military compared with the civilian component of the Central Organization of Defense, as well as that of the army by comparison with the other two services. However, the reform increased the actual powers and influence of the chief of defense staff and the general secretary of defense, two offices held at the time, respectively, by General Giuseppe Aloia and General Giraudo. Both men belonged to the Andreotti circle.

At the same time, the 1962–1966 reform also improved the real importance of the other chiefs of staff within their respective armed services, thereby transforming them into effective armed force commanders rather than mere figureheads. The effect, however, was to give rise to structural tension between the defense staff and other staffs. Moreover, the concentration of so much military power in the hands of the chief of defense staff was believed to be a danger to Italian democracy as well as a constraint to the political control of the Defense Ministry by both the minister and Parliament. The reform produced much criticism from both the press and the left-wing political parties. In Maurice Duverger's opinion,[5] the best way to control the military was *divide et impera*, an opinion that was frequently quoted by the Communist Senator Arrigo Boldrini. In fact, the reform seems to have followed this advice. In 1966 rivalry among the generals and staffs had already become evident, most noticeably between Generals Aloia and De Lorenzo.

General De Lorenzo, a former commander of the Carabinieri and subsequently chief of army staff, led the opposition of the chiefs of the armed forces staffs by refusing to accept Aloia's directives ordering an extension of the anti-Communist psychological warfare and counter-guerrilla commando training (corsi d'ardimento) in each of the Italian armed forces. He took the initiative and abolished this training in the army. However, during the same year De Lorenzo himself became involved in the SIFAR affair, which concerned irregularities within the intelligence service; he was later dismissed as the result of an unprecedented Cabinet decision based on his apparent involvement in the supposed 1964 military coup d'etat attempt.

In 1967, for the first time, a Socialist, Roberto Tremelloni, held the position of defense minister. The navy and air force received from him a ministerial circular ordering that the annual defense budget was to be shared among the army, navy, air force, Carabinieri, and Central Defense Administration, thereby reducing the coordination powers of the chief of defense staff and reversing the interservice trend of the years between 1962 and 1966.

According to Law No. 200 (March 8, 1968), a new Joint Chiefs of Staff Committee, including the chiefs of defense and armed forces staffs, as well as the general secretary, was appointed to act as a "highest advisory board" to the minister. Matters of responsibility and operational procedures for the committee were described in detail by Decree No. 781 (October 13, 1972).

The responsibility for the committee's proposals was collegial: Proposals and opinions addressed to the minister of defense were to be decided by the majority, and any disagreements were to be included, on request, by members holding differing opinions. Decisions concerning matters under the jurisdiction of one of the members were to be considered as directives of action emanating from the committee itself. The committee was involved in operational planning, financial programming, structural organization of the armed forces and interservice coordination, and the central and territorial organization of the Defense Department. The institution of the Joint Chiefs of Staff Committee has strongly reduced, if not altogether abolished, the coordinating powers and authority of the chief of defense staff. The latter is able to issue directives only through his committee's chairman, but the chairman himself is only a "primus inter pares" (first among equals).

The supporters of this *primus inter pares* arrangement, mostly navy officers, affirm that the Joint Committee follows the British model and is based on a "collegial" settlement of interservice coordination. Its opponents would prefer a West German model based on an "individual" arrangement, which would make chiefs of staff the commanders of their own services and thereby place them under the official powers of the chief of defense staff, who acts as commander of all the armed forces.

From 1950 to 1972 the chief of defense staff—namely, Generals Luigi Marras, Giuseppe Mancinelli, Aldo Rossi, Giuseppe Aloia, Guido Vedovato, and Enzo Marchesi—had been selected from the army. Generals Marras, Aloia, Vedovato, and Marchesi had previously been chiefs of army staff, whereas Generals Mancinelli and Rossi acted on behalf of and as substitutes for the chief of army staff, who were Generals Giorgio Liuzzi (1954–1959) and Giuseppe Aloia (1962–1965), respectively. In this way, the highest Italian military office became, in effect, the army's mechanism to exert hegemony over the other two services.

Since 1972, two navy admirals, Eugenio Henke (1972–1975) and Giovanni Torrisi (1980–1981), and two air force generals, Francesco Cavalera (1977–1980) and Lamberto Bartolucci (since 1983), have held the position of chief of defense staff along with two army generals, Andrea Viglione (1975–1977) and Vittorio Santini (1981–1983).

Admiral Henke, a former director of the intelligence service (SID), later became involved in the so-called State slaughter affair and was indicted for alleged collusion between neo-Fascist terrorism and the intelligence services. Admiral Torrisi, during his term in office, was charged with membership in a secret Freemasonic Lodge, P2, which attempted to exert hidden political power, and thus was obliged to resign.[6]

The two admirals, however, were the only chiefs of defense staff who exerted any significant influence on Italian military policy, and hence greatly increased the role of the navy. It soon became evident that the collegial approach to the responsibility for military policy, as well as the alternation of the three armed services represented on the Defense Staff, was not able to guarantee complete interservice coordination. In 1972–1973 the navy, in spite of its chairmanship of the Joint Committee, forwarded the details of its decennial naval program, Legge Navale, directly to the minister, requesting expenditures for 1973–1982 of 1,000 billion lire, without first submitting it for the committee's agreement. In this way, the Joint Chiefs of Staff Committee could not carry out a real interservice program; moreover, along with the renunciation of the PPBS/SFUD and the 1967 ministerial circular concerning the annual sharing of the defense budget, the Joint Committee's function was reduced to that of a mere clearinghouse.

Procurement Procedures and the Military Industrial Complex

Italian military industrial production has mostly been in the hands of the private sector, but the military departments have developed their own arsenals and workshops, officially called the "defense industrial area," for the main purpose of repairs and the manufacture of small arms, engineering and maintenance, and vehicle parts.

During World Wars I and II, two separate departments were created to coordinate war production—namely, the Undersecretariat (later termed Ministry) for Arms and Munitions, directed by General Alfredo Dallolio from 1915 to 1918, and the Undersecretariat for War Production, directed by General Carlo Favagrossa from 1940 to 1944.[7] In the period immediately following World War II, the Italian military industry was largely closed down, except for the naval sector, due largely to the after-effects of the war, the technical obsolescence of the equipment, and the demobilization of the armed forces. The survival of the ground and air sectors of the Italian military industry and the growth of the electronic sector were both assisted, however, by the need for repairs of obsolete equipment, both national and allied, and the procurement of weapons for the Italian Armed Forces produced under license from the United States and Britain. The Italian Armed Forces, however, were for the most part equipped in 1948–1953 by direct supply of U.S. surplus weaponry under the Mutual Defense Aid Program (MDAP).[8]

Since the early 1970s, however, the Italian military industry has grown mainly due to exports to the Third World. At present, Italy is the fifth largest armament exporter of the world, after the United States, the USSR, France, and the United Kingdom. Nevertheless, the Italian Armed Forces account for only 30 to 40 percent of the national military production, and are equipped only partly with weapons and materials of national origin. The exception is the navy, which has commissioned the naval shipbuilding industry to build ships suitable for both Italian and Third World navies.

The Italian defense industry comprises approximately 150 firms, of which only 40 are able to produce off-shore "key-in-hands." All of the firms are grouped in part into public financial holdings (EFIM, IRI). The defense industry employs about 100,000 persons (1982), and has a turnover of 6,000 billion lire (U.S.$4 billion), at least 50 percent of which is exported. During the decade from 1970 to 1980, the growth rate was 100 percent, compared with a 5 percent growth rate in manufacturing and an 11 percent growth in the oil industry.[9]

Unfortunately, this industrial sector lacks the necessary inner coordination and a sole interlocutor at the government and defense levels. Consequently, the structure of the Italian defense industry is unbalanced, with scarcities in major sectors and superabundances elsewhere, monopolies in some cases and unrestrained competition in others. In addition, there are rivalries, expensive duplications, and complicated industrial relations with the Ministry of Defense, which in certain instances have caused the failure of important initiatives. In the long run, these discrepancies damage research and development, cut down the acquisition of advanced technologies, and hamper standardization and coordination at the national, European, and Atlantic levels.

In this way, the Italian military industry has become increasingly dependent on foreign countries for acquiring patents and know-how, and continues to run the risk of being excluded from the Western and European defense markets. The "European option," with the formation of a European Armament Agency as interlocutor for the European Defense Improvement Program (EDIP), is at present an unrealistic one, notwithstanding the "Tornado," FH-70, and other such programs.[10] More realistic, however, is the "Third World option," which depends on U.S. approval concerning know-how, patents, exported weapons, and technology. This goal has been reached with the decennial and renewable Memorandum of Understanding (MOU) between Italy and the United States, which was signed in Washington on September 11, 1978, by Minister of Defense Attilio Ruffini and U.S. Secretary of Defense Harold Brown.

Nonetheless, the government's coordination of the military industry is still lacking. Absent in the ministry of defense is any representative in the Interministerial Committee for Industrial Policy (CIPI); this is also the case in the Ministry of Public Sharing, in spite of its public holdings (IRI, EFIM). Only the general director of Allesdife is a member of the Board of Directors of IRI.

The functions of the former Ministry for War Production have been transferred to the Ministry of Industry and Trade by Decree No. 24, passed on January 27, 1944. No special structure for the defense industry has yet been created, except for the permanent military representative (a colonel, in fact) in the Ministry of Industry and Trade. The latter is also the secretary of the defense industry's Interministerial Technical

Committee, chaired by the chief deputy of the defense staff. Created by the decrees of October 1, 1964, and April 16, 1971, this committee is responsible for the coordination of the activities of the two aforementioned ministries in the areas of defense research, development, and production. The decree of February 28, 1967, introduced by the minister of industry, provided for an interministerial committee for the study and planning of industrial mobilization in time of war. However, given that the responsibilities of such a committee are somewhat hypothetical in this era of deterrence, it has effectively ceased its activities since 1974, without ever having produced any significant studies.

As a group of Institute for International Affairs (IAI) researchers have pointed out, the Italian procurement policy has developed under a previous agreement with the Atlantic Alliance:

> [D]ecisions and evaluations, made by national administrations and duly approved by Governments, are discussed at the Alliance level and retransmitted as allied "force goals" to national administrations. "Force goals" thus become "force proposals" which are submitted for approval to the Alliance's political organs, the Atlantic Council and Defence Council. Once these have been discussed and approved at a political level they return to National Administrations as "force goals" which have to be put into practice.[11]

In the absence of a true interservice program, each single armed service elaborates its own requirements, assuming "that the annual budget allocated for defence expenditures will correspond to the budget assigned to it in previous years, with upward and downward variations according to the country's economical situation.[12] Each staff usually proposes its programs to the Joint Chiefs of Staff Committee, which, according to the above-mentioned 1967 Ministerial Circular, is reponsible for sharing the annual defense budget among the services, the Carabinieri, and the Central Defense Administration. Following its approval, each proposed program is included in the Interservice Procurement Program, and the fourth Reparto of each service staff gives instructions to the proper general directorate, which defines its technical features and contractual terms and prices, and later tests the product and reviews its effectiveness.

Customarily, the procedures for defense contracts are competitive, with calls for tender and bidding. These procedures are explicitly required both by the Memorandum of Understanding between Italy and the United States and by Law No. 113 (March 30, 1981), which enforces European Economic Community Directive No. 77/62 (December 31, 1976) concerning public contracting procedures allowing competition of European firms. But Italian law also permits private negotiations, which are considered more appropriate and even more economical, in the long run, than the open ones. The FH-70 program, for example, was contracted to the OTO-Melara company following private negotiations emanating from the Terrarmimuni. It is generally accepted that the current contracting procedures are too bureaucratic and involved. A study by the Center for Social Research (CENSIS) underscores the fact that a contract between a private firm and the Ministry of Defense must pass through fifteen stages at different executive and control levels.[13]

Since 1978, the competence of Segredifesa in procurement and contracting procedures has significantly improved as a result of the delegation of the office of national armament director to the general secretary. The duties of the general secretary are to (1) oversee the fulfillment of major programs so as to clarify the eventual decisions made by the Joint Chiefs of Staff Committee regarding the prosecution of these programs; (2) oversee and coordinate expenditures in foreign countries, stimulate cooperation and coproduction governed by international agreements, order national industry to coordinate industrial clearances, royalties, and relations between the Ministry of Defense and national industry; and (3) propose, at the proper levels, activities necessary for harmonizing Defense Ministry goals in the fields of research, development, production, and procurement with the policies of the national economic industry and technical-scientific research.

Remodernization and renewal programs of the armed forces are financed by Chapters 4011 (army), 4031 (navy), and 4051 (air force) of the defense budget. Major programs, however, have been financed over a period of ten years by the so-called Promotional Laws of the navy (1973), air force (1975), and army (1977), which are aimed at promoting Italian industrial relations and supporting the national economy.[14] These laws are not programming acts but only financial acts, and the programs themselves have had to be refinanced by new laws and, at times, reduced because of inflation. Each law provides ten annual shares, which were inserted yearly in the above-mentioned chapters of the defense budget, as well as a committee for its fulfillment, chaired by an undersecretary of state in addition to two magistrates from the Council of State and the Court of Accounts. Members of the committee also include the chairman of the corresponding section of the Armed Forces High Council; the general directors of Terrarmimuni, Motordife, Telecomdife, Naval-costarmi, and Costarmaereo; the general director of industrial production from the Ministry of Industry; and a representative from the staff of each service chief of staff.

The Communist Proposals (1983)

A wide reform of the Italian Central Organization of Defense has been proposed in a bill dated August 10, 1983, sent by the Communist deputy M. P. Cerquetti, who is also the official reporter of the Inquiring Parliamentary Commission on armaments and military procurement.[15]

The principal proposals are as follows: first, to allocate, again to the Parliament, the responsibility for any decision regarding the employment, mobilization, and external deployment of men and units of the armed forces in time of peace. For this purpose, the bill forbids the government to execute in a provisional way the international military treaties that have not yet been ratified by the Parliament, and provides for the appointment of special inquiring commissions in each instance of actual employment.

A second proposal was to attribute to the Cabinet a quinquennial strategic and military planning competence, and to the premier the responsibility for its execution with the power to coordinate civil and military defense in peace and war. According to this proposal, an interministerial committee would be appointed for procurement activities, and in cases of emergency the ministers of defense and civil protection would assume command, respectively, for both military and civil defense. In case of military emergency an operational center would be activated by the office of the president of the Cabinet.

Third, the chief of defense staff was to be transformed into the higher military adviser to all the political authorities (Parliament, premier, Cabinet, and minister of defense), with direct competence in military policy, forces planning, programming and budgeting, interservice training, operations intelligence, and doctrine of employment. The chiefs of armed forces staff would keep competence only in personnel, training, and R&D activities, whereas the Joint Chiefs of Staff Committee would be reduced to that of a mere chief of defense staff advisory board, with opinions considered necessary but not binding. Further, according to Cerquetti, the importance of the Armed Forces High Council would be emphasized, thus permitting its transformation into a higher military advisory board to the minister of defense.

The fourth and final proposal was to separate operational from administrative technical competences, attributing the latter ones to the general secretary of defense, who would become the technical reporter of the Interministerial Committee for Procurement. The competence to determine procurement procedures and contractual arrangements within the limits of the laws governing public accounts and international agreements would be transferred to the Cabinet under parliamentary control.

Conclusions

In sum, the problem of the Italian high command is characterized, first, by the artificial distinction between the *constitutional* and the effective *political* contexts. The former consists of the president of the Republic as commander of the armed forces and chairman of the Supreme Defense Council, which is ruled by law but lacks any actual power. The latter, consisting of the domain of the government, the minister of defense, and the Parliament, obtains its power from existing practices and is reinforced by its functional relevance. However, as a consequence of this domain's lack of legal formalization, political agencies are not fully able to take part in national defense or military decisionmaking policy. In this political context, theoreticians point out the need to support the executive branch of government with an interministerial political and strategic committee.

Second, in the technical or military context, there is no clear distinction made between the *operational* high command and the *logistical* command. As a result, three different military high commands continue to exist— the army, navy, and air force staffs, all concerned with both logistical and operational fields. Interservice coordination is not sufficiently ensured by the chief of defense staff, the responsibilities of which have progressively diminished since 1968, or by the Joint Chief of Staff Committee, which acts, above all, as an interservice clearinghouse in the logistic field.

There are presently two trends of reform concerning the technical and military levels of the high command. The first trend is perceived by scholars and young officers (e.g., Bess, Schwarzenberg and Luigi Caligaris) who would like to see a complete separation of the operational command from the logistical one, such that the logistic responsibilities are removed from the service staffs and concentrated in the hands of the general secretary of defense. They envisage that the general secretary of defense would eventually be assisted by two or three deputies for personnel, budget, and procurement. Caligaris has suggested the necessity for a collegial advisory board for the minister of defense, with the status of a defense committee and composed of the four chiefs of staff, the general secretary, and his deputies. He also recommends a joint committee consisting exclusively of the four chiefs of staff as a collegial high command for operations.

Another completely different reform has been suggested by the Giannini Panel—namely, to keep the present structure and increase only the coordinating powers of the general secretary by introducing a dual system for interservice coordination, that is, one administration for peacetime, with a collegial structure ensured by the Joint Chief of Staff Committee, and another for wartime, with an individual structure controlled by the chief of defense staff as general commander of the operational forces. It is interesting to note that the past minister of defense, Lelio Lagorio, preferred the same structure for both peacetime and wartime—specifically, the vertical structure exerted by the chief of defense staff.

The plurality of issues makes it very difficult to envisage an early rationalization of the Italian High Command, but external and inner political pressures could encourage or even suddenly quicken the pace of reform.

Notes

1. The Jupiter missiles were withdrawn in 1962 by the fourth Fanfani cabinet, as a counter-item for the withdrawal of USSR missiles from Cuba. On May 26, 1983, after his meeting with President Reagan in Washington, Premier

Fanfani stated that with such a decision Italy had helped the United States to avoid a nuclear war.

2. See V. Ilari, *Le Forze armate tra politica e potere (1943–1976)* (Firenze: Vallecchi, 1979), pp. 58ff., 96ff., 159ff.

3. See V. Ilari, in *Politica Militare*, no. 12 (April-May 1982), pp. 37–46.

4. See V. Ilari, in *Rivista Militare*, no. 2 (March-April 1983), pp. 13–26.

5. Maurice Duverger, *The Idea of Politics* (London, 1966).

6. Prefect Pelosi (General Secretary of CESIS), the Republican under-secretary of state at the Ministry Defense, Pasquale Bandiera, and Generals Giuseppe Santovito, Giulio Grassini, and Orazio Giannini, the directors, respectively, of the military (SISMI), State Intelligence (SIDE), and the Revenue Guard were charged with the same illegal involvement and were obliged to resign their office. Approximately 150 armed forces, Carabinieri, revenue guard, and state police officers were also charged with "P2" membership.

7. See Massimo Mazzetti, *L'industria italiana nella grande guerra* (Rome: Ufficiostorico dello SME, 1979); C. Favagrossa, *Perche perdemmo la guerra* (Milan: Rizzoli, 1946); F. Minniti, in *Storia Contemporanea*, no. 4 (December 1975), pp. 849–879, and no. 1 (February 1978), pp. 5–51; see also *Clio*, no. 4 (October-December 1977), pp. 305–340, and no. 1 (January-March 1979), pp. 79–126.

8. Something like 13 to 14 thousand billion 1981 lire from the sale of armaments were transferred to the United States from Italy. See Giuseppe Mayer, *Le ripercussioni economiche e finanziarie delle spese militari italiane in dieci anni de Alleanza atlantica* (Rome: Stabililmento Fotomeccanico, 1959).

9. See Fabrizio Battistelli, *Armi: nuovo modellow di sviluppo? L'indusstria militare in Italia* (Torino: Einaudi, 1980); Antonio Colomba, *Analisi del settorre militare italiano e delle spese paer la difesa (1945–1982)* (graduate thesis, Faculty of Economics, Rome University, 1982); AA.VV., *Il complesso militare industriale in Italia* (Rome: Convegno FLM-LOC, April 15-16, 1978); Rosenberg and Sellier, Turin, 1979; CNR, *L'attività aerospaziale in Italia*, (Indagine SORIS, Torino-Milano 1971); EFIM, *Ammodernamento dei sistemi di difesa e sua correlazione con lo sviluppo dell'industria, dell'occupazione e dell'esportazione* (August 1976); *Catalogo della produzione militare industriale italiana* [Italian Defense Production catalogue] (Rome: Societa Edizioni propaganda Aria-Mare-Terra, 1981); Sergio A. Rossi, in *Défense Nationale* (April 1982), pp. 85–94; C. Romiti and Michele Nones, in *Informazioni Parlamentari Difesa*, no. 9 (1983); Camera dei Deputati, *Relazione della commissione parlamentare di inchiesta e di studio sulle commesse di armi e mezzi ad uso militare* [Hon. Enea Cerquetti, Communist party of Italy] (Rome, 1983).

10. See European Parliament, Political Commission, Statement by Egon Klepsch on European Cooperation in the Armament Procurement (May 8, 1978); Italian translation by La Pietra, editor (Milan, 1979).

11. R. Aliboni, M. Cremasco, F. Gusmarolli, and S. Silvestri, in *Lo Spettatore Internationale*, no. 2 (April-June 1980), p. 169.

12. Ibid., p. 176.

13. See *Espansione*, no. 12 (April 1970), p. 102.

14. In this context, the Defense Ministry and its staffs have supported initiatives such as the Genoa Naval Exposition since 1976.

15. The report was published in November 1983. Cerquetti also published in 1975—*Le Forze armate italiane dal 1945 al 1975: Structure e dottrine* (Milan: Feltrinelli, 1975)—and has announced a new book on the Italian Army.

7

The Japanese Central Organization of Defense

Masashi Nishihara

Product of the Cold War

Born out of the Korean War

The Japanese Defense Agency, Japan's defense ministry, and the Japanese Self-Defense Forces (JSDF), Japan's armed forces, were officially established on July 1, 1954. They were born after long "labor pains," and even today, after thirty years of existence, they are still suffering from the after-effects. The old Imperial Army and Navy, defeated by the Allied powers, were completely demobilized in the immediate postwar years under the Allied occupation authorities headed by General Douglas MacArthur (Supreme Commander for the Allied Powers, or SCAP). Their high-ranking officers were tried and purged from public office by the Allies; some were executed. The victorious U.S. forces, which came to occupy the defeated nation, fulfilled their dual goal of the complete demobilization and democratization of Japan.

However, the demilitarization process ended abruptly in June 1950, when the cold war turned into a hot war in the Korean Peninsula. Washington quickly reversed the policy of demilitarization and pressed Tokyo to rearm. By then, the Japanese, both leaders and the masses, had been so effectively educated by the U.S. occupiers about their "guilt" in starting the "immoral" Pacific war, and about the paramount importance of a moral commitment to pacifism, that it was politically very difficult for Tokyo to adopt a rearmament policy. As will soon be discussed, the new Constitution of 1946, which denounced war, had been drafted by MacArthur's SCAP headquarters, and many Japanese thought that their country would no longer have to possess a military force.

The Japanese rearmament process thus began with a euphemistic name: the Police Reserve Force. On July 8, 1950, within two weeks after the Korean War broke out, MacArthur instructed Prime Minister Shigeru Yoshida's government to organize a Police Reserve Force of 75,000 men to replace the same number of U.S. occupation forces (four infantry divisions) as a force to maintain internal security, since the U.S. forces had to be transferred to the Korean Peninsula. The Police Reserve Force was established on August 10 by a government ordinance, not by a law adopted through the parliamentary process, in order to avoid possible parliamentary filibusters. Most of the equipment required was provided by the United States, and the recruitment and training of reserves were carried out under the supervision of the U.S. Military Advisory Group. The Police Reserve Force was not under the existing police organizations but was a separate force, although initial recruitment was conducted by the police organizations. At first, officers were recruited from among wartime nonregular officers; later they came directly from among prewar and wartime professionals, of ranks from major to colonel, as they began to be removed from the purge list by the SCAP.

Japan regained its sovereignty on April 28, 1952. Six months later, on October 15, 1952, the name of the Police Reserve Force was changed by law to the Security Force, a step closer to the image of the armed forces. The law passed the Diet on July 31, 1952, and the Police Reserve Force Headquarters was renamed the Security Agency on the following day. The new agency was placed directly under the Prime Minister's Office rather than given a separate ministerial rank. It also integrated the armed coast guard forces of the Maritime Safety Agency, a branch of the Ministry of Transportation. These armed coast guard forces were soon to become the Maritime Self-Defense Force. By this time the Security Force had some 110,000 ground troups and 8,000 maritime troops. More prewar regular officers, now depurged, occupied leading positions in the Security Force.

On September 27, 1953, Prime Minister Yoshida made the important decision that Japan should form a long-term defense plan; he thus proposed to change the name of the Security Force again. This time his colleagues suggested the "Self-Defense Force" (SDF) as a name. It was some nine months before the new name was officially adopted. In the meantime, an air force wing was established within the Coast Guard Force of the Maritime Safety Agency in September 1953. And in October a study was initiated to consider adding another air force wing to the security force, which would be designed to develop later into a full-fledged Air Self-Defense Force. Thus, after heated debates the laws passed in the National Diet on June 9, 1954, allowing for the establishment of the Defense Agency and the services of the Self-Defense Force. These organizations were officially inaugurated on July 1, 1954. The SDF began with an authorized size of 152,112 service personnel. By 1983 it had grown to 272,162 men, with 180,000 in the land force, 45,199 for the sea, 46,834 for the air, and 129 for the joint staff.

Between Washington's Demands and Pacifist Claims

The basic framework for the Defense Agency has remained unchanged for the subsequent three decades. The development of the Japanese defense establishment as a whole has two distinguishing characteristics. First, the major postwar defense policies have been under the strong influence of, if not dictated directly by, Washington. In August 1945, the United States ordered Japan to demilitarize itself and then, after the 1950 Korean War, to begin rearmament. Washington wanted to decide the size and type of the rearmed forces. After the 1960s, the United States began to reduce the size of its military presence in Japan, but it continued to watch how much Japan spent for defense and what arms Japan bought from the United States. This tendency still persists today. The Carter administration attempted to dictate to Japan the proportion of defense spending to GNP and the size of the annual increase in defense spending, and the Reagan administration has prescribed certain roles and missions for Japan to take up. Thus the government's defense policy has been one that assumes the existence of the U.S. protective umbrella and at the same time resists U.S. pressures.

Second, the government, which since 1945 (except for a short period in 1947–1948) has been consistently controlled by the same political party, the Liberal Democratic party (or its antecedents), has had to accommodate persistent pacifist sentiment opposed to rearmament programs, U.S. bases in Japan, and U.S. warships with nuclear bombs visiting ports in Japan. Consequently, the government has resorted to the use of many euphemisms to weaken political opposition. Most of the prewar and normal military nomenclature has been avoided in postwar practice: The Self-Defense Force substituted for the armed forces, the Ground Self-Defense Force for the army, the Maritime Self-Defense Force for the navy, the Air Self-Defense Force for the air force, the "ordinary troops" for the infantry, "special cars" for tanks, the director-general of the Defense Agency for a minister of defense, the Defense Academy for the military academy, and so forth.

Constitutional and Legal Bases

A Realistic Interpretation of Article 9

The Japanese defense organization has constantly suffered from constitutional ambiguity as to its very existence, and this ambiguity has caused a major postwar political controversy. Article 9 of the 1946 Constitution stipulates as follows:

> Aspiring sincerely to an international peace based on justice and order, the Japanese people forever renounce war as a sovereign right of the nation, and the threat or use of war as means of settling international disputes.
>
> In order to accomplish this aim of the preceding paragraph, land, sea, and air forces, as well as other war potential, will never be maintained. The right of belligerency of the state will not be recognized.

This very short article has been an object of political tension throughout nearly the last four decades. Does this article state that Japan can have a defense organization, or does it not? When the constitution was first promulgated in 1946, the Yoshida government explained that Japan should have no fighting forces, not even for defensive purposes. And in 1950 when the Police Reserve Force was formed, the same government justified the force by saying that "it had no fighting capabilities." Faced with strong pacifist demands to the effect that Article 9 prohibited any rearmament, the government claimed that Article 9 actually allowed Japan to exercise its right of self-defense.

It was a new interpretation, based on a new emphasis placed on the first ten words of the second paragraph of the article. In other words, the new interpretation was that Japan might have a force as long as it would use it *not* "as means of settling international disputes" but simply as a means of self-defense. The new justification was also based on Article 51 of the United Nations Charter, which refers to the right of self-defense as an inherent right of any nation. Hence the euphemism known as the "Self-Defense Force."

In a 1981 poll, as many as 82 percent of the Japanese people regarded the SDF as constitutional and thus supported it; only 8 percent opposed the SDF. Yet, the Socialist party, the largest opposition party, continues to regard the SDF as unconstitutional. On the whole, the government has been cautious in making bold moves on defense issues, for it knows that Japan's political culture is such that consensual decisions, not majority decisions, are what matter.

Legal Approaches

Despite constitutional ambiguity and public controversy as to the status of the Self-Defense Force, the government on July 1, 1954, enacted two fundamental laws concerning the force, as mentioned earlier: the Law on the Establishment of the Defense Agency (hereafter referred to as the Defense Agency Law) and the Law on the Self-Defense Force (the SDF Law). The Constitution and these laws provide the basic legal provisions for the Japanese central organization of defense.

The postwar political leaders, both in and out of power, strongly concerned about the lack of civilian control over prewar and wartime military decisions, have made extra efforts to bind defense and security issues through rigorous legalistic approaches. Opposition party leaders have often challenged the government on legal grounds. For instance, they questioned the constitutionality of F-15 fighters equipped with in-flight refueling devices. They argued that to possess such fighters able to fly over a longer range went beyond the exercise of the constitutional right to self-defense. They also opposed the government's suspected plan to have an SDF contingent participate in UN peacekeeping operations, on the grounds that sending SDF men abroad is not specified in Article 3 of the Self-Defense Force Law, which relates the purpose of the SDF. These legalistic arguments, in turn, compel the ruling party to try to find legal justifications, which are often strained, for what the SDF actually does.

Other than these legalistic arguments over such issues of a controversial nature, the laws clearly specify how the central organization of defense should operate. First, the Defense Agency Law provides that the Agency must come under the prime minister's office (Article 2) and that the director-general of the Agency must be a state minister, who must be a civilian (Article 3, and Constitution, Article 66). Second, the Agency controls and supervises the three services of the SDF (Article 4). Third, the authorized numbers and compositions of the three services are stipulated in the same law (Article 7). Fourth, the defense budget is decided upon every year by the Diet as a part of the Budget Law (Constitution, Articles 83–86). Fifth, the civilian director-general of the Agency appoints the highest-ranking officers, including the chairman of the Joint Staff Council (a four-star general or admiral) and the chiefs of staff of the three services (two- or three-star generals or admirals). The director-general, in turn, is appointed by the prime minister, who also must be a civilian and a member of the Diet, and his appointment is attested by the emperor (Constitution, Articles 66, 68). General Hiromi Kurisu, who was chief of staff of the Ground SDF, remarked in October 1977 that the chairman of the Joint Staff Council should be "attested" by the emperor, in keeping with the prewar practice for high military officers. He was severely criticized in the mass media for trying to revive militarism. The emperor under the current constitution performs only "with the advice and approval of the Cabinet" (Constitution, Article 7). The government did not consider that there was popular support for Kurisu's view.

Under the old constitution (1889–1946), the emperor exercised strong power over military matters: He had the "supreme command" of the army and navy; he determined the "organization and peace standing" of the army and navy; and he declared war, made peace, and concluded treaties. The postwar emperor was deprived of all of these powers. The postwar constitution, having denounced war, naturally gives no one the power to declare a war. It does not even include any references to whether the prime minister can declare the choice to exercise the right to self-defense. Only the SDF Law stipulates that "the Prime Minister on behalf of the Cabinet exercises the supreme 'control and supervision' over the SDF" (Article 7). This "control and supervision" is a vague though common term in the Japanese bureaucracy; it is used to denote "responsibility," which includes, in this case, "command" and "management" of the SDF.

Neither the present constitution nor the two laws just mentioned refer to conscription, by contrast to the previous constitition, which stipulated that "Japanese subjects are amenable to service in the army or navy" (Article 20). Although the current SDF members are all volunteers, there has been discussion concerning the constitutionality of a future conscription system. On this issue the government and all the opposition parties agree. Referring to Article 18 of the Constitution ("Involuntary servitude, except as punishment for crime, is prohibited") and Article 13 ("All of the people shall be respected as individuals; their right to life, liberty and the pursuit of happiness shall be, to the extent that it does not interfere with public welfare, the supreme consideration in legislation and in other governmental affairs"), they consider conscription unconstitutional. But some conservative business leaders and constitutional lawyers support the constitutionality of such a system. The SDF Law allows for reserves, but their authorized size as of 1983 was 41,600. There are no civil defense systems and no militias in Japan today.

The Structures of the Central Organization

The Structure of the Command for Operations

The Japanese central organization of defense, having dual functions of operations and administration, consists of two structures, which naturally overlap with each other. The operational command structure is intended to function as follows:

1. The prime minister bears the ultimate authority to give "orders to move troops" (SDF Law, Article 8). He gives such orders to the director-general of the Defense Agency, who in turn gives the orders to the highest-level commanders of the three services, namely, territorial army commanders of the Ground SDF, the commander of the Self-Defense Fleet and the district commanders of the Maritime SDF, and the air defense commanders of the Air SDF. These orders are given through the chiefs of staff of the three services and, in addition, to the chairman of the Joint Staff Council (JSC) in the event that integrated units need to be formed. Neither the prime minister nor the director-general "command" the troops; they simply give orders. The chiefs of staff and the Chairman of the Joint Staff Council (JSC) do not command the troops, either. They simply see to it that the director-general's orders to the highest-level commanders have been carried out. The chiefs of staff, as the highest professional advisers, assist the director-general (SDF Law, Article 9) (see Figure 7.1).

2. When a situation begins to *look* dangerous, even if the danger is not imminent, the director-general can initiate and, with the prime minister's approval, issue "orders to standby to move troops." The rest of the process for operational action is the same as that described in the previous paragraph.

3. The prime minister, in deciding to issue "orders to move troops," must obtain prior approval from the Diet or, if the Diet is not in session, must obtain an *ex post facto* approval from the Diet as soon as its next session opens (SDF Law, Article 76). He must also consult with the National Defense Council (NDC), as the highest consultative body, which is placed in the Cabinet. The NDC is composed of six civilian cabinet ministers. Other than the prime minister, who chairs the council, these

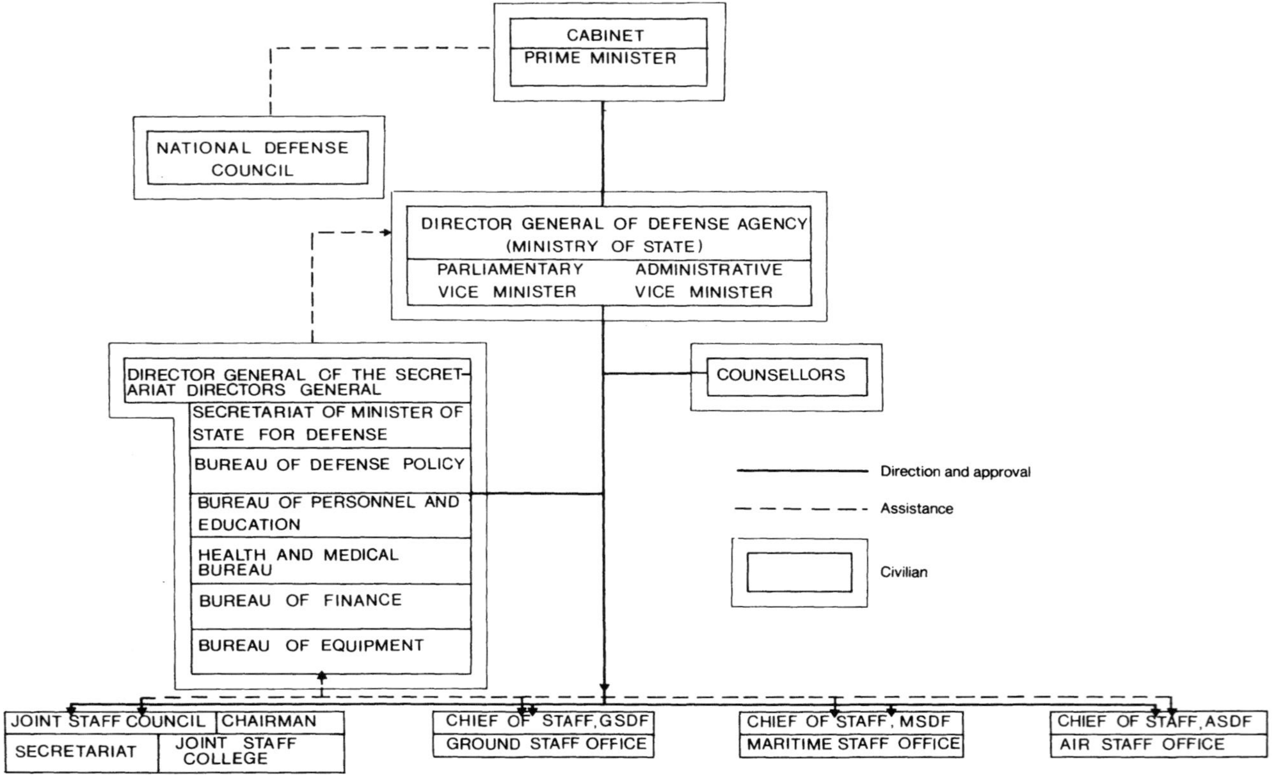

Figure 7.1 Japanese Central Organization of Defense: Process for Order, Command, and Assistance

are the deputy prime minister, the foreign minister, the finance minister, the director-general of the Defense Agency, and the director-general of the Economic Planning Agency (NDC Law, 1956, Article 4). The JSC chairman and other cabinet ministers can be present only by invitation from the chairman.

4. How fast the prime minister's orders will be executed at the battle site depends not only upon the smooth flow of orders from the top to the commanders and to the local troops, but also upon the speedy flow of communications from the local commanders to the top in an effort to seek appropriate orders. In 1976 a Soviet MiG-25 pilot flew in suddenly and landed in Hokkaido, the northernmost island, to seek political asylum. About two hours passed before the incident was reported to the director-general of the Defense Agency, and over three and a half hours before he started an emergency session in his operation room. This lesson led in 1983 to the establishment of a Central Command Post in the SDF headquarters.

The Structure of Management for Administration

Administrative matters for the SDF are being managed both by civilian sections of the Defense Agency, which are called "internal bureaus" (naikyoku), and by the general staff offices of the three services. There are five internal bureaus: the bureaus of Defense Policy, of Personnel and Education, of Finance, and of Equipment, as well as the Health and Medical Bureau. They are coordinated by the director-general (chief secretary) of the Secretariat of the Defense Agency and the administrative vice-minister serving the director-general (minister of state) of the Agency. The chief secretary and the chiefs of the five internal bureaus assume specific tasks to assist the director-general in issuing general directions concerning what is to be done by the three services and in giving approval for what has been done by them.

On administrative matters, it is thus to the chiefs of staff of the three services and the JSC chairman, not directly to the commanders of the services, that the director-general gives "directions and approvals." Both the civilian internal bureaus and the staff offices of the three services serve to assist the director-general, but the civilian wing prevails over the uniform wing (see Figure 7.2).

This is basically how administrative matters are being managed, although the exact procedures vary according to the nature of the matters in question. The National Defense Program Outline (NDPO), which currently serves as the master defense buildup plan, was adopted in 1976. Concerning the planning of defense programs, yearly and long-term, the three services formulate their draft proposals separately and, in some cases, through the Joint Staff Council, according to the directions given by the director-general of the Agency. The draft programs then go to the Bureau of Defense Policy, with whose recommendation and coordination the director-general of the Agency approves the defense programs. On this basic defense plan, the director-general consults with

140

Figure 7.2 Japanese Central Organization of Defense: Process for Direction, Approval, and Assistance

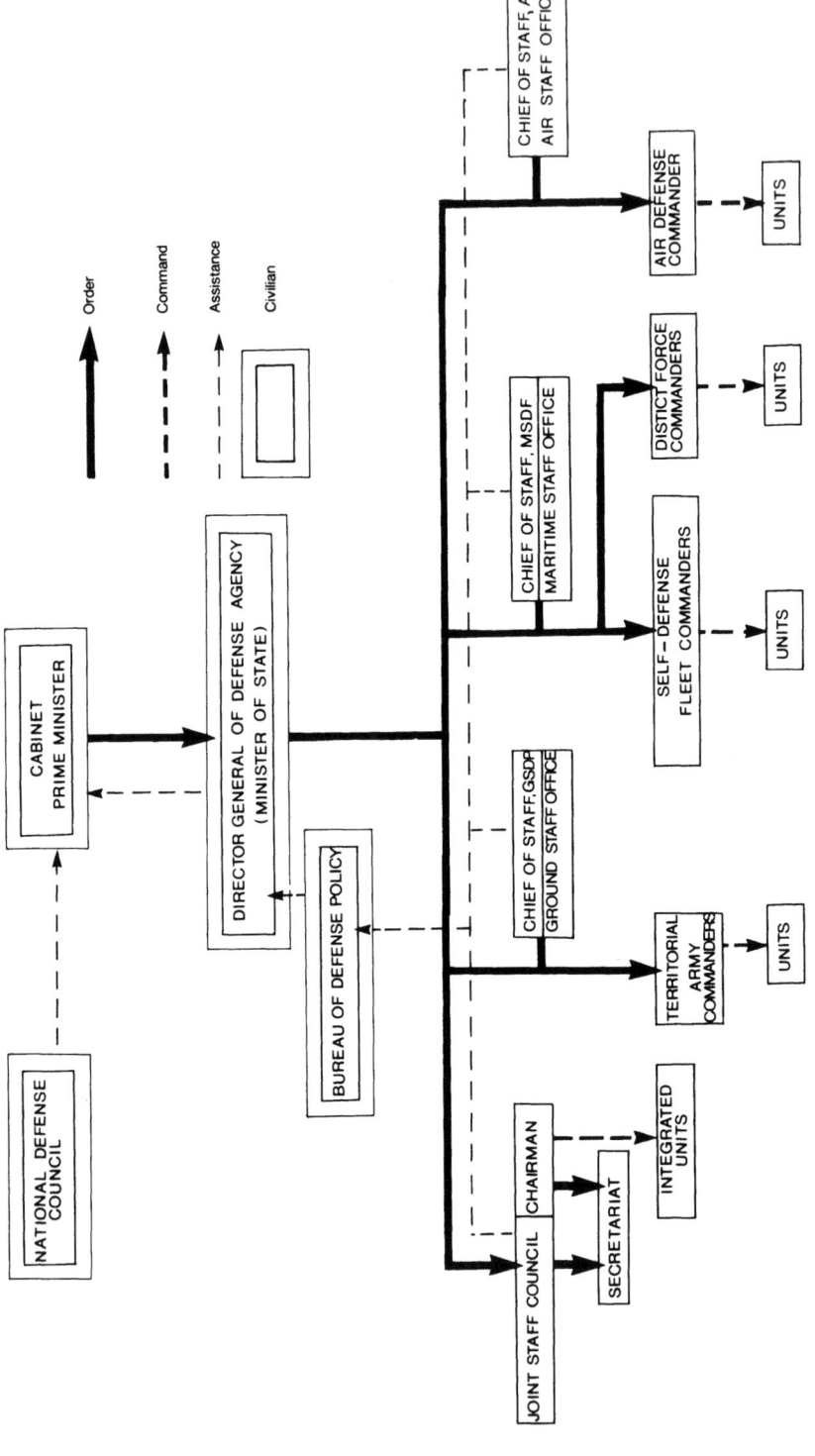

the prime minister and the National Defense Council. In this way the National Defense Program Outline was formulated in 1976, as were subsequent modified plans.

There are detailed provisions in the SDF Law and its related ordinances concerning promotions, experience, and retirement age. In accordance with these provisions, directions are issued on a regular basis by the director-general to the three chiefs of staff for whom their respective staff offices work. The latter propose their personnel plans, for instance, and submit them to the Bureau of Personnel and Education. The bureau examines them and, with modifications if necessary, recommends them to the director-general for approval. The personnel plans go neither to the National Defense Council nor to the prime minister for endorsement.

Issues of a politically sensitive nature, however, require different procedures. The selection of jet fighters has been such an issue. In the past, the Defense Agency sent survey missions of civilian and military specialists to foreign countries—the United States and Europe, in particular—and recommended the desired type of jet fighter to the director-general, who, with the prime minister, made the final decision, subject only to the agreement of the National Defense Council.

Perhaps the most complicated and politicized matter of all is the defense budget. Following tense battles within the Agency as to which service should get how much, the Agency's head must fight within the Cabinet, particularly with the minister of finance. What counts here is the prime minister's leadership and the influence he can carry over the ruling party and often over the opposition parties as well.

Informal Structures

The formal structures of command for operations and of management for administration, as described earlier, do not reveal precisely how the process actually works. Most organizations feature informal means of communication and decisionmaking. The approximately 500 civil servants in the internal bureaus of the Defense Agency and the 40,000 or so commissioned officers of the SDF alone constitute a huge and complex organization, in which "informal" processes affecting command and management are bound to be present.

Because the Japanese Self-Defense Force has never been engaged in an armed conflict, it is difficult to say what kind of informal processes will emerge in a future crisis, at a time when the chain of command will really have to work. But it is often suggested that, although the formal process requires the director-general of the Agency to issue orders to service commanders in a crisis, he would have to consult in advance with the chiefs of staff as to the nature and scope of desirable orders to be issued. The Bureau of Defense Policy, which, formally, is supposed to assist the director-general, might also be likely to consult with the military professionals. Thus, in terms of operational effectiveness, the command structure is likely to look different in a crisis when the military will have more say over what is to be done, although the principle of civilian supremacy will still be retained.

Informal processes are in operation today, particularly with respect to the management of administrative matters. Japanese people prefer informal consultations to formal ones, and consider it most important to keep personal conflicts to a minimum. The National Defense Council meetings and Joint Staff Council meetings are usually little more than ceremonial procedures. The members neither expect nor like to discuss matters, but prefer simply to approve what has already been settled beforehand by the staff. Japan's decisionmaking culture is consensual rather than majoritarian, thus signifying the importance of informal and substantive discussions at the staff level. Such a culture requires the active building of a network of personal ties crossing organizational boundaries. People try to develop their common bonds based on such factors as schooling at the same prefectures, high schools, or colleges, or at the Defense Academy itself, the same year of entering public service, and the like. These personal ties—whether cross-organizational, horizontal, or vertical—naturally facilitate informal but frank communications. Hence staff-level consultations, often not reported in the media, frequently settle major issues such as the budget, procurement, supplies, promotion, and so forth. This process is called "digging around the root of a tree" (nemawashi). Here again, the director-general actually consults with the chiefs of staff before he gives directions to them.

Civil-Military Relations

The Central Organization of Defense

On the whole, the civil-military relations in the central organization of defense are in acceptable condition, although in several critical areas the relationship appears tense. The problem is that the civilian members of the Defense Agency feel that they have to maintain control over the military officers in order to prevent any repetition of the prewar high-handed behavior of the military, whereas the officers feel they are receiving undue disrespect.

When a chief of staff of a given service receives communications from his subordinate commanders regarding external attacks or approaching dangers, he is to report not to the chairman of the JSC but directly to the head of the Bureau of Defense Policy, who in turn reports to the director-general of the Agency. The latter then reports to the prime minister. Neither the chiefs of staff nor the chairman of the JSC has direct access to the director-general of the Agency and the prime minister. Hence professional military officers, because they must go through two civilians to reach the prime minister, tend to be frustrated and often voice their unhappiness.

The chairman of the JSC has severely limited powers. He cannot initiate decisions on behalf of the Joint Staff Council. The director-general of the Agency decides the agenda for a JSC meeting; the JSC chairman only presides over such meetings. He cannot order the chiefs of staff of the three services. He can only command integrated units, provided that such units have been formed. The JSC does not function as a *joint* staff council. What is more, the JSC chairman is not an *ex officio* member of the National Defense Council.

Yet, in recent years, the "uniform" side seems to be increasing its ability to influence the "civilian" side. The budgetary process, for example, requires professional assessments of sophisticated modern weapons systems. The civilian staff of the Agency's Bureau of Finance must rely on the officers' help. In planning joint military exercises with its U.S. counterpart, the civilian Bureau of Defense policy cannot be competent without close cooperation from the officers. In fact, the arrangements at the officer's level for U.S.-Japan defense cooperation tend to take priority over the civilian side of discussions.

Democratic Control

In a democracy like Japan, civilian control over the armed forces is desirable. Because of the unhappy military behavior of the past, postwar Japan has become excessively sensitive to "democratic" control, although such control has often been taken to mean "disrespect" for the armed forces.

No officers have ever been given an opportunity to testify before the Diet and express their professional opinions about the military situations abroad and Japan's defense capability. Most such military analyses are given to the Diet members by Foreign Ministry officials and the International Affairs counsellor for the director-general of the Agency, who is also seconded by the Foreign Ministry. The position of director-general of the Agency similarly needs to be enhanced. His position is not yet renamed the minister of defense, and his post is not a powerful one among the Cabinet ministers. Among the most powerful are the minister of finance, the minister of international trade and industry, and the foreign minister. The position of the Defense Agency's head tends to be less significant. During the period from 1954 to 1983, as many as thirty-six men were appointed to this position, each with an average tenure of only ten months. Nakasone is the only prime minister to have served as the director-general of the Defense Agency.

Efforts to keep the SDF weak and disrespected do not constitute an effective method of control, for the SDF may become rebellious out of frustration and might even move to destroy the democracy. Given a proper place within the system and a proper role to play, it could become a healthy force. In this context, the Special Committees on Security, which both the Upper and Lower Houses of the Diet have established, represent a step in the appropriate direction. The committees eventually should be expected to invite service officers to their sessions.

All political leaders who are concerned about their electoral votes must be careful not to alienate strong pacifist groups around the country;

these are exploited by the Socialist party with a large degree of success. Some leading daily newspapers also exploit the pacifist sentiment. Because of Japan's consensus-oriented political culture, the government party is reluctant to take confrontational postures on defense. The LDP leaders who feel that Japan should more quickly strengthen its defense capability must accommodate themselves to such a political reality. Thus Japanese political leaders tend to follow public opinion rather than to lead it. They are responsive to public opinion rather than being responsible for it. In a Japanese-style democracy where consensus has paramount importance, perhaps there is political wisdom in not making clearcut decisions on defense issues, the responsibility of the SDF officers, nuclear issues, and so on. To live in political ambiguity, including the constitutional ambiguity of the status of the SDF itself, is a generally accepted fact of life for many Japanese.

Yet this is not to suggest such political ambiguity would survive a national crisis that might reveal its inherent contradictions. A crisis management plan, now so severely lacking in Japan, has to be based on clear analyses of likely crisis scenarios—thus ultimately demanding a clearly specified and more respected role for the defense organization.

8
Norway

Reidar Lauritz Godø

Historical Background

The origin of the central organization for defense in Norway is founded on the Constitution (Grundlov) of 1814. This is one of the oldest written constitutions in the world—second only to that of the United States. The Constitution states that the king has the highest command authority over the armed forces. Although the wording of the Constitution remains the same today, the interpretation of the wording has undergone considerable change, as will be explained later.

Until the end of the nineteenth century, the wording "the King" meant the king in person, and the successive kings in question were the kings Norway had to share with Sweden in the union Norway was forced into at the peace settlement in Kiel in 1814. The transition from Danish rule to the union with Sweden was based on the condition that the Norwegian Constitution, which had been independently developed by a Norwegian Constitutional Assembly at Eidsvold in 1814, was adopted. This arrangement gave Norway a considerable degree of independence within the union. The king's position as the highest command authority stemmed from the traditional idea of the time that leading military forces in battle was a task for the sovereign or his/her direct representative. Perhaps this royal role recalled to the Norwegians the image from their sagas of the Norse kings as leaders of their warriors. It may nevertheless seem strange today that the highest command authority was left with a king Norway had to share with a country with which it had been forced to be united and which it regarded as a potential military opponent. But as in so many situations in history, the countries were left to choose between undesirable options.

Luckily, the Constitution also contained some built-in limitations on the king's exclusive power, especially when it came to the use of military forces outside the country, the size and composition of forces, and the like—functions that were left to the Norwegian Parliament (Storting) to decide. The original command arrangement of 1814 was thus, not surprisingly, the cause of considerable conflict between the king and the Storting. This general friction was accentuated by a clause in the

Constitution that allowed military commanders to deal directly with the king on military matters; in other words, they could bypass the political authorities. This special provision remained unchanged until 1893, when the Storting decided that it was the responsibility of the minister of defense, and not of the military commanders, to deal with matters of military command in conjunction with the king.

This change of procedure followed a wider change in the relationship between the king and the Storting. Up to 1884, the members of the government were "the king's men" (the king's advisers), selected and appointed by him. In 1884, a parliamentary system of government was introduced, and from that date, the government had to answer to the Storting. In addition, the countersignature of the minister of defence was necessary for decisions on matters of military command to become valid.

The initial arrangement when Norway entered the union with Sweden did not provide for an independent Norwegian command system at all. Separate ministries for the army and the navy were established in the government of 1814, but commanders for the army and the navy were not appointed until 1830. In the meantime, the highest command authority under the king was exercised by the Statholder (governor) as the king's representative in Norway. The two ministries for the army and the navy were merged into one Ministry of Defense in 1886, and since then there have been no separate ministries for the individual services in the government. The Norwegian Ministry of Defense is nearing its hundredth anniversary—among the oldest, if not the oldest, department of its kind anywhere in the world.

As will be seen from the historical survey, it was not until the end of the nineteenth century that the government and the Storting gained full control over defense, and at that time the union with Sweden was nearing its end. Toward the end of the century there was also a considerable strengthening of Norway's defense posture, which, in the main, was aimed at establishing a defense of the Norwegian rights and interests within the union against Swedish interference. This development established a foundation for a peaceful Norwegian withdrawal from the union in 1905. Thus Norway developed into a fully independent country, with a monarchy and a king elected by a general referendum and with a constitutional system founded on the Grundlov of 1814.

In the period from the absolution of the union with Sweden in 1905 up to World War II, many organizational changes occurred within the defense complex, but these are of little significance in relation to today's command structure. Toward the end of this period there was a growing interest in civil-military cooperation in the preparations for defense, as well as an increasing recognition of the need for permanent bodies for high-level consultation and exchange of information on matters of security and defense. A special Defense Council (Forsvarsradet) was established in 1934, with the prime minister as chairman and the minister of foreign affairs, the minister of defense, the commanders of the army and the navy, and some others as members. The role of this body was, however, of little practical importance, although in the troubled decade of the 1930s, it was nevertheless a visible sign of a recognition of the need for high-level exchange of information and coordination within the fields of security and defense. Unfortunately, as in so many countries in Europe, the attempts to produce a defense posture to match the military threat did not come about. The effort may best be described as "too little and too late."

The German invasion of Norway in 1940 resulted in a number of valuable lessons. The sudden attack drove the king, the Storting, and the government into retreat, which left the central military command system in a state of disruption during the first crucial moments of the invasion. During the two months of fighting (April 9 to June 7, 1940), the central leadership of the nation had to rely on improvisation. Wherever the king and the government moved, the bombers followed. The lessons learned from this experience focused attention on the need to establish a crisis managment organization and, equally important, to make arrangements for a system of leadership with a good survival capability. During the fighting, the government appointed, for the first time in modern Norwegian history, a supreme military commander over all the military forces—a chief of defense. This position was continued when the government went into exile in London.

Norwegian Strategic Defense Philosophy

In an attempt to create a basis of understanding for the Norwegian central organization for defense of today, some remarks on the country's defense philosophy may help, given that the central organization has to fit the apparatus it is going to lead and the conditions under which it has to operate.

The strategic position of Norway is, in the main, governed by its geographic position. Not only does Norway have a common border with the Soviet Union of almost 200 kilometers, but the Norwegian border is also close to the largest military base in the world, on the Kola peninsula. The southern part of the country has a similar strategic position in relation to the outlets from the Baltic. The elongated shape of the country is also an important element in this connection. If the country were to be rotated around its southern tip, the northern tip would reach the Mediterranean. Moreover, the country is isolated geographically in relation to the other countries in the NATO alliance. Norway's very exposed strategic position in today's world needs no detailed elaboration.

Norway's geographic position, and the strategic position associated with it, means that Norway will be in the frontline, from the very outset, in any possible East-West military conflict. If to this consideration the country's small population of only 4 million is added, the problems of establishing a viable defense posture should become clear. Further, the existing policy whereby no allied forces are permanently stationed in Norway in peacetime—except for periodic training—should make it obvious that the challenge of establishing a viable defense posture calls for special solutions.

One solution lies in the Total Defense Concept (TDC). For Norway, this concept is both a philosophy and a reality. The philosophy lies in the acknowledgment that the defense of the country is everybody's concern, and that all resources have to be made available for the fight for survival. The reality lies in the fact that quite far-reaching steps have been taken in order to transfer this philosophy into positive action. This may be illustrated with two concrete examples. First there is the conscription system, a long-time tradition in Norway, which makes it possible to utilize in the fighting forces all males in the population from 20 to 45 years of age. Only vagrants and those medically unfit are exempted. Both a rapid mobilization system, organized and tested after long experience, and refresher training for those called up make it possible in a short time to raise a military force of over 300,000 men— approximately 16 percent of the total male population.

Second is the policy of nonmilitary defense, which calls for the use of the ordinary civilian apparatus to the maximum extent possible to support the fight for survival. As the military forces will have to fight within their own country, they can rely on the nonmilitary defense for a number of support functions, thereby cutting their own administrative tail to the benefit of the "shooting forces." The civilian apparatus has been supplemented with the necessary elements required for war— provisions such as the Civil Defense, shelters, medical supplies, and so on. In addition, considerable extra organizing and training have been arranged to secure a rapid transfer of activity from peace to war.

The responsibilities for the necessary preparations rest in principle with the ministry concerned. Thus all government ministries are drawn into the organization for defense. Although this organization makes clear the responsibilities for defense preparations, experience has shown that some extra bodies, both central and regional, are still needed to perform the sole function of controlling and coordinating them, particularly among the various ministries. The organization for defense will be dealt with more fully later.

The interdependence between the military and nonmilitary defense efforts requires special attention because of its importance for the total defense effort. The personnel mobilized into the fighting units must be assured that their families are taken care of while they are away from home fighting the war. Hence there must be a back-up organization to take care of their families. To a large extent this is a function for the Civil Defense. A force of over 1,000,000 men and women have been trained for this task, and a large proportion of the population has been provided room in underground shelters. The civilian authorities at every level—central, regional, and local—also have clear responsibilities in this respect. Among the many other functions that could be mentioned to illustrate the importance of a balanced total defense effort and the interdependence between the military and the nonmilitary efforts is of such importance that it calls for special attention—namely, the arrangement made by the leaders of the nation that enables them to keep the population informed in order to maintain morale and the will to continue fighting.

Overall, civil defense provisions require special preparations designed to function under wartime conditions. Good protection of the most vital facilities and utilities must be provided, as must alternative solutions meant to counteract the destruction of war (e.g., careful location and "hardening" of vital facilities, etc.).

The background just outlined aims at creating a foundation for understanding the central organization for defense in Norway. The historical survey gives a picture of the constitutional evolution leading up to the present-day relationship between the king, the Storting, the government, and the military leaders. The evolution leading up to this relationship—whether formal or informal—is very important, as it gives the central organization of defense a solid foundation that is undisputed and generally accepted. Further, the hard lessons of World War II and the tense situation in the postwar period, in combination with a general awareness of the country's exposed strategic position, have created a base for political consensus on the major issues concerning security and defense. This consensus has again created a solid foundation for establishing a viable organization for defense, together with Norway's allies in NATO.

The Organizational Structure

First, we look to the top of the organization, with particular emphasis on the decisionmaking process concerning defense policy and activity in peacetime in addition to the special provisions for crisis and war. The three central bodies in the organizational structure that come immediately into focus in this context are the Storting, the government, and the central military organization under the control of the chief of defense and the Defense Command.

The relationship between the Storting and the government generally follows the pattern common to most democratic countries whose government is based on a parliamentary system. The Storting keeps a firm control over the direction of the defense policy as an element in the country's security policy. The international situation is regularly debated, as is Norway's involvement in NATO. Items concerning arms control and disarmament are regularly on the agenda.

The appropriation of funds is the prerogative of the Storting. In practice, the Storting goes into great detail on matters of organizational structure, "manning" (i.e., personnel and numbers), location of defense facilities, procurement of equipment, length of military service, and so forth. The reasons for this are obvious, as most of the defense-related activity has significant political implications. It follows from this that the handling of matters relating to defense calls for a close relationship between the government and the Storting. The maintenance of the consensus atmosphere between the political parties on the major issues of defense and security policy mentioned earlier requires that special attention be given the relationship between the government and the Storting when dealing with these matters.

The Defense Committee (Forsvarskomiteen) is the special committee in the Storting established specifically for handling defense matters. It consists of representatives from most of the political parties in the Storting. The normal procedure is that the government, as the executive body, presents its proposals to the Storting for decision. In the course of considering these proposals within the Storting, the Ministry of Defense is usually called upon to provide additional information for the Defense Committee and to discuss alternative solutions with it. The military establishment is also usually called upon to assist in this process. The relationship between the Storting, the government, and the defense establishment is further broadened by regular visits on the part of the Defense Committee to military units and installations, where the committee can obtain on-the-spot information concerning the state of affairs within the military.

The government constitutes the highest executive leadership. The ministers in the government usually number between fourteen and sixteen. They are formally equal to one another, and there is no inner cabinet. As earlier indicated, it is laid down in the Constitution that the government is the highest command authority over the armed forces. The fact that decisions have to be made formally by "the king in council," which means the king in council accompanied by the ministers in the government, does not alter this reality. The Constitution allows for military command matters to be dealt with through a special procedure, one aimed primarily at dealing with matters requiring special protection for security reasons (defense plans, etc.). Under this procedure, proposals are presented to the king by the minister of defense in the presence of the prime minister and the minister of foreign affairs. The decisions are signed by the king, but they require the countersignature of the minister of defense to become valid.

The executive command authority is, to a large extent, delegated by royal decree (Kongelig resolusjon) to the chief of defense as the superior military commander. Command authority may also be delegated to a NATO commander, as will be discussed later. The total defense organization brings all of the ministries directly into the responsibility for defense planning and execution. The prime minister, as head of the government, is the overall organizer and leader of the total defense effort. As this entails a very complex task, the internal organization of the government becomes an important matter.

To assist in the peacetime tasks, the prime minister's office has been afforded additional staff specifically for this purpose. Each of the other ministries, in the same way, has been supplemented with special staff elements, in proportion to the extra work represented by the defense-related activity. To assist the government in its total effort in taking initiatives and as the coordinating authority, a special directorate (Direktoratet for sivilt beredskap) has been established. These special staff elements together form a web within and among the ministries, with the purpose of promoting and coordinating the total defense effort—an activity that must be performed in such a way as to avoid disrupting the division of responsibility for defense preparation work within the government.

The control and coordination of the preparations within this very complex apparatus require special, high-level attention. The ultimate responsibility lies with the prime minister and the government. To assist them in this task, a Coordinating Council (Koordineringsradet) consisting of senior civil servants from the most affected ministries has been established. The chairman is the senior civil servant on the prime minister's staff responsible for preparedness work. The chief of staff, Defense Command, who is also the deputy chief of defense, is a member of the Coordinating Council, which is designed to safeguard military-civilian coordination at the top level. Due to the dependency of the military defense for its functioning on the support from the nonmilitary defense, and as an extra safeguard measure, the chief of defense has been charged with the task of following the preparations on the civilian side of the total defense and to report on the situation to the minister of defense and/or the prime minister.

The Military Structure

The organization for defense has to fit the tasks with which it is confronted and the situation under which it has to function—hence the relevance of the survey of the strategic situation of Norway and the defense philosophy designed to meet the challenge. In Norway, as in most other countries, the three armed services—army, navy, and air force—have been established as almost autonomous bodies within the military complex. Although the need for close cooperation between the services in the execution of military operations has long been recognized, the services have generally retained a great measure of independence in their development and conduct. For countries with large military resources and with considerable military commitments outside their boundaries, such a situation can be well understood and justified. But for Norway, with small resources for military defense relative to its strategic position and with no declared military commitments outside its own territory, the situation is somewhat different. In keeping with its defense philosophy, Norway has attempted to tailor its defense to meet the fight for survival. On this point no compromise or alternative strategy has been offered.

In line with this basic defense philosophy, the central defense organization underwent an extensive restructuring in the early 1960s. Before this reshuffle, there was a general feeling—perhaps mostly in influential quarters outside defense—that the existing defense structure (1) was top heavy, (2) had large resource-demanding staffs whose benefits came at the expense of the fighting forces, (3) encouraged unnecessary compartmentalization, and so on. These were arguments that were also being debated in many other countries at the time.

The Norwegian military establishment was certainly ready to accept traditional military organizational structures. It preserved order within each individual service. The personnel were recruited into and trained within a given service, and their careers were tied to the same service. In other words, there were strong centripetal forces acting to prevent a breakup of the existing order and structure characterizing each of the separate services.

Although the need for close cooperation among the services was fully recognized, at least in theory, the question of how this need could best be realized was a difficult one to answer. A chiefs of staffs system had been employed since World War II to ensure interservice cooperation at the top level, but there remained the general feeling that this system, as practiced in Norway, did not meet the requirements. Too often, when controversial military questions involving more than one service were raised, the matter was either resolved by compromise, which made none of the services very happy, or passed over to the politicians for decision.

The main factors that brought about the circumstances in the early 1960s were, first, the adverse changes in the country's defense position, which, at that time, were due to the accelerated Soviet buildup of military power, mainly sea power centered on the Kola area; and, second, the cessation of the weapons aid programs from abroad. Something radical needed to be done, therefore, in order to keep up with this new strategic situation. There was no room for any extravagance. Old inhibitions had to be abandoned and drastic measures developed in an effort to keep up a viable defense posture. Accordingly, the compartmentalization of the three services had to be broken down in order to open opportunities for improved utilization of the most important element in a military system—the personnel. This called for extended use of integrated (interservice) staffs in the planning process, so that military forces could be designed to work together at the staff level as well as in the fighting units.

The Chief of Defense and the Defense Command

In the top echelons of the present military command structure, the Defense Command encompasses all the central military staffs: namely, the Defense Staff, the central staffs of the three services, and the Home Guard. All are organized under a joint staff system called the Defense Command. The central position of the Defense Command can be clearly seen in Figure 8.1.

The basic principle governing this command structure is that matters concerning more than one of the armed services are to be dealt with by integrated staff elements within the Defense Command. The chief of defense has been given a dominant position over the whole military structure. Second in command to the chief of defense is the chief of staff of the Defense Command, who is also the deputy chief of defense. A third key position in the Defense Command with overall defense responsibilities is the chief of the Operations Staff. The officers holding these positions will always come from different services.

Service commanders who have been relieved of some of their military functions and who, with their staffs, have been incorporated into the Defense Command as inspector generals of their respective services have the main functions of "producing forces" within their own services. An important function for the inspector generals and their staffs is to provide advice and assistance to the chief of defense and the integrated staff system.

The chief of defense is, by royal decree, charged with full-command authority over military defense and is also the senior military adviser to the government. He is directly answerable to the government and responsible for the overall planning and conduct of military affairs, although somewhat limited in authority with regard to administrative matters. He is also charged with the responsibility for long-term planning and budgeting. The linkup between the chief of defense and the NATO Command System is illustrated in Figure 8.1.

It should be noted in Figure 8.1 that there are two regional commands, one for the northern part of the country and one for the southern part. These are integrated commands. There is also a subdivision into lower regional commands (although this is not shown on the chart). Thus the national chain of command is as follows: (1) The Constitution (Grundlov) states that the government (the government in council with the king) has supreme command authority over the armed forces. (2) The government, by royal decree, has delegated executive command authority to the chief of defense. (3) The two commanders over north Norway and south Norway, respectively, have, by royal decree, been charged with command authority over the forces within their region, under the supreme leadership of the chief of defense. (4) Within these regions, separate service commanders exercise operational control over the forces of their own service branch in accordance with plans and decisions determined by the regional commander, with whom they are colocated.

Procedures

In the formal structure described thus far, there are three main bodies with a decisive influence on the formulation of defense policy and within the decisionmaking process itself—Parliament, the government, and the chief of defense. Within Parliament, the Defense Committee, consisting of representatives from most of the political parties in the Assembly, is the committee specifically charged with dealing with defense-related

Figure 8.1   Norway: Central Command Structure

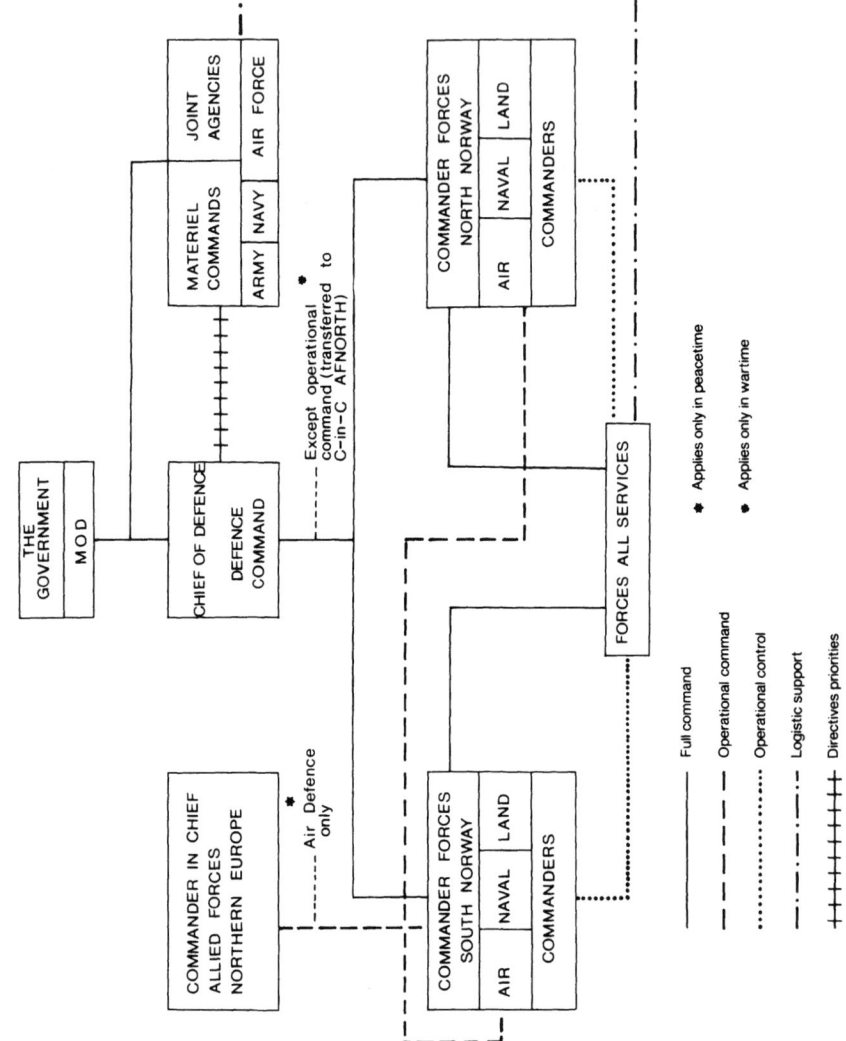

matters. The Foreign Relations Committee may also be called on to deal with such matters; on occasion it is supplemented by members of the Defense Committee. Within the government itself, the minister of defense is not only responsible for defense affairs but also serves as the link between the chief of defense and the government.

Before looking at the decisionmaking process, it is important to note that the procedures in the postwar period have largely been influenced by the fact that defense policy has not been a source of major disagreement between the main political parties—at least not until now. This consensus has generally been considered a defense asset and held to be of the utmost importance in preserving the general consensus between the political parties. This belief, which has prevailed up to the present day, reflects the attitude of the majority of the people in the country. Therefore, in order to maintain this situation, successive governments have attempted to establish and maintain procedures designed to preserve the atmosphere of consensus. This has called for a certain flexibility in procedures relative to the political (party) groupings prevailing at the time. As a consequence, the established procedure in the decisionmaking process between the government and Parliament, which, of course, must always be followed as it is part of the constitutional process, may be supplemented by ad hoc arrangements. And these, in turn, can have a decisive influence on the policy outcome.

One such flexible procedure is to invite the political parties in Parliament to select groups of representatives—usually the top party leaders—to meet with the minister of defense for briefings and informal discussions on the military situation and to consider alternative courses for the long-term development of the defense structure. The chief of defense and his staff usually assist on these occasions in both the briefings and the discussions.

No formal decisions are made under this procedure, but an understanding may be determined between the government and the political groupings in Parliament on certain major issues concerning the long-term development of the defense structure. The formal decisions have to be made under the ordinary procedure described earlier. This flexible process serves to reduce the temptation to use the defense budget as a means of bargaining between the parties in favor of more popular policy decisions, while at the same time leaving room for open debate about defense issues over which the political parties may hold differing opinions.

The debate on Norwegian defense and security issues that continues within and between the political parties and is supplemented by information and debate in the public media plays an important role in the shaping of political attitudes toward defense policy. Independent political groupings and protest movements have also played a role in this context, especially to the extent that they have succeeded in channeling their influence into and through the major political parties. Their efforts have mainly concentrated on issues connected with nuclear weapons, arms control, and disarmament. To a certain extent, this activity has also thrown a shadow over the more traditional defense provisions and cooperative spirit that hitherto prevailed.

Another flexible process involves the use of independent, ad hoc defense commissions. There have been two such commissions in the period after World War II, the latter in effect from 1974 until 1978. This commission consisted of thirteen members, the majority of whom were politicians appointed by the major political parties. After working for four years, it presented a proposal covering the period from 1979 to 1985 with an additional long-term perspective covering a 15-year period from 1979 to 1993. The commission's proposals, which in the main were unanimous, have been the subject of hearings and discussions by a number of bodies and organizations from inside as well as outside the defense sphere.

The advantage of this procedure, in addition to the direct value it gives to the defense planning process, is the insight it provides the political parties into defense problems and the workings of the armed forces. It also affords them a more direct influence in the development of defense policy and, with it, perhaps, a stronger feeling of responsibility for and involvement in the nation's security and defense policy. Planning through the use of defense commissions is very time-consuming; for practical reasons, it can be managed only within comparatively long time intervals. But the long-term effects of the work done by such commissions are both considerable and beneficial—primarily because the politicians have a guarantee that the money they have to provide will go into a defense establishment that they themselves helped to shape. The acid test of the commission's proposals comes when they have to be implemented through the ordinary processes in government and Parliament. Good intentions are not always enough to carry the proposals through the hard bargaining over priorities where the yearly budgetary allocations in government and Parliament are concerned.

Defense Planning

The main element determining the development of the defense policy is the process of long-term planning, which sets the "course and speed" of the development of the defense structure. Because it is a very complicated process, and a very important one as well, it requires close cooperation between the military and the political authorities at various stages within the process.

The chief of defense is charged with producing a "rolling" long-term plan. That is, at the outset he has a free hand in stating his opinion on the need for forces, their composition, the required funding, and the like within a long-term perspective. As the defense establishment is an already-existing organization, the long-term plan will have to determine modifications to the existing force structure, according to changes in the perceived threat, technological developments, alliance strategy, and so on. The chief of defense may be given some political inputs into such factors as the future state of the economy and the length of military service within which to plan; however, he is also called upon to state his opinion on the consequences of the country's defense posture as a function of the political perspectives given him by the government of the day.

The long-term plan ultimately presented by the chief of defense will encompass not only the whole defense structure, but also those defense-related elements that fall outside his chain of command. The complicated process of elaborating such a plan requires a joint effort within the staff complex of the Defense Command, where the estimates and evaluations from the armed services constitute important inputs. No service has ever received the resources it considers itself entitled to, or believes to be necessary, and there are bound to be differences of opinion in the process of working out the final details of the long-term plan.

The long-term plan therefore calls for high-quality staff work. It is especially important that all the interested parties are made to understand the reasons behind the final proposals as well as the essential inter-dependency between all the various elements that go toward meeting the overall aims of defense policy. Although the way is still open for the services to take their separate requests directly to the political authorities, this right has not constituted any significant problem in recent years. The long-term plan presented by the chief of defense is subject to change by the government of the day. In the event of such change, the chief of defense and his staff are called upon to assist in finding a compromise solution. However, it is standing procedure for the chief of defense to present his proposal after the government's proposal on defense has been presented to Parliament, so that Parliament can see whether or not the government's proposal differs from that presented by the chief of defense. In turn, the government's proposals on defense may also be subject to change in the course of the discussions and questioning that take place within the Defense Committee in Parliament; here again, the chief of defense and his staff may be called upon to provide additional information or assist in the search for alternative solutions.

To the present day (1985), this process has been characterized by a remarkable degree of unanimity, regarding the course to follow, among the military authorities, the government, Parliament, and even the Norwegian people. The main reason for this is to be found in the atmosphere of consensus that has existed between the political parties on the main issues of security and defense; but it is also the result of the open and thorough planning process inherent in the military ap-paratus, the government and the Parliament. This process gives little room for "solo plays" (i.e., unilateral decisions made by any of the parties concerned). Neither does it cover up the differences that usually exist between the military as a whole over service requirements, as expressed through the proposals of the chief of defense, and the defense spending and policies that those in political authority are willing to entertain. Finally, the annual defense budget is, in reality, an implementation of the long-term plan; in the main, it follows the same procedure as that governing the submission and acceptance of the long-term plan.

The Link with NATO

A study of Norway's central organization for defense and the defense decisionmaking process would be incomplete without some discussion of the link-up with the NATO central command structure. It is a well established fact that NATO is an organization of sovereign states but with no supranational structure to dictate to member countries how they should act on the various issues of defense. The NATO command system looks at defense problems from an overall international position within the Alliance, but each individual country within NATO is probably more influenced by the defense problems in its own sphere. The interaction between the views emerging from the different perspectives represents a valuable asset in the process of developing defense plans for each individual country, an interaction that, in turn, helps to structure the military forces that constitute the defense posture of the Alliance as a whole.

The political melting pot in this process is either the NATO Council or the Defense Planning Committee, in which the ministers of foreign affairs and/or the defense ministers have the final say. On the military plane it is the NATO Military Committee in which the chiefs of defense of the member countries have the final say on military and tactical matters. NATO planning and the defense review process within NATO provide valuable inputs into national defense planning, thus constituting an important element in the decisionmaking process in the individual member countries. Relevant in this context are the decisions made at the summit meeting of the NATO Council in Washington in 1978 concerning the fifteen-year plan for the Alliance.

As for the linkup between the national command system and the NATO system, Norway comes under the European Command (SACEUR) through the Commander-in-Chief Allied Forces Northern Europe (CINCNORTH), whose headquarters are located in Norway. In peacetime, CINCNORTH's command authority over Norwegian forces is limited to air defense only. The Defense Plan for Norway, thus provided, is first subject to the approval of the Norwegian government. Formally, this approval is obtained through the special procedure, previously mentioned, by which the minister of defense presents the plan to the king in the presence of the prime minister and the minister of foreign affairs.

Norway has also declared its obligation to transfer operational command authority to CINCNORTH in wartime (again, see Figure 8.1). In accordance with the existing agreement, CINCNORTH has to exercise his command over the forces in Norway through the commanders for north Norway and south Norway, respectively. As will be noted in the organizational chart, the transfer of command will not require any changes in the chain of command below this level. A third command under CINCNORTH—the Baltic Command, which encompasses Denmark and the northern part of Germany—covers the remaining part of NATO's Northern European command.

Special Provisions for Crisis and War

As already mentioned, Norway underwent some costly experiences during the invasion in 1940, from which many lessons were learned. One was the necessity for organizing the state's leadership for normal times (i.e., peace). Another called for a system of leadership with a potential for survival and the ability to function under the extreme conditions of crisis and war. As Norway must plan on being in the frontline from the outset in a possible future East-West conflict, the acknowledgment of this assumption becomes a decisive factor in the defense planning of the country. The most obvious defense requirement is special physical protection for the most vital installations, which are of both strategic and national importance, including naval bases, early air warning systems, communications networks, command posts, and public utilities. Additional arrangements must be made to counteract the consequences of societal breakdown following war.

In modern war, however, such arrangements are unlikely to be sufficient. Even with significant protection, the system of leadership is likely to break down—either temporarily or permanently, and with disastrous consequences for the defense of Norway. In order to counteract such a breakdown, a system of delegated authority has been introduced into the Norwegian defense structure. This comes into effect automatically if the situation calls for it. This delegation of authority goes from top to bottom, within both the military and the civilian structures. The instructions to military commanders go so far as to require them to disregard orders issued in the name of the government if the commanders have any reason to believe that the orders are false or issued under the dictates of an invader.

From Norway's past experience, given the existence of its central organization of defense, one lesson above all is clear: A system of leadership with good survival capability represents the vital element in the process of establishing and maintaining a viable defense posture in peace and war.

9
Central Organizations of Defense in the Soviet Union

Robert H. Baker

The contemporary character of the central organization and structures of Soviet defense may best be understood by locating their origins in the year 1953. That is not, of course, to deny the influence of earlier times, but 1953 was a watershed in Soviet history. The death of Joseph Stalin in March of that year affected all political structures and processes, not least the defense sector, which also experienced a final reunification of the various service ministries into the Ministry of Defense.

The comprehension of any area of Soviet policymaking is impeded by the complications and uncertainties of the bifurcated administrative/political system, in which responsibilities are divided between the party and state structures. At its simplest, the Soviet Union can be regarded as administered by governmental or state bodies, such as ministries or state committees, which constitute an executive branch responsible to the elected legislature, the Supreme Soviet.

The policy formulated and implemented by this executive will fall within the terms and requirements of the general political line as established by the highest organs of the Communist party of the Soviet Union (CPSU). The CPSU maintains an administrative hierarchy parallel to that of the executive in order to oversee supervision of policy and ensure that it follows the general line. In so doing, it is required by its own statutes to avoid "the merging of the functions of Party and other bodies or undue parallelism in work."[1] Party organizations, then, are proscribed from acting "in place of government, trade union, cooperative, or other public organizations of the working people" (Statute no. 42).[2] The administrative supervisory hierarchical apparatus of the CPSU is responsible to the quinquennial delegate Congress of the CPSU, through its Central Committee, for both its own and the government's performance.

This administrative separateness has proved unattainable, largely because of the experience of Stalinism, but also because of the logical implausibility of the supervisory relationship.[3] Instead, an integrated administrative structure with blurred lines of responsibility has developed, and particularly at the highest political levels, the two functions are frequently embodied in the same office-holder.

The endemic secrecy that characterizes Soviet political relations, coupled with the integrationist tendency noted above, makes the establishment of unequivocal relations of authority and responsibility a less precise exercise than that in more open polities. However, the precision attainable has increased since Stalin's death as the political system has gradually evolved. The evolution has been from a system that is characterized by totally arbitrary control, as an expression of Stalin's will, to one that is largely rule-governed. The rules themselves are for the most part unwritten and dependent for their observation upon an unspoken commitment to them by those in power. They are commonly understood by those in power because they have been developed through a common political experience since 1953. Since 1970, the results of this common experience have been increasingly embodied in constitutional and legal provisions that are generally acknowledged as authoritative.

The point is crucial to a historical understanding of Soviet defense policy and the character and relationships of defense institutions. Their history, for a quarter of a century after Stalin's death, was the reflection of a political system developing a *modus operandi*. Change and variation of policy or organization in other polities may be explicable, and the more easily understood for it, in terms of rules, established procedures, permissible deviations from the constitutional position, and the like; in the Soviet case such an explanatory framework is only now becoming available as the Soviet Union moves from an arbitrary to a constitutional polity.

At the time of Stalin's death in March 1953, the constitutional position was that the Supreme Soviet was charged with the "organization of the defence of the USSR, direction of the Armed Forces of the USSR, and determination of the directing principles governing the organization of the military formations of the Union Republics."[4] These responsibilities devolved to the Presidium of the Supreme Soviet, and their formulation into practical policy and its implementation came to be the responsibility of the service ministries (within the overall structure of the Council of Ministers), each of which had a Main Military Council consisting of a commander-in-chief and his subordinates. This Main Military Council was responsible for the administration and combat-readiness of the service. Each was responsible to the Higher Military Council, which was the peacetime equivalent of the Stavka, or Supreme Command, and as such, functioned at the ministerial level with military representation. The Higher Military Council's responsibility was to coordinate the armed forces with the political-strategic and economic constraints and capabilities of the state.

In theory, the Higher Military Council was responsible to the Council of Ministers and, through it, to the Politburo. In fact, responsibility was direct to Stalin. Indeed, the reorganization of the Armed Forces' ministry in the four years after World War II was designed largely to reduce the military potential for political action that might have threatened Stalin's position.

With Stalin's death, the need to divide in order to rule the military became less critical, and a more rational integrated ministerial system was reintroduced. This system provided for ministerial responsibility for defense as a whole, with a Higher Military Council operating at the ministerial level; it exercised the same responsibilities as had existed before the reunification, with a Main Military Council within the Ministry of Defense responsible for service coordination and planning. Indeed, far from being "ruled," the military was now being involved by Stalin's successors in the process of determining what the postdictatorship political rules should be. The first task the military leaders were called upon to perform was to provide the muscle for the attack on the security organs— namely, the Ministry of State Security and the Ministry of Internal Affairs, or MGB/MVD). In this task the military's role was vital. The forces that the interior/security ministries had at their disposal were of substantial proportions.[5] Even though no physical clash occurred between them and the regular armed forces of the state, the latter were an essential political and psychological constraint. Subsequently, the military played its part as an interest group in the struggle for succession.

In this promotional role, the armed forces were most closely identified with the first secretary of the CPSU, Nikita Khrushchev, who, in 1958, also became prime minister. This identification was achieved through the simple, and typically Khrushchevian, expedient of his saying what the military wished to hear.[6] Khrushchev sided with the military in opposing his main contender for the leadership, Georgi Malenkov, whose policies could be seen as, and were in fact perceived to be, detrimental to military interests.

In addition to gaining military support, Khrushchev was eager to reestablish the supreme political authority of the CPSU as an institution— an authority that had waned during the years of autocratic authority. In particular, he needed to reaffirm the Leninist principle under which government bodies were responsible to the party bodies if he was to check the power of his rivals within the state apparatus. It is this need that has led to a persistent difficulty on the part of students of Soviet military affairs in understanding the party/state relationship where defense is concerned, particularly with respect to the position of the new Defense Council.

Article 119 of the 1977 Soviet Constitution lays an obligation on the Supreme Soviet to "form the Council of Defence of the USSR and approve its composition." This was the first authoritative Soviet reference to the council. In fact, its roots can be traced back to Khrushchev, even though it did not assume its final form under him; rather, it evolved over a twenty-year period. This lengthy gestation is one reason why there has been so much confusion and uncertainty about the institution,[7] and why a close examination of its evolution is necessary to an understanding of its relevance.

In the 1950s and early 1960s, reference were beginning to be made in both Soviet and Western literature to the emergence of a Supreme Military Council of Defense in the USSR. It was evidently different from the Main Military Council of the Ministry of Defense, but it was not immediately clear whether or not it was the same institution as the Higher Military Council. In fact, it was a developing form of the latter. Khrushchev's need to establish party dominance led to his intrusion into this sphere of government, although after 1958, of course, as prime minister he could involve himself *ex officio*. His chairmanship of the Higher Military Council gave him direct access to the policymaking structures in the defense area, as well as immediate access to the service chiefs. In this way, Khrushchev was able to bypass the Defense Ministry bureaucracy and increase his political flexibility.

Although speculation in the West continued throughout the 1960s and early 1970s, the Supreme Defense Council subsequently came to be seen as a subcommittee of the Politburo, chaired by Leonid Brezhnev, the general secretary of the CPSU; it also included senior party and government figures, as well as a number of high-ranking military officers, among whom was the chief of the General Staff.

In fact, the Defense Council was not, in any formal sense, a subcommittee of the Politburo; as the provisions of the 1977 Constitution made clear, it was the Higher Military Council going through a transformation process. At the time when it attracted most attention among Western observers, from the early to the mid-1970s, a general rationalization of the central policymaking process was occurring in the USSR. In effect, what had happened was that Khrushchev's struggle to assert the dominance of party institutions had succeeded completely. The Politburo became, and has remained, the highest policymaking body within the Soviet political system, but Khrushchev's desire for personal dominance had also produced a number of anomalies—anomalies compounded after 1964 by Brezhnev's machinations to achieve his own preeminence. The most glaring of these was that the ministers responsible for foreign affairs and defense were excluded from the supreme policymaking body of one of the world's two superpowers, as was the chairman of the department responsible for internal security.[8] The absence of these three key portfolios made patent nonsense of any pretensions to a rational decisionmaking process, for which reason, in 1973, all three were incorporated into the Politburo.

This integration of party and state was most clearly apparent in two ways: First, it was manifest in the person of Marshal Andrei Grechko, who held the post of minister of defense from 1967 until his death in 1976; the second was the full institutionalization of the Defense Council (the designation "Supreme" had been dropped), a development that was widely commented on in 1976 and finally embodied in the Constitution of the following year. Given lead times in drafting constitutions, it is reasonable to conclude that the Defense Council had therefore been functioning in something very much like its present form for several years and, most probably, between the years 1953 and (approximately) 1960.

The Constitution makes clear that the Defense Council is a state (or government) body rather than a party body. That it was viewed in the past as a subcommittee of the Politburo can be explained by its being chaired by the CPSU first secretary, Khrushchev, and, after him, by the successive CPSU general secretaries, Leonid Brezhnev, Yuri Andropov, Konstantin Chernenko and today, Mikhail Gorbachev. In all of these cases, however, the secretaryship was combined with a government post that would justify its inclusion of the chairmanship of the Higher Military Council or the Defense Council. In Khrushchev's case, the post was that of premier; in the case of his successors, the chairmanship of the Defense Council was legitimized by their each having become, in their own right, the chairman of the Presidium of the Supreme Soviet and, as president, also the head of state.

The importance of the Defense Council, therefore, lies in its being the linchpin of the Soviet defense establishment (see Figure 9.1). Through its personnel and functions, it integrates the highest officials of the CPSU and the Council of Ministers with the highest-ranking military personnel. As such, it is at the apex of military/administrative coordination. The council is also the defense-specific policymaking body in the USSR. Final decisions are ultimately taken by the Politburo, and the general political line is established by it; but within the parameters of that general line, defense policy is formulated by the Defense Council. It is difficult to see how the Politburo can do much more than ratify recommendations coming from a body that contains a number of its leading members—a body, moreover, that is serviced both by the expert secretarial departments of the Central Committee and, in some cases, by Defense Ministry officials. The Defense Council also receives advice and information via the chief of the General Staff, who reflects military expertise and enjoys a monopoly of technical information.

If the Defense Council, which is responsible to the Politburo, effectively formulates defense policy, that policy is actually administered through the Ministry of Defense. Ultimate responsibility within the ministry itself is formally exercised through the institution of the Main Military Council, which is concerned with the integration and coordination of the armed services. It also reviews the General Staff operational and force planning for the armed forces, which has been drawn up according to the general criteria for military development defined by the Politburo and the Defense Council. The Main Military Council is chaired by the minister of defense and includes the chief of the General Staff, the commander-in-chief of the Warsaw Treaty Organization Forces, the chief of the Main Political Administration, the first deputy minister for General Affairs, the five service commanders-in-chief, the inspector general, the deputy ministers for Armaments and Electronics, the chief of the Rear

Figure 9.1   The Military and Political Infrastructure of the Soviet Union

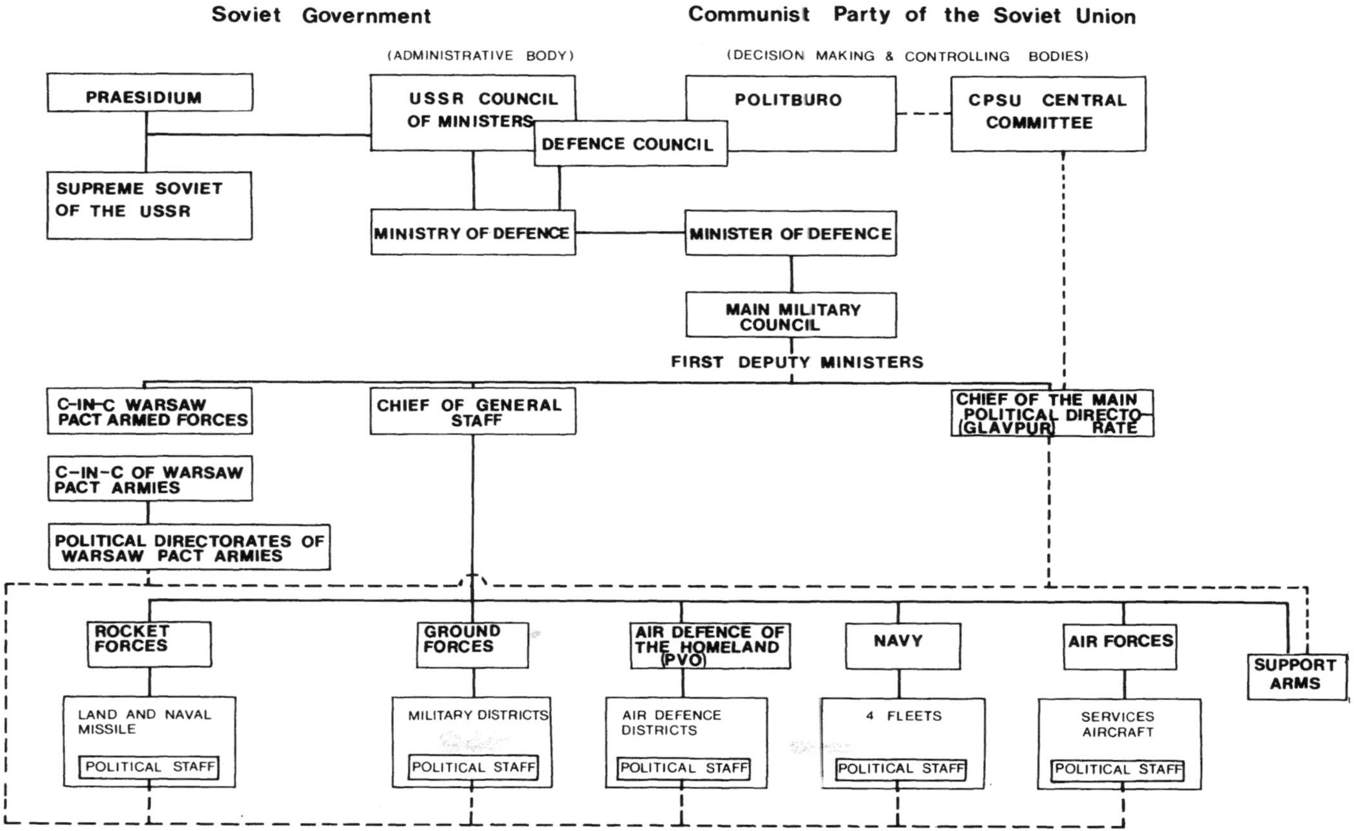

Soviet Government	Communist Party of the Soviet Union

(ADMINISTRATIVE BODY)   (DECISION MAKING & CONTROLLING BODIES)

PRAESIDIUM

SUPREME SOVIET OF THE USSR

USSR COUNCIL OF MINISTERS

DEFENCE COUNCIL

MINISTRY OF DEFENCE

POLITBURO

CPSU CENTRAL COMMITTEE

MINISTER OF DEFENCE

MAIN MILITARY COUNCIL

FIRST DEPUTY MINISTERS

CHIEF OF GENERAL STAFF

CHIEF OF THE MAIN POLITICAL DIRECTORATE (GLAVPUR)

C-IN-C WARSAW PACT ARMED FORCES

C-IN-C OF WARSAW PACT ARMIES

POLITICAL DIRECTORATES OF WARSAW PACT ARMIES

ROCKET FORCES

LAND AND NAVAL MISSILE

POLITICAL STAFF

GROUND FORCES

MILITARY DISTRICTS

POLITICAL STAFF

AIR DEFENCE OF THE HOMELAND (PVO)

AIR DEFENCE DISTRICTS

POLITICAL STAFF

NAVY

4 FLEETS

POLITICAL STAFF

AIR FORCES

SERVICES AIRCRAFT

POLITICAL STAFF

SUPPORT ARMS

Services, the chief of Civil Defense, and the deputy minister for Construction. It is formally accountable to the Supreme Soviet or its Presidium. In practice, the Main Military Council will answer to the Defense Council and, through it, to the Politburo. Significantly, there is considerable overlap between the members of these various bodies.

In 1984, the minister of defense, Marshal Dimitri Ustinov, was also chairman of the Main Military Council, a member of the Defense Council, a secretary of the Central Committee, and a member of the Politburo. With him on the Defense Council was Marshal Nikolai V. Ogarkov, the chief of the General Staff. Today their posts are held by Sergei Sokolov and Marshal Sergei Akhromeyev, respectively. Depending on circumstances, the Defense Council is also likely to include, on occasion, others from among the highest-ranking members of the Main Military Council (e.g., Marshal V. G. Kulikov, commander-in-chief of the Warsaw Treaty Organization military forces).

The constituent branches of the Soviet Armed Forces have the principles of defense policy translated into specific roles and missions for them by the General Staff, the chief of which, *ex officio*, is also a first deputy minister of defense. The General Staff controls the five Soviet armed services, and acts as the main administrative link between the more rarified atmosphere of policymaking, on the one hand, and the service activity in which that policy finds practical expression, on the other. In particular, it has the task of coordinating the five services into an integrated defense structure as might be required by the formulation of military strategy and the preparations for possible military conflict.

Interservice disputes arising from this process will normally be settled within the General Staff structure itself. Where they are too divisive to be reconciled within a purely military framework, they will go to the Main Military Council for resolution: The presence, *ex officio*, of each of the service commanders-in-chief on that body ensures representation of competing service views. However, the importance of the General Staff in the Soviet defense organization goes well beyond its central function as the main link between the armed services and their political masters.

The General Staff has under it a wide range of functional directorates, including those responsible for strategic planning for possible future conflict, troop exercises, and the maintenance of a military operational command center in the Kremlin, the Main Operations Directorate. The Intelligence Directorate—or the GRU, as it is now more commonly known in the West—deals with military intelligence and thus serves as an alternative to the KGB as a source of information. The General Staff's Military Science Administration is a particularly important institution, since it is central to the development of military science and doctrine. Moreover, it is probably the only institution in the Soviet Union that can devote itself to the study of military affairs with the knowledge that it has full and accurate information upon which to base its theoretical work. This monopoly of military technical information by the armed forces is virtually complete in the USSR.

In the event of war, the General Staff will effectively become the executive agency of the Supreme High Command, as it was during the Great Patriotic War. The Supreme High Command itself is likely to be formed from the Main Military Council of the Ministry of Defense.[9] Overall direction of the war effort would fall to the Defense Council, as in the case of its predecessor, the State Defense Committee, which supervised and directed the conduct of war between 1941 and 1945.

Within the Ministry of Defense there are the five separate services: the ground forces, the navy, the air forces, the strategic rocket forces, and the national air defense forces. Each service has a military council composed of its commander-in-chief and a Higher Command Staff, which is responsible for efficiency and combat readiness. Through the controlling agency of the General Staff, each military council is responsible to the Main Military Council.

Until the development of nuclear forces, the ground forces formed the basis of Soviet military might and the elite of the military establishment. In the late 1950s and early 1960s, as Soviet rocketry enhanced the country's nuclear capability, Khrushchev took the view that the ground forces had significantly diminished in importance. In 1955, 640,000 men were demobilized; in 1957, 1958, and 1960, there were further reductions of 1.2 million, 300,000, and 1.2 million men, respectively. The bulk of these cuts were borne by the ground forces, and in 1964 Khrushchev went a step further and abolished their High Command, a decision that was later reversed in 1967.

The reorganization, if not reconstitution, of the ground forces in 1967 was an important and integral part of the balanced force structure that came with the more creative approach to strategy in the nuclear age introduced after the removal of Khrushchev. Today, there are five combat sections in the ground forces: the tank/armored forces, the motorized infantry, the airborne troops, the troop air defense, and the rocket and artillery forces. Operational control, under the authority of the Ministry of Defense, is exercised through the commanders of the sixteen military districts.

From the primarily coastal defense force that emerged at the end of the Great Patriotic War, the Soviet Navy has expanded and developed since the 1960s under the leadership of Admiral Sergei Gorshkov into a balanced attack support, interdiction, and intervention force. The inadequacies of Soviet naval capability had become apparent before the Cuban Crisis of 1962, which exposed them glaringly. Decisions to embark on the program of expansion that took place in the 1960s and 1970s, however, were most likely taken by Khrushchev, possibly as early as 1961, given the lead times in naval production and the emergence of the first naval vessels involved at the end of 1964.

This decision, and the naval expansion that followed it, indicates the developing sophistication of Soviet strategic thinking that occurred near the end of Khrushchev's period in office. His attitude toward the ground forces notwithstanding, Khrushchev came to realize, or was persuaded, that total reliance on a doctrine of massive retaliation was not only politically constraining in the pursuit of Soviet foreign policy interests but questionable as well, given Soviet problems with missile degradation and an increasing vulnerability to a U.S. first-strike after the Kennedy assured deterrence procurement program began to take effect.

The combination of political inflexibility and strategic inadequacy led to the development of both a strategic and a general maritime capability. Operationally, the navy divides into the Baltic Fleet, Black Sea Fleet, the Northern Fleet, and the Pacific Fleet. There is also a flotilla in the Caspian Sea. Operational command is exercised by the fleet commanders, under the direction of the naval headquarters in Moscow, which is answerable in turn to the Ministry of Defense.

The National Air Defense Force, or PVO-Strany, became an independent service after World War II. From an early responsibility for anti-aircraft defense, it has developed capabilities required to meet the demands of both endo- and exo-atmospheric missile defense. PVO-Strany is divided into three branches: interception aviation, surface-to-air missile forces, and radar. Operational control under the Ministry of Defense is exercised by the heads of the three branches through the National Air Defense Force Military Council and its commander-in-chief.

The character of the Soviet Air Force derives largely from its initial role as air support for the ground forces—the traditional focus of Soviet military strategists in the prenuclear age. Although the air force is an independent service like the other four, its roles and responsibilities are seen more as support functions in relation to the other services. One of its three branches, Frontal Aviation, is responsible for tactical air combat and will be commanded in time of war by the appropriate ground forces command. Military Transport Aviation, following precedent, will be controlled directly by the Ministry of Defense, thereby strengthening the coordination, control, and optimum use of resources. Long-Range Aviation, the third branch, comprises the manned nuclear bomber force. This will also be directly controlled by the Ministry of Defense in the event of hostilities. Peacetime operational command of the Soviet Air Force is by force commander through his commander-in-chief, who acts under the authority of the Ministry of Defense.

The Strategic Rocket Forces, the last of the five services, officially came into being in 1959. Missile development had an intensive postwar history in the Soviet Union, as the launching of Sputnik in 1957 had made clear to the West. But the problems associated with putting "showpiece" rocket technology into military production continued for some time. They were compounded by the Soviet Union's inability to produce miniaturized thermonuclear, long-range missile-portable warheads until the mid-1960s. The Strategic Rocket Forces were introduced later than the Soviet leaders would have liked, but their arrival and expansion during the 1960s did mean that less emphasis on manned bomber development for strategic purposes was needed.[10] The development of this strategic missile capability also offered the illusory promise of being able to leapfrog the United States technologically and thereby offer a guarantee of Soviet security.

One much-noted feature of the Strategic Rocket Forces is the influence of Soviet artillery and artillerymen and the lessons drawn from their experience. Initial missile development was supervised by Marshal of Artillery M. D. Yakovlev, who was succeeded by Marshal of Artillery M. I. Nedelin. In addition, the Dzerzhinsky Artillery School has become the Dzerzhinsky Military Engineering Academy, which is responsible for the design and development of missile systems. It is argued, convincingly, that this artillery connection has been instrumental in producing the emphasis on preemption that characterizes much of the strategic thinking about nuclear weapons, and that the preemptive strike is the nuclear equivalent of the "disruptive strike" of artillery theory.[11]

There are no known subdivisions of the Strategic Rocket Forces,[12] and peacetime operational command, under the Ministry of Defense, is exercised through its commander-in-chief and deputies. However, so far as strategic nuclear weapons are concerned, the controlling function of the minister of defense, acting with and for the Defense Council and/ or the Politburo, cuts across service boundaries. Direct operational command of the land-based missiles of the Strategic Rocket Forces, of the missiles of the SSBN fleets in the north and east, and of the nuclear weapons of the Long-Range Aviation forces is exercised by the minister of defense.

One unique feature of the Soviet Central Administration is that it contains within it an institution specifically designed to guarantee the political reliability, and indeed controllability, of the armed forces. Although its organization and function have varied since its inception in 1918, its title and purpose have not. This institution is the Main Political Administration (MPA). Not only is it unique to the Soviet Union, but it is also unique within it. It is a hybrid body that, at the same time, is both a department of the Central Committee of the Communist party and a directorate of the Ministry of Defense. Its current head, and the publicly responsible official, is General A. A. Yepishev, who is supported in his duties by a collegial bureau comprising the heads of the administrative divisions within the directorate. These divisions in turn are primarily responsible for political education, in the form of agitation and propaganda; the organization of party cadres within the armed forces; party and Komsomol organizations; military publications; and general cultural work. The MPA's responsibility goes right through the defense system from the highest to the lowest levels, from the Ministry of Defense itself down to the basic military units. It also includes institutions that deal with military research and education. It does not, however, deal with defense industries; these are overseen by their own specific Central Committee departments.

The MPA's precise terms of reference are that it is accountable for its work to the Central Committee—effectively the Secretariat—but that it reports to the minister of defense on the political and moral condition of service personnel and on all aspects of political work in the armed forces.[13] Its actual responsibility is unclear, largely because of its hybrid nature. As a directorate of the Ministry of Defense, its chain of responsibility ought to proceed through the ministerial structure to the Presidium of the Supreme Soviet and, from there, transinstitutionally to the Politburo; but as a Central Committee department, its responsibility is directly to the Politburo and, nominally, to the Central Committee itself. Given the task of the MPA to supervise and "check" on the military, its party association is the more important one.

However, the character of the MPA itself points up one of the dilemmas of Soviet public administration alluded to earlier—that of the CPSU's task of supervision without substituting itself for the state. In the case of the MPA, it is both a party and a state organ. The paradox is readily apparent: In order to do its job of education and supervision effectively, the MPA has to be a part of that which it supervises. In becoming a part of it, it runs the risk of "going native" and adopting the values and mores of the host institution, to the extent that they differ from those of the governing body.[14]

The institutional schizophrenia that is inherent in the character of the MPA has been countered largely through the policy of personnel selection and management. It provides its own training schools and schemes and operates its own promotion system. Its present head embodies both the problem and the remedy—General A. A. Yepishev has an extensive record in CPSU work, has spent time in the KGB, and has also held state posts at the ambassadorial level in Eastern Europe. His military career includes work as a political commissar at the front between 1941 and 1943 as well as conventional military service and education before the war. In short, he is ideally qualified to be both gamekeeper and poacher simultaneously. Clearly his political masters must believe that he has these qualifications, for they have kept him in the post for some twenty-two years. However, Yepishev's tenure as chief of the MPA does not indicate only the approval of the political elite; it also indicates the stability of central institutional relationships between the military and the politicians.

The institutional, ideological, and political incompatibility of the military and CPSU establishments has been much exaggerated.[15] By the end of the Great Patriotic War, the integration of the CPSU, the Soviet Armed Forces, and Soviet socialism was fully and irrevocably established. This did not, of course, prevent incidents of internecine institutional conflict, such as those that surfaced as a result of Stalin's paranoid megalomania; nor could it guarantee institutional harmony in the face of Khrushchev's idiosyncratic and personalized style of rule. However, these were relatively short-term political traumas, and since the highly personal style of rule that had caused them came to an end in 1964, a party/military institutional symbiosis has become increasingly apparent in terms of both a structural stability and the relationships between the personnel who served in either. There have been no significant political clashes between the military and the CPSU since Khrushchev was removed from office in 1964. But there certainly has been disagreement and debate over policy—for example, over such questions as what to do about Czechoslovakia, arms control, and Afghanistan.[16] Yet the phrase "disagreement and debate over policy," itself, indicates both an integrated policymaking structure, within which the opinions of the armed services are incorporated as a matter of right, and the end to competition for power and influence over defense decisions between military and party leaders.

Given this relative institutional harmony over the past twenty years and the systemic integration achieved by 1945, it is quite clear that the role of the MPA has changed radically since its inception and principally since the death of Stalin. It is now no longer a body dealing with questions of political loyalty, except to the extent that it embraces such considerations as morale, party-mindedness, patriotism, and so on. Understood systemically, political (i.e., party) loyalty is absolute and, since the end of personal politics in 1964, cannot be interpreted as loyalty to any individual, political leader, or faction.

Ambiguity about the chain of responsibility for the MPA, then, is not a matter of any real moment. In the first place, institutional symbiosis means there are no political security issues involved in its role; there are only issues of efficiency. In the second place, the chain of responsibility, or the process of accountability, connect to a common integrated party/state structure, constructed, so far as the constraints of the Soviet system will allow, to be a rational decisionmaking organization.

The quality of decisionmaking in defense is crucially dependent upon the quality and quantity of information available to the decisionmakers. Soviet concern to achieve optimum decisionmaking and policy-formu lating procedures since 1964 has been most evident in the area of information resources, in addition to purely structural adjustment. In particular, the monopoly of technical information so jealously guarded by the military has inhibited the development of the strategic civil/military dialogue that provides much of the dynamic to Western military and strategic thought. The reasons for the military's maintenance of such a monopoly are quite clear: Information in a highly bureaucratized system is a political resource; its possession is an advantage in the process of bureaucratic manipulation, and its absence is a distinct disadvantage. The military, as one group, competes with others for resources within such a system and will not make its own position of advantage freely available to competitors. The implications of any such monopoly, particularly if it was managed in the self-interest of the institution exercising it, were obvious, and attempts to remedy the pattern were begun under Brezhnev when he succeeded Khrushchev in 1964.

First, the style of policymaking was radically changed. Unlike Khrushchev, Brezhnev was not concerned with excluding special-interest groups from the policy center for fear that his political position might be undermined. Since he saw no challenge either to his authority or to his policies coming from the military, and since the technical information the armed forces monopolized was essential to rational policymaking, the military was integrated into a civil/military administrative and policy structure, as outlined earlier. However, even before his position was formalized in 1973, Marshal Andrei Grechko was consulted by, and had access to, the Politburo.

Through integration of this kind, the self-interested and defensive character of the military's monopoly of information could be minimized and its worst effects mitigated. Nonetheless, the monopoly largely remained, and the content of strategic thought and form of doctrinal development naturally reflected an institutional perspective.[17] In an attempt to resolve this problem, Brezhnev attempted to revive two major research institutions as alternative sources of military science and strategy information and expertise. The Institute for the Study of the U.S.A. and Canada, and the Institute for the Study of World Economy (IMEMO) have both been largely unsuccessful in this task.[18] Both found that alternative perspectives from those of the military could not be developed if the military was not prepared to release the information upon which they might be constructed. This general military attitude was made abundantly clear in Marshal Nikolai Ogarkov's famous request to U.S. SALT negotiators not to disclose the details of Soviet weapons systems in front of Soviet civilian negotiators. So long as IMEMO depends on the *Military Balance* published by the International Institute for Strategic Studies (IISS) for some of its information on the Soviet Union, it is unlikely to prove a credible alternative source of strategic thinking to that of the military.[19]

An integrated part of the central organization of defense, though standing outside the Ministry of Defense proper, are the defense industries. Nine ministries have been identified in the defense industry group,[20] as follows: the Ministry of Aviation Industry (aircraft and aircraft parts); the Defense Industry (conventional army material); the Ministry of Shipbuilding Industry (ships); the Ministry of Electronics Industry; the Ministry of Radio Industry and the Ministry of Means of Communication (electric components and equipment); the Ministry of Medium Machine Building (nuclear weapons); the Ministry of General Machine Building (strategic missiles); and the Ministry of Machine Building (ammunition). Each department has, as its title suggests, ministerial status with responsibility through the Council of Ministers to the Presidium of the Supreme Soviet.

Defense production itself is incorporated into the National Five Year Economic Plan and its annual constituents as drawn up by the Soviet State Planning Commission (GOSPLAN). The requirements of defense production are established on the basis of service bids for money, facilities, and weapons systems as determined by the General Staff working in conjunction with the Defense Ministry's Main Financial Directorate. The individual services formulate their plans and bids in liaison with the relevant defense-production ministries. Interservice competition that proves irreconcilable at the General Staff level is resolved within the Main Military Council of the Defense Ministry.

Decisions on what the armed services want, and what the defense budget can afford, are determined by the Military-Industrial Commission (M-IC). This body is a commission of the Council of Ministers and is chaired by a deputy premier, who, currently (1984), is L. V. Smirnov. It is composed of the chairman and of representatives from the Ministry of Defense, the defense production ministries, GOSPLAN, and the Central Committee Secretariat. The M-IC is probably the penultimate stage in the process of generating and coordinating defense requirements before the Main Military Council of the Ministry of Defense conducts a final review. These requirements are then passed to the Defense Council (and possibly the Politburo) for a final decision.

The presence of representatives of GOSPLAN and of the Central Committee Secretariat on the Military-Industrial Commission is important. The GOSPLAN representatives come from a defense section that is both attached to the Central Committee Secretariat and exercises a CPSU supervisory function. As part of its supervisory responsibility, the Central Committee of the CPSU has two departments that are specifically concerned with the defense industry ministries; these are the departments of Defense Industry and of Machine Construction. Together, they are responsible to the Central Committee and the Politburo for the effectiveness and efficiency of all the defense ministries. Their work is supervised by the secretary for defense management, currently Sergei Sokolov, who is also minister of defense. The M-IC is thus a vitally important central defense organ, providing as it does an interdepartmental technical forum for the integration of service needs and the general national industrial and economic capacity, within the more general policy lines established by the Politburo and the Defense Council.

Less professionally central, but nonetheless structurally within the Ministry of Defense, are the directorates of the various logistic requirements of the services (e.g., fuel, personnel, clothing, etc.). These requirements, and the relevant directorates, are coordinated by the Rear Service, headed by a chief of the Rear Service (who is normally of the rank of general) and based on the Soviet Military Districts. In the same category is Civil Defense, for which the Ministry of Defense assumes administrative responsibility, with the chief of civil defense having the status of deputy minister of defense. The Central Civil Defense Staff are responsible for providing plans for protection and recovery of the population. They are also responsible for providing training procedures and directives for the civilian groups that make up the major part of the Soviet civil defense effort.

It is quite clear that since the death of Stalin in March 1953, the central organization and policymaking processes of Soviet defense have developed a highly integrated and rational structure. The confusions and impediments that some commentators saw as inevitable, given the bifurcated party/state division of responsibility and the cyclical and inherent conflicts predetermined by the inimical nature of the professional ethos of the military and the political objectives of the CPSU, have, where they might once have existed, largely been resolved.

When Stalin died, the political institutions he left behind were without any clear knowledge of their proper relationship to one another, simply because their relationship had been subordinated to Stalin's political will. The establishment of commonly understood political relationships emerged as a consequence of political conflict among Stalin's successors, using party and state institutions and policies as their weapons.[21] The political and institutional hierarchy that emerged when Khrushchev gained control was essentially unstable, because it was predicated on the belief that power was a personal attribute and institutional relationships reflected personal power relationships. Moreover, it took as a working principle a zero-sum understanding of political power. The institutional hierarchy, therefore, was not a hierarchy of authority, although in its stress on the Leninist principle of the policy primacy of the CPSU it might have seemed so; it was, in reality, a hierarchy of dominance.

Khrushchevian politics were a step away from Stalin's, but they embodied too extensively the arbitrary character of the dictator's political style, given the complexities of decisionmaking in the modern nuclear age. The fall of Khrushchev did not end institutional hierarchy; rather, it allowed this hierarchy to become constitutional, and to abandon the zero-sum concept of political power. As a result, hierarchy has become based on authority and responsibility with constitutionally and legally defined relationships that bear a recognizable relationship in practice to their theoretical delineation. At the same time, the concept of political power has become variable sum; within the hierarchy of authority today there is a high degree of functional integration without a concomitant diminution or blurring of that authority or power. The incorporation into the Politburo of a serving officer, Marshal Grechko, as minister of defense was not, in the post-Khrushchev world, an indication of the armed forces' enhanced power vis-à-vis their political masters. On the contrary, it was an indication that the issue of where authority lay had finally been settled, and that the question of interdepartmental power did not, therefore, arise within the Soviet hierarchy.

By the same token, any view that saw the replacement of Marshal Grechko with Marshal Dmitri Ustinov, who was not a serving officer, as some form of demotion or setback for the armed forces misses the point entirely. Ustinov had a heavily militarily-oriented background and was likely to be disposed to the military point of view. But even if that were not the case, his appointment meant little in terms of the exercise of political "influence" by the military. The armed forces are adequately represented, as a matter of constitutional right, at all levels of the defense establishment and decisionmaking process. The same argument applies to the present defense minister, Sergei Sokolov. To talk of "advances" or "setbacks" in institutional terms is to revert to the language and concepts of the Khrushchev era, when institutional relationships were reflections of personal political relationships and it was necessary for personal contacts and promotion to protect against, and compensate for, institutional disadvantages. In the arbitrary political system of Stalin, a military leader, like Grigori Zhukov, needed to be close to the relevant political actors in order to accommodate the institutional interest of the armed forces. In the post-Khrushchev era, constitutional and legally regulated institutional relations have obviated the need for such personal intervention and projection.

In conclusion, the central organization of Soviet defense is, today, relatively straightforward. The general political line, insofar as it deals with the security interests of the USSR, is established by the Politburo. Its shape and content, as a generally delineated defense policy, is determined by the Defense Council. Further details and the more general stages of transforming broad policy into specific administrative programs occur in the Main Military Council of the Ministry of Defense. The General Staff constitutes the final link in an administrative chain that carries policy down, consistently refining and detailing it en route. This path, reversed, provides for the cybernetic character of the policy-cum-administrative process. Alongside this military chain, similar cybernetic linkages provide for the production of defense materiel, for the political and moral education and welfare of the services, for the coordination of logistics, and for the Civil Defense program.

The whole process is stable, integrated, rational, and rule-governed; it conforms to the bulk of the criteria of a rational/legal system of authority. Concentration on the institutional overlap between party and state in the USSR is irrelevant to contemporary defense structures and defense policy. So far as the higher levels of policy and administration are concerned, the existence of two institutions—state and party—with the government subject to the authority of the CPSU, is no more remarkable (and is certainly of less consequence to the continuity of policy) than the episodic capture and loss of departments of state by political parties engaged in the adversarial politics of democratic societies.

Notes

1. *Ustav Kommunisticheskoi Partii Sovietskogo Soyuz*, no. 42 (Moscow: Politizdat, 1966), pp. 70ff.
2. Ibid.
3. See R. H. Baker, "Clientelism in the Post Revolutionary State: The Soviet Union," in C. Clapham (ed.), *Private Patronage and Public Power* (London: Frances Pinter, 1982).

4. Constitution of the USSR, Article 14(g), in J. N. Hazard, *The Soviet System of Government*, 3rd ed. (Chicago and London: University of Chicago Press, 1964).

5. Two days after Stalin's death it was announced that the Ministry of International Affairs and the Ministry of State Security had been amalgamated into a single Ministry of Internal Affairs, of which L. Beria became minister. This put both the Frontier Troops and the Special Purpose Units directly under Beria's control. He used both to provide leverage against his colleagues in the earlier stages of the succession struggle. See R. Hingley, *The Russian Secret Police* (London: Hutchinson, 1970).

6. Khrushchev simply denounced Malenkov's assertion that war was no longer fatalistically inevitable between capitalism and socialism. Yet once Malenkov was out of the way, Khrushchev took up the assertion and practiced much more of Malenkov's "consumer communism" himself.

7. *Konstitutsia S.S.S.R.*, Article 119 (13), Partinaia Zhiizn, no. 12 (June 1977).

8. The character of Khrushchev's political tenure had made it essential that he retain full control of defense policy and foreign affairs. His control of these policy areas was maximized by the absence of the responsible ministers from the Politburo in that he remained the authoritative source of information for his nominal peers within the Politburo. He also remained the link between the Politburo and the two ministries. In this position his control was, he believed, guaranteed, and the danger of military independent-mindedness, as evidenced in Marshal Zhukov's brief membership of the Politburo in 1957, was avoided.

9. This seems particularly likely, given that the Supreme Military Command was replaced in 1946 by the Higher Military Council (attached to the Ministry of the Armed Forces), which has evolved into the present Main Military Council.

10. Cf. R. H. Baker, "Understanding Soviet Foreign Policy," *Royal United Services Institute Journal for Defence Studies* (March 1978).

11. See D. Holloway, *The Soviet Union and the Arms Race*, ch. 7 (New Haven, Conn., and London: Yale University Press, 1983); and J. Erickson, "The Soviet View of Deterrence: A General Survey," *Survival* (November/December 1982).

12. E. L. Warner, *The Military in Contemporary Soviet Politics* (New York: Praeger Publishers, 1977), p. 27.

13. T. J. Colton, *Commissars, Commanders, and Civilian Authority: The Structure of Soviet Military Politics* (Cambridge, Mass., and London: Harvard University Press, 1979), p. 24.

14. The problem has been evident since the time of the Civil War (1918–1920), when political commissars frequently found themselves unable to judge between the political and purely military realms of command or, with amateurs' zeal, decided that they enjoyed the purely military side of affairs more than the political task to which they had been set. Another graphic example is to be found in the 1930s, when the MPA under U. B. Gamarnik actually allied itself with the military in seeking to shelter its members from Stalin's purges.

15. See W. E. Odom, "Party Ties," *Problems of Communism* (September/October 1973).

16. M. Mackintosh, "The Soviet Military Influence on Foreign Policy," ibid.

17. In the field of strategic thought in the USSR a distinction has to be drawn between military doctrine and military science. The former is concerned with the state's evaluation of questions of war and of military policy, insofar as the military policy is a reflection of the state's evaluation of the correlation of forces and its present and future implications. The latter deals with war and how to fight it.

Doctrine is essentially the task of the politicians and military science, the task of the soldiers. This division gives rise to institutional contradiction, with Soviet military writers discussing disruptive or preemptive nuclear strikes at the same time as their political leaders are proposing policies of détente and proclaiming themselves committed to "no first use" of nuclear weapons.

18. See O. Eran, *The Mezhdunarodniki* (Ramat Gan, Israel: Turtledove Publishing, 1979); and the author's private conversations with émigrés and with Soviet officials.

19. A. J. Alexander, "Decision Making in Soviet Weapons Procurement," *Adelphi Papers*, nos. 147 and 148 (London: International Institute for Strategic Studies, 1978).

20. Holloway, *The Soviet Union and the Arms Race*, pp. 117–120.

21. For an excellent brief treatment, see M. Frankland, *Khrushchev* (London: Penguin, 1966).

10
The Central Organization of Defense in Spain

José-Maria Comas

The morphology of the central structures of defense reflects the nature of the existing political regime. Recent Spanish experience is a prime example. The expression of political demands by military spokesmen reflects to some degree the spirit that governs civil-military relations.

After General Francisco Franco's death on November 20, 1975, a new popular consensus and desire for reform led the country to move from a dictatorship to the establishment of a pluralist regime similar to the liberal democracies of the Western world. The personal autocratic regime that had emerged after the military victory of 1939, putting an end to three years of civil war, centered on Franco himself. He himself held the mainspring of power, so that the institutional machinery that was progressively introduced over a period of forty years of personal government never succeeded in gaining a true organizational and functional independence. Decisions ultimately always reverted to the person who represented the legitimacy of the regime and who had the charisma of a politico-military "caudillo."

The Franco dictatorship, as with all other such regimes, needed force to maintain itself, which explains its strict control over the armed forces, and was bound to serve particular ideological interests. Franco's control over the armed forces during his "reign" represented a new departure for a country whose strong tradition of military intervention in politics had rendered it unstable. The euphoria of victory, his role as general of the armed forces, and the maintenance of the army's unity earned Franco the support of the officer corps, which in turn reinforced the personal control he was able to exercise over the armed services as a whole. However, this was possible only at the price of a carefully maintained blurring of the distinction between the political domain and the military arena—a confusion of roles that infringed as much the principle of political subordination as the autonomy of the military institutions.

The advent of a democratic regime, institutionalized by the Constitution of December 29, 1978, did not fail to transform fundamentally the institutional order of the state. In the terms of the first two articles of the Constitution, the Spanish state is structured along the lines of a parliamentary monarchy within the framework of a national unity that recognizes the right of self-determination for other regions and nationalities, with specific reference to the historic rights of the Basques, the Catalans, and Galicians, The principle of one central authority and one central coordinating function, so dear to Franco's followers, has been replaced by a separation of powers and by a national sovereignty emanating from the people.

Political change in Spain went hand in hand with a reorganization of the state structure, following a model far removed from the centralizing yoke of a country whose very geography and history had promoted autonomy. After Franco, the dual democracy/regional autonomy structure appeared to be the two sides of the same popular demand. The real challenge facing the young Spanish democracy is how to complete the construction of a new state without damaging the unity of the country— a unity nearly five centuries old.

The new Constitution established a principle concerning the relationship between political institutions and the military High Command. It is significant to note here that the architects of the 1978 Spanish Constitution remained faithful to the long tradition of a people who want the Constitution to contain a reference to the role of the armed forces. Article 8 defines their functions: On the one hand there is the defense of sovereignty and of the territorial integrity of the state; on the other there is the political function of the defense of the Constitution. The armed forces could be used, under the terms and conditions set out in law, in the practical defense of the Constitution. Legal defense belongs solely to the judicial courts—and particularly to the Constitutional Court—created for this purpose by the Constitution itself.

Under the specified functions outlined, it was necessary to establish the basis for the Organization of Defense and for the armed forces in accordance with the rules laid down in paragraph 2 of Article 8 mentioned above. This was the Law of July 1, 1980, the contents of which determined, among other things, the range of competence between political and military bodies at the heart of the central administration for defense.[1] This law was the continuation of the institutionalization of new agencies in the management and running of defense and, in particular, the creation in July 1977 of a Ministry of Defense, which replaced the three existing ministries.

The replacement of an autocratic regime, whose leader had been general of the armed forces, by a parliamentary regime raised a number of problems concerning the mechanism for politico-military decisions. The aim of all the reforms introduced since 1976 was to reach political unification of defense at the central management and administrative levels. As far as management was concerned, the conceptual distinctions between political decisions and the military's execution of those decisions had to be made clear, while taking into account the absence of a

"Generalissimo." In the field of administration, unification would have to be conducted in accordance with the powers delegated to the new Ministry of Defense. The responsibilities of the higher bodies for defense were therefore revealed in a new perspective in post-Franco Spain.

Institutionalization of Defense Management (1978–1983)

The Spanish legislators differentiated between the state's power over the armed forces and the state's power in the armed forces by making military appointments dependent on distinct bodies, in accordance with the judicial principles of subordination to political power. The operation of this principle corresponds to the period from the introduction of the constitutional decree of December 29, 1978, and developed by the Law of July 1, 1980, which introduced the new structure for defense. Certainly before—and especially since—1976, a few normative texts had outlined in draft form the future organization for central defense. The structures that were established have been reformed very recently (1984) and are analyzed in the next section.

Power over the Military

This power is that of the political decisionmakers whose function is to determine the occasion and the form of action by the armed forces within the context of the functions ascribed to them in the Constitution. The decision to use force is, by its nature, a political one. We are concerned here with an original and basic power that must belong to those offices that constitute the legitimate embodiment of popular sovereignty. In a democratic society this power belongs to political institutions that are the representatives of national sovereignty. By law, the military authorities are not independent, and thus do not decide on their courses of action. They remain subordinate to the decisions of political authorities.

The decision to use force remains a political one. Authority is derived from the Constitution, which bestows this power. Article 97 grants the Spanish government the responsibility for the armed forces and the defense of the state, in a very real sense. We should also note that matters of national defense are vested in the central administration, and not with the various autonomous regions.

The authority of the central government must be examined in the light of the content of Article 62 of the Constitution; this grants the king, as the head of state, certain powers concerning the military and the defense sector. The king confirms military appointments (Figure 10.1) and is supreme commander of the armed forces (Article 62). In Article 64, paragraph 3, the monarch can, with the prior authorization of Parliament (the "Cortes") declare war and sign a peace treaty. The formal role of the king in matters of defense gives him the right to

Figure 10.1 Spain: Central Defense Organization

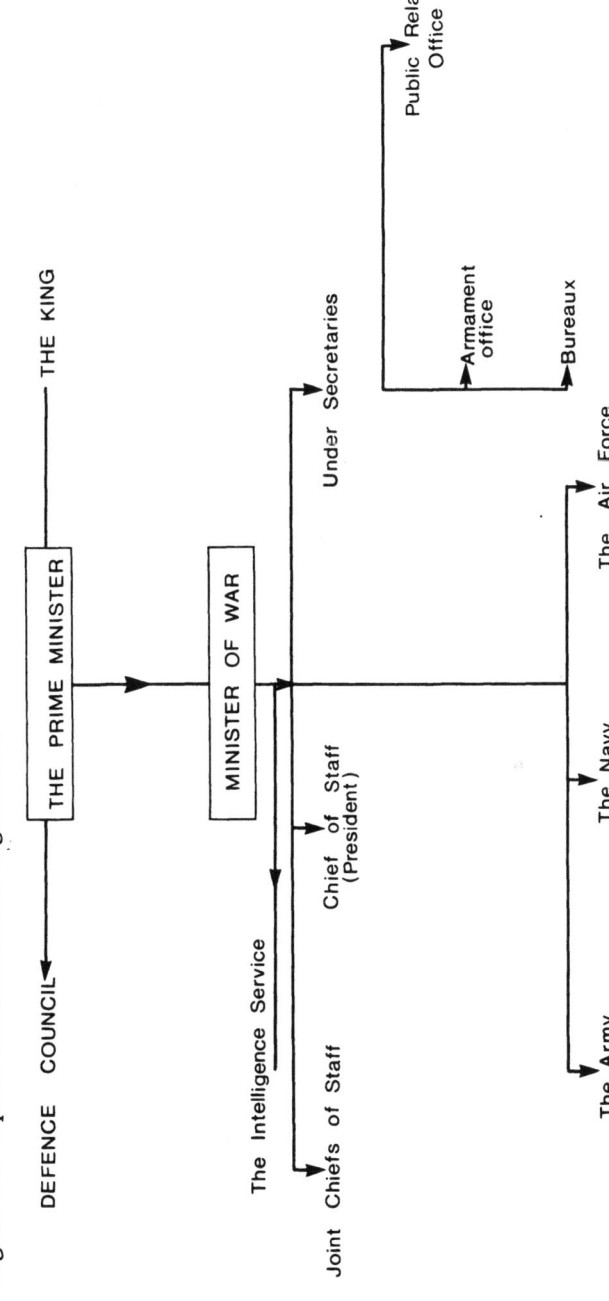

Source: Adapted from C. Donnelly, "Military/Political Infrastructure," in R. Bonds (ed.), *The Soviet War Machine* (London: Hamlyn, 1976). p. 32.

preside, if he so wishes, over the Council for National Defense, an advisory and initiating body at the center of national defense policy-making.

The king's role is more than simply a formal one; he would appear, in fact, to exercise a wide range of powers that undoubtedly are more extensive than those of his counterparts in parliamentary monarchies or of presidents in democratic republics. However, the powers that the Constitution grants him are not absolute. To exercise them, the king needs the countersignature of the prime minister and of competent ministers, in particular that of the defense minister. Article 64 of the Constitution specifies in paragraph 2 that the king is ultimately not accountable and that the political responsibility for his actions falls on those ministers who are countersignatories. Spain is therefore a parliamentary monarchy and not a limited monarchy in which the king can independently exercise certain residual powers. In this respect, were a Spanish monarch to act illegally, political sanction would necessarily be imposed—a situation that, in a limited monarchy, would threaten the very stability of that kind of system.

In any case, the supreme commander of the armed forces fulfills a constitutional function; as monarch he is not their Generalissimo. In status, therefore, he is very different from his predecessor as head of state. General Franco was the head of state, and even the head of government, until the appointment of Admiral Carrero Blanco as prime minister in June 1973; he was also the Generalissimo of the armed forces, a position he occupied on October 1, 1936, when the generals who rose against the Republic in a putsch appointed him as such. When Franco left this position, the armed forces were left without a leader; despite the fact that the present holder of the Crown is recognized by the majority of the officers as being Franco's successor, his position is not the same. The supreme command of the armed forces is no longer in the hands of the head of state and a general who governed without reigning, but now resides with the constitutional monarch who reigns without governing. This new situation implies that the armed forces have, in theory, lost the political influence they enjoyed under Franco, their leader, who was concurrently both the formulator of military policy and the person responsible for the general policies of the state.

In the structural provisions detailed in the 1978 Constitution, the king is not so much a political figure as an arbitrator and a mediator; it is this fact that throws a new light on the exercise of his responsibilities: Article 56 determines that the king, as head of state, is "symbol of its unity and of its permanency, who arbitrates and mediates in the day to day running of its institutions." The monarch therefore holds a moral position, but he can nevertheless bring about political results, as the institutional practices of the last few years have demonstrated.

In Article 62 of the Constitution, the king must be informed of affairs of state, including military and defense matters. He receives this information during his regular meetings with the prime minister and with the minister of defense. If he so wishes, the king can ask the prime minister to reconsider any measure with which he may disagree, and may express his view on any measure that the government is considering. In these respects the king would use his moral influence and the dialogue would be conducted in secret, informally and off the record. In any event, the king has to limit himself to expressing his opinion, or to making a proposal using his moral authority, in persuading the head of the executive of the validity of his point of view. Ultimately, the government has the last say. The king's role with regard to the armed forces does not, therefore, imply his involvement with the government in their management. As supreme commander he has a symbolic and honorific title, in the same sense as that governing, for example, his role as representative of the state in international affairs. It should not be forgotten, however, that this symbolic role can have real scope.

It is reasonable to ask, then, what forms the basis of the influence that the king exerts over the armed forces. In reality, the monarch has inherited this influence from a tradition grounded in contemporary experience that demands that the head of state appear as a neutral spokesman for the Spanish Armed Forces. The stability and prestige of the title of head of state have certainly made dialogue with the armed forces easier; nevertheless, it is necessary to place the origins of this practice in its historical context, known as "the Restauracion," which, from 1879, saw the establishment of a stable political regime until 1923 under the reigns of Alphonso XII and Alphonso XIII. The Constitution of 1876 granted the Crown control of the armed forces as well as the right to use this power as it liked, thus representing a delegation of power that has been undeclared in the constitutional history of Spain since 1812—the date of the first Constitution. The close links between the king and the armed forces led to the idea of a military monarch; it was an idea that became especially accentuated during the reign of Alphonso XII, who interpreted his constitutional role literally—that is, as a commander who could do exactly as he wanted with the armed forces.

The Restauracion left an imprint on the twentieth century of a close and personal link between the head of state and the armed forces that reached its zenith under Franco. King Juan Carlos was made a "spokesman for the army" under very different circumstances, which were divorced from ideological references to any historical precedent. His military background enabled him to better understand the problems of the armed forces.

However, the acceptance of the reality of the closeness of the king to the armed forces does not imply that the armed forces must be led by the monarch; on the contrary, they remain under the government's jurisdiction. Nevertheless, in a time of crisis, when political bodies have been unable to act—such as on the night of February 23, 1981, the date of the coup d'etat attempt—the king, who must abide by and make others adhere to the Constitution, can order the armed forces to defend the constitutional order that is being threatened. This he did on February 23, limiting himself to the role the Constitution had granted him.

Apart from this exceptional situation, it is the government's responsibility to issue instructions to the armed forces when necessary and to determine their aims and objectives. Therefore, the armed forces' intervention in defense of the Constitution should be decided by the government either according to the procedure of a Declaration of Emergency—if the government and the Parliament feel that such action is necessary—or under other legal requirements. The armed forces' intervention can be implemented outside a state of emergency, given that the law defining this eventuality ascribes the possibility of proposing that a state of emergency exists only to the Congress of Deputies, one of the Spanish parliamentary chambers. Then as long as the suggested measures are in accordance with its accepted and customary role, the government can decide on a course of action for the armed forces in defense of the Constitution without any preliminary declaration from the Congress. However, this would happen only in exceptional circumstances; normally the armed forces would act in the event of a declared state of emergency.

Even in this context, however, any decision regarding intervention and the subsequent control over the armed forces still belongs in the political domain. It is the Cortes, with its obligatory declaration of a state of emergency, that determines the extent of possible measures; and it is the Cortes, not the military authorities, nor even the government, that decides on the number of offenses that can eventually be placed under military jurisdiction during an emergency (see Article 35 of the law ruling on a state of emergency).[2]

The government must nominate the military authority that, under its control, implements a state of emergency. It must therefore publish and distribute proclamations on the necessary courses of action, in accordance with the Constitution, the laws governing a state of emergency, and the conditions laid down by Parliament.

The management and control of the armed forces in this exceptional situation are concerned only with the defense of the constitutional order. The same conditions apply when necessary measures have to be taken for the defense of the territory. The Cortes must authorize both a Declaration of War and the signing of a peace treaty. In the event of an armed conflict, it is the prime minister who is responsible for the direction of the war; he would be helped in this function by the Council for National Defense, of which he is the chairman, unless the king decides to preside.

This body plays a key role in the provision of national defense, in that it becomes the center for defense decisionmaking, in wartime especially. In defining defense policy it suggests the main principles of national defense, and even proposes and formulates military policy and issues instructions that must be followed regarding the potential contribution of nonmilitary aspects of overall national defense. This institutional function is linked to both a counseling role and one of assistance to the prime minister, as much in time of peace as in time of war. The composition of the council is mixed, given that there are political representatives—namely, the prime minister, the minister of defense, the heads of other ministerial departments who are invited to attend, along with their technical representatives, and those who hold senior rank in the armed forces, specifically, the chiefs of staff.

At the center of government, two people share the main responsibility for defense: the prime minister and the minister of defense. The former is undoubtedly the more important, especially in time of war, since he exercises all the powers governing the management of armed conflict. Yet, during time of peace, the defense minister's role becomes more clearly defined and significant as a consequence not only of his own terms of reference, but also of the responsibilities delegated to him by the prime minister. The latter leads and coordinates the government's policies in matters of defense and is able to delegate certain functions in the management of defense policy to the minister of defense. In this way, the role of the defense minister, who oversees the management, coordination, and implementation of defense policy, is extended to all those defense functions that the prime minister has not reserved exclusively for himself or has not, himself, actually decided to exercise.

With respect to military policies, once the prime minister has delegated authority, the defense minister can exercise political authority over military commanders—the Chiefs of Staff Committee—as well as those matters over which the prime minister has not assumed responsibility. Extensive delegated authority in the hands of the minister of defense can prove to be a political risk, both for the defense minister, because he does not have the same authority as the prime minister, and for the prime minister himself.[3]

Authority over the armed forces also carries with it the responsibility for their control—and this is specifically the task of the parliamentary assembly known as the Cortes. This responsibility is exercised in three ways: It has, above all, a legislative role; then, to the extent it is able, it has the power of control over the executive; and, last, it acts in an advisory and deliberative capacity.

In its legislative role, the Cortes approves laws dealing with defense as well as budgetary allocations. In its controlling capacity, the Cortes holds the government and the military administration accountable, using the whole arsenal of institutional means permitted by the Constitution, such as the questioning of the government by parliamentary committees of inquiry or even motions of censure. In addition to its role in declarations of war and peace, the Cortes must authorize the completion of treaties or international agreements that contain references to the military. In its deliberative capacity, the Cortes discusses the major outline of defense policy as well as short-, medium-, and long-term armament programs, including ratification of the laws required for the respective policies of essential expenditure, which in turn are necessary for the modernization of the armed forces.

Nevertheless, the power and influence of the Cortes remain unclear as long as the executive fails to define adequately or precisely its defense policy or fails to present in any detail the alternatives and choices between the means it will use and the objectives to be achieved. This shortcoming has been one of the constant factors in Spanish politics in recent years. Those who exercise power over the armed forces are also the political decisionmakers. Their action must be related to those who, in turn, exercise authority within the armed forces.

Authority in the Armed Forces

Authority in the Spanish Armed Forces—that is, operational command—is legally only an executive function derived from, and subordinated to, the decisions of the political authorities. The military command is limited to carrying out a defense strategy and a military policy that are defined and decided upon by civil bodies outside the institution of the armed forces, and whose power and authority are based upon and derived from popular consent.

Under Franco's regime, political power and military power were concentrated in the hands of the same people. This inevitably meant that the military would become involved in political affairs, such as those of the government or the Legislative Assembly. Moreover, by granting the heads of the armed forces' ministries respective command over each branch of the armed forces, Franco confused the relationship between politics and the military so that it became difficult to distinguish whether the armed forces' ministers were acting in a political capacity or, alternatively, in their capacity as the heads of one or another of the armed services. This practice led after Franco's death to the establishment by the political leadership of appropriate agencies with the sole responsibility of exercising military command. As early as 1976, many bodies designed to exercise military control from the center were created. Two elements characterized this matter: the establishment, first, of a collective body in the form of a Chiefs of Staff Committee and, then, of separate bodies comprising the senior staffs of each of the armed services.

The Chiefs of Staff Committee was officially created by the Decree of February 8, 1977, even though certain basic texts had referred to it previously.[4] Known by its acronym, JUJEM, this committee was the highest combined committee of military command and authority responsible for the operational efficiency of the armed forces as well as for the resources allocated to them. The formation of the JUJEM answered the need for a unification of command in order to increase the efficiency of military action and the general state of readiness of the armed forces. Its goal was to gain a fuller understanding of the possibilities and needs of the armed services in order to allow decisions to be taken while at the same time coordinating the exercise of command and furthering the eventual integration of the armed forces. The JUJEM's role was dictated by the need for planning and coordination. Its formation was an innovation in a tradition of Spanish military politics that, until then, had had a distinct German influence. The joint composition of this new body reflected more an American influence, of which the precedent was the U.S. Joint Chiefs of Staff, first established in 1942.

The historical precedent of the JUJEM within Spain was the creation of a Senior Defense Staff at the end of the Spanish Civil War of 1936 by the Decree of August 30, 1939. The decree defined the Senior Defense Staff as being an administrative agent for national defense, as well as coordinator of the three chiefs of staff from the army, navy, and air force. This body was directly responsible to the head of state. Later, in 1967, Article 39 of the General Law of the State—the last of Franco's Fundamental Laws—defined the Senior Defense Staff as being a technical body for national defense, which, under the prime minister, was to coordinate the activities of the service chiefs of staff. Since its inception, the Senior Defense Staff has seemed more a personal staff to the head of state than a real armed forces, Chiefs of Staff Committee. Having become institutionalized, the Senior Defense Staff—far from moderating the influence of Franco on the armed services—only reinforced it.

The Senior Defense Staff also often seemed more a link in the chain of the president's decisions than an autonomous expression of the management of the armed forces. The new clause, which in 1967 established this body's dependence on the prime minister, made little significant difference given that the two posts were in fact held by the same person until 1973. The experiment lasted too short a time to provide any indication of its long-term consequences. The Senior Defense Staff's dependence on the head of state was only one of the negative aspects of its situation. Its coordinating role over the services' staffs was not easy to exercise. The fact that these staffs separately depended on a superior of ministerial rank made the desired coordination virtually impossible to implement. Under such conditions it was difficult to form a structure in which those involved found themselves on the same level in the hierarchy, since the chiefs of staff depended hierarchically on their service ministers.

Manipulated by the ex-head of state, and in the face of chiefs of staff who were not dependent on it, the Senior Defense Staff could not effectively carry out the role it had been given. Despite these difficulties, the staff did fulfill one important function: It marked the starting point of a differentiation between political bodies and the higher echelons of the armed forces' commands. In a sense, the Senior Defense Staff foreshadowed the integration of military command.

The experience of the Senior Defense Staff served as a guide when the reorganization of the central defense administration necessitated the introduction of new institutions. The excessive dependence on the ex-holders of office by the Senior Defense Staff indicated the need for defining much more clearly the subordination of any new body to executive power; moreover, the search for efficiency implied that the encumbants of this new body should be hierarchically senior to and more powerful than the chiefs of staff of each of the armed forces. The conclusions drawn from this experience were only partially followed when the structure and role of the new body were being defined.

The old Senior Defense Staff was reorganized under two provisions of the prime minister dated April 8 and July 2, 1976. It disappeared for good in a law passed on May 19, 1980, and its functions were divided between the body that replaced it—the JUJEM—and the Ministry of Defense.[5]

Incorporated completely within the Defense Ministry, the Chief of Staffs Committee is subordinate to the prime minister, who exercises authority through the defense minister except in matters over which he reserves the right to handle himself. The committee consists of a chairman and the three chiefs of staff from each of the armed services. The chairman is appointed by decree, having first been approved by the Council of Ministers on the nomination of the prime minister. The post must be held by a lieutenant-general or an admiral on active service. While exercising his duties, this chairman is considered the most senior figure in terms of the promotion lists of the three services. Since the creation of this committee in 1977, one may note a certain tendency to favor members of the air force for selection to the chairmanship of the JUJEM. However, following the events of February 23, 1981, political reasons have led to the selection of an army officer; specifically, in January 1982, Lieutenant-General Lacalle-Leloup succeeded Lieutenant-General Altaro Arregui from the air force.

However, the personal standing of the chairman of the JUJEM was one more of symbolic status than of real command at the center of the armed forces. Indeed, the novelty of the position lay in the fact that the chairman neither exerted superior authority over the other members of the committee nor held any direct military command. He was only *primus inter pares*, and his role was merely one of coordinator and arbitrator. Even so, this role was a difficult one to carry out; given that the chairman had no superior authority, his vote did not count when he arbitrated the differences that arose within the JUJEM. Even then, the law determined that arbitration could be referred to the prime minister if a solution were not to be found within the military itself.

The chairman's lack of real power was such that his position risked being turned into a sort of "backwater" useful only in "neutralizing" the influence of a military personality who became awkward, while at the same time according him the prestige associated with the office—primarily because his formal statutory powers limited him to certain courses of action after he had ceased to serve as chairman of the JUJEM. The chairman could cease to hold office for one of the following reasons: (1) upon resignation, once accepted by the head of state; (2) following a decision taken by the Council of Ministers on the recommendation of the head of state; and (3) upon his appointment to the reserves. In January 1982, the government took the initiative and replaced the chairman and the other members of the JUJEM a few months before they were due to be appointed to the reserves. The reason for this decision was a political one; the objective was related to the fact that the court case against those who had planned the military putsch of February 23, 1981, had to be heard quickly, and that the government wished to reform the structure of the senior ranks of the services' High Command. As soon as he had been removed from office, the chairman of the JUJEM was prevented from holding a position subordinate in authority to the committee or to one of its members, which meant, in effect, that any post of command in the armed forces was closed to him (even if he had not been in the reserve) regardless of the caliber of the members of the committee and the positions they held.

From the JUJEM's creation until 1984—the period during which it was the commanding body—it never managed to reach the intended level of effectiveness; it also failed to impose its authority as the obvious center of armed forces management. This was due to the chairman's position as a mere representative figure, a situation that mitigated the coordinating function he should have played. Despite the fact that the JUJEM had a chief of staff from each of the armed services, the chairman's relative lack of seniority made his task more difficult to perform.

Yet even with these structural faults, the JUJEM served a useful function during the period from 1978 to 1983.[6] It was well placed in the defense policymaking and planning process, and it took an active part. Even before the government had defined its defense policy objectives, the JUJEM had considered a document containing a range of strategic alternatives. Later, when the government was drawing up its directives for national defense, the JUJEM gave technical advice to the Council on National Defense. Still in the planning stage, the JUJEM finally drew up the interservice strategic plans; these contained a first part that identified in outline the underlying principles and direction of military strategy, and a second part that defined the means deemed necessary to achieve those strategic ends. It was then left to the government itself to approve both the overall plans and the military means.

During the planning phase, the JUJEM intervened to determine the timing of the joint services' strategic plan by dividing it into various stages and identifying within each the priorities to meet the requirements, respectively, of the army, navy, and air force. Thus, the JUJEM determined the implementation of strategy and coordinated the various plans of each of the services based on that strategy by defining the preparation and organization that each was required to meet. The JUJEM had the responsibility, in effect, to coordinate the logistics of the three services as well as the systems of communication and electronic warfare necessary for overall command and control.

The JUJEM also performed roles more directly concerned with the organizational aspects of the armed forces. In this capacity, it suggested to the prime minister the creation of unified and specialized commands. It also planned maneuvers and combined-services exercises. Furthermore, it was responsible for checking on the discipline and morale of the armed forces as a whole. Finally, the JUJEM established a doctrine of unified action; its objective was to promote, with the help of the National Mobilization Service, the preparation of plans for general mobilization.

Outside this operational and coordinating role, the JUJEM performed one other function that had been delegated to it under the Law of November 6, 1980—namely, the reform of the military penal code. Under its provisions, the JUJEM could propose to the minister of defense the introduction of a new procedure by which general officers could be transferred to the reserves when they had been negligent, undisciplined, or incapable of exercising effective command over their units or subordinates. The final decision was to be made in all cases by decree, endorsed by the Council of Ministers on the recommendation of the minister of defense, and even then only after the Supreme Council of Military Justice, the highest-ranking military court, had given its judgment. Once the decision had been taken, the interested party would have no other recourse than to make a special appeal to the king as head of the armed services.

Command of each branch of the armed services is vested in its respective chief of staff. The law defines them as being those who exercise military command over each service, under the authority of the minister of defense. The institutionalization of these positions of command is a very recent phenomenon. Until 1976, the admiral serving as chief of the naval staff was the principal military authority in his service. In the other two services (the army and the air force) the respective holders of ministerial office assumed command. These were high-ranking officers who carried out their ministerial duties in complete harmony with their role as commanders-in-chief of their service, for which they had political, as well as managerial, responsibility.

The Decree of December 23, 1976, institutionalized the post of the chief of staff of the army; by this change of title, he replaced the previous chief of the general staff.[7] Owing to his subordination to the military office-holder at the head of the ministry of the army, the latter has never been able to gain the necessary authority to establish himself as the senior commanding officer. His role has been limited, instead, to that of an auxiliary in the military chain of command. In the same way, the Decree of February 8, 1977, created the position of the chief of staff of the air force.[8] However, the navy chief of staff, whose status had been determined by the Navy Law of July 4, 1970, saw his authority extended by the Decree of August 25, 1978.[9]

Regarding the application of these laws and decrees, the three chiefs of staff are nominated by the government and proposed by the minister of defense once the respective superior councils have given their nonbinding advice. The minister is at liberty to disregard this advice. Those nominated would exercise all the powers of command as well as the responsibility to ensure that the maximum operational capability of their service is maintained with respect to the resources allocated to them.

Similarly, the chiefs of staff are responsible for the development and implementation of joint strategic plans to the extent that they apply to the service under their command. They must therefore establish, and execute, the entirety of the operational, logistical, preparative, and formulative plans of their particular service. They also define the military policy of their respective services and ensure that this policy is adhered to along with those issues pertaining to the morale and discipline of the men under their command.

The chiefs of staff have an advisory and intelligence responsibility to the minister of defense. They must give him continuous and reliable information in the following areas: the general strategic situation and potential threats; the requirements of the armed forces to enable them to carry out their roles effectively; and, finally, the implications of any of these issues for military policy and the defense policies of the state.

Socialist Reforms: The Law of January 5, 1984

The victory of the Socialist party (PSOE) in the parliamentary elections of October 28, 1982, confirmed the swing in Spanish political opinion. The government of Felipe Gonzalez continued and accelerated the structural and operational modernization of the Spanish Armed Forces. In the autumn of 1983, Defense Minister Narcis Serra Serra presented a proposal for the reform of the central organization of defense, which altered Title 1 of the law governing the principles underlying defense and the organization of the armed forces of July 1, 1980. Following debate in the Cortes, the bill was passed by a large majority in the Congress of Deputies at the second reading, and it became law on January 5, 1984.

The reform contained in the law had two principal objectives. First, there was the military objective to establish better coordination among the military commanders; second, there was above all the political objective of reaffirming the supremacy of civil control over the direction of the armed forces. The implementation of this second objective gives the government authorities the immediate responsibility for politico-military decisions, whereas the former objective is still to be achieved through a thorough reexamination of the military High Command.

The principles that had determined the introduction of the institutional structure of defense since 1978 affirmed the preeminence of civil power within the framework of a divison of competence between the political and military authorities. This differentiation of authority put an end to the theoretical distinction between the exercise of "power" within the armed forces—the latter being subordinate to the former—at a time when nobody could ignore the subordination of the military both to civil control and, in particular, to executive authority.

However, in spite of these declared principles, the text of the Law of July 1, 1980, was not sufficiently precise in defining the competences of the military apparatus and the political decisionmakers. Certain relationships had been left hazy and ill defined, particularly the one concerned with the triangular relationship between the king, the government, and the armed forces. On the pretext of a lack of definition in the law, anyone could point to a sketch outline of the theory of military autonomy in such a way as to set back the interests of the armed forces' subordination to political authority.

In the late 1970s, certain reactionary military circles were putting forward the idea of establishing a direct link between the armed forces and the king, thereby allowing them to circumvent the exercise of civil authority. Toward this end, the proponents of such a view were appealing to the hierarchical chain of command with the king at the top, in order to leave the government with only a political role divorced from military command. Since then, the envisaged set of arrangements has required the full involvement of the monarch with the armed forces—ideally, a two-headed arrangement, with the civil authorities left to play only a secondary role.

This approach recognized the armed forces as a sort of "fourth power" residing above the executive and in total contradiction to the letter and intent of the 1978 Constitution. These theoretical constructions were not bereft of ulterior political motives. In effect, were it accepted that the armed forces could not receive valid orders except from the king, then, by manipulating the position of the monarchy, the generals would be able to manufacture the grounds for military intervention without the need to seek public approval. Thus, according to this thesis, anything would be possible, from a constitutional point of view, in any hypothetical situation in which national sovereignty, territorial integrity, or the constitutional order was deemed to be under serious threat. Therefore, the JUJEM—inasmuch as it is the collective instrument of military command—would decide whether the government had ceased to be effective or was able to exercise authority, and thereby allow the armed forces to assume their constitutional role as defined in Article 8 of the Constitution. This fallacious reasoning would have allowed, and legitimated, a military coup d'etat, should the situation arise.

In this risky situation, where the stability of the democratic system was concerned, the Socialist government determined to bring forward the reform of the armed forces in the sense of making a clear and precise reaffirmation of the principle of the supremacy of civil power in the politico-military decisionmaking process. Under the provisions of the Law of January 5, 1984, the decision to use the armed forces and to exercise effective command belongs to the prime minister, with the king restricted to a formal and honorific position while retaining the title of commander-in-chief of the armed forces. The Law of 1984 not only confirmed the letter and spirit of the Law of 1980, but it was also in accordance with the Constitution of 1978.

Article 8 of the Law of 1980, modified on January 5, defined the functions and powers of the prime minister with regard to defense matters. His list of powers clearly demonstrates the strengthening of the role of prime minister. He determines national defense policy and, above all, has authority over all command, coordination, and operational matters concerning the armed forces. Paragraphs 2 and 3 of the same article outline the powers of the prime minister regarding the direction of defense policy and of the armed forces. The prime minister is also responsible for the conduct and direction of war in the event of armed hostilities, formulates the directions in foreign negotiations, and defines the overall orientation of military strategy. In this last respect, he is responsible for the determination of overall, grand strategic objectives and endorses strategic plans, the deployment of forces, and the necessary measures to meet the requirements of the armed forces. Finally, he can delegate the function of defense policy formulation and the control of the armed forces to the minister of defense.

The defense minister's role vis-à-vis the armed forces has been strengthened by a number of explicitly defined powers. The minister, under the provision of Article 10, submits to the government the objectives of defense policy and elaborates, defines, and executes military policy. He formulates the combined strategic plan and defines the overall objective of the armed forces, both of which have to be endorsed by the government. He also directs, coordinates, and controls the personnel policies of the services, and exercises the right of inspection over military education and training. At the same time, he submits economic and financial programs to the government and has responsibility for their execution. The minister also coordinates and directs the administration of resources, decides on arms production, and coordinates and initiates scientific and technical research programs relevant to national defense matters. Finally, the minister directs the military administration on behalf of the government.

Thus it has been confirmed that defense strategy and military policy, in all their various aspects, reside with the political authorities, and that politico-military decisionmaking rests in the hands of the prime minister and, through delegation, those of the minister of defense. No doubt can remain regarding the subordination of the objectives, the means, and the operational actions of the armed forces to the civil authorities at any given time.

However, it is not enough merely to detail powers and principles; we must also see how they operate in practice. Accordingly, both the functions and the structures must be analyzed. Above all, it should be noted that the expansion of power in the political context has gone hand in hand with more extensive reforms in the structures and functions of the military High Command.

The Law of January 5, 1984, introduced a substantial change in the structure of the military High Command through the effect of a change in the nature of the Chiefs of Staff Committee and by means of the establishment of a new post, that of the chief of defense staff, or JEMAD.

The chairman of the JUJEM was replaced by a chief of defense staff, who is directly responsible to and a close collaborator with the minister of defense; he is also military adviser to the minister of defense. This new post, established under Article 11(2) of the new law, was designed to improve communications between the minister and the military authorities and thereby achieve a quicker and more efficient response from the military High Command.

With regard to his statutory position, the JEMAD is appointed by decree and endorsed by the Council of Ministers. He is nominated by the prime minister, although in carrying out his duties he is responsible to the minister of defense. The position must be filled by a lieutenant-general or an admiral in active service and in an administrative post in command of military units. In January 1984, the government appointed as chief of defense staff Admiral Liberal Lucini, who had previously served as under-secretary for defense in the first government under the new monarchy. The grounds for dismissal of the JEMAD are the same as those noted above regarding the previous position of the chairman of the JUJEM.

The JEMAD does not hold a position of command in the armed forces during peacetime—a decision that demonstrates the political concern of Spanish legislators not to give to the military a single chief of the armed forces who could be interpreted as being, or becoming, a Generalissimo. However, Article 11(2), paragraph 3, stipulates that in time of war, the government is empowered to appoint him commander-in-chief of the operational forces under the authority of the prime minister, with the responsibility for the conduct of military operations.

Among the other responsibilities of the JEMAD it is important to note certain command functions that he exercises in conjunction with the minister of defense. Specifically, he can exercise joint command and take over any specific command that may be created from time to time. If the situation warrants it, he may delegate this responsibility to the chief of staff of the relevant service. Moreover, in his capacity as collaborator with the minister of defense, the JEMAD participates in the analysis, implementation, and operational aspects of military policy. He submits for the minister's approval operational and interservice logistical plans, and once these are approved, he is responsible for their implementation. In the same way, he submits to the minister, after consultation with the JUJEM, any plans for standardization of the armed services, the purpose of which should not be to the advantage of any particular branch, but, rather, should improve efficiency and economy overall. Even so, as a consequence of certain features of the law concerning the JUJEM's membership and the status within it of the chairman have had a detrimental effect on the search for better coordination at the center of the armed forces.

In the absence of the prime minister or the minister of defense, the chief of defense staff chairs the meetings of the JUJEM. He also takes responsibility for convening the JUJEM on the instructions of the minister of defense, arranges the agenda, and supplies the minister with details of reports and recommendations submitted by the JUJEM. For assistance in his duties, the JEMAD relies on a defense staff headed by an officer of division general rank, or a vice-admiral equivalent, appointed by the minister on the JEMAD's recommendation.

The chief of defense staff has no direct command over the armed forces. Each service has its own chief of staff, who exercises command under the aegis of the minister of defense. The restructuring of the JUJEM constituted one of the essential elements in the reform exercise that culminated in the law of January 5, 1984. The JUJEM remained in existence but ceased to be a joint command, becoming instead a consultative organ restricted to giving military advice to the government and to the minister of defense on all matters concerning the strategic aspects of military operations and the necessary measures to ensure the operational effectiveness of the armed forces. Its lack of influence, due to a certain punctiliousness in line with the best traditions of military subservience to political authority, has persuaded the legislators to redefine the JUJEM's role and to limit it to its current consultative position. This restructuring has caused the JUJEM to lose many of its former powers, which are now reallocated to the JEMAD and, above all, to the minister of defense.

Within the new legally defined framework, the JUJEM has the authority to take advice and offer its opinion on the general strategic situation, notably with respect to both the joint strategic plan and the assessment of the external threat. In the same way, the JUJEM draws up the guidelines of joint military action and coordinates the plans of the three branches of the armed services. The JUJEM's composition has not undergone any radical alteration except for the addition of the JEMAD as a fourth member.

The reform has also affected the composition of the National Defense Council and the nature of its responsibilities. According to Article 9, as modified by the Law of January 5, 1984, this council is defined as an advisory and consultative body of the government in the field of national defense. Previously, it performed the additional function of formulating and proposing the overall direction of defense policy. Today, however, it advises on all matters of national defense referred to it by the government, whereas the general direction of policy is formulated by the minister of defense. The council, moreover, examines and proposes to the government any measures concerning certain aspects of defense that could have implications for other ministries. It retains its role as adviser to the prime minister regarding the conduct of war, and may also advise the king and the prime minister directly.

The composition of the National Defense Council is now more limited. It comprises the prime minister and, in due course, the deputy prime minister(s), the minister of defense, the JEMAD, and the three service chiefs, as well as the ministers of foreign affairs and of the interior. Other ministers may attend on the invitation of the chairman, who is normally the prime minister, unless the king attends.

The wish to emphasize the supremacy of political decisionmaking over the military authorities, which was reaffirmed in the Law of January 1984, has gone hand in hand with the urge to unify the management of defense at the highest level of political responsibility.

The Unification of the Armed Forces

The setting up of new management structures has accompanied the efforts since 1977 to establish, once and for all, a unified military management structure within the central organization of defense. Spain adopted a unified form of defense management while it was reorganizing the central administration in July 1977. The creation of a Defense Ministry, however, had to overcome historical tradition; the government wanted to fulfill certain aims, but the majority of these are yet to be realized (as of 1984). The Defense Ministry, created on July 4, 1977, is historically the successor to three previous armed forces ministries—those of the army, navy, and air force.[10] The origins of the Ministry for the Army, as well as that of the navy, date back to the reign of Philip V at the start of the eighteenth century. The Air Force Ministry was established on August 8, 1939, after the Spanish Civil War.

The present Ministry of Defense was originally created under the same name by Franco during the 1936–1939 conflict, on January 30, 1938. The nearest precedents were the creation of the post of deputy prime minister for Defense Affairs during the first government under the reign of King Juan Carlos in November 1975 and the reorganization of the Armed Forces High Command. The deputy prime minister charged with defense affairs was considered to be the precursor of the future minister of defense as well as a first step toward the unification of the armed services. However, this latter step had to overcome obstacles that resulted, on the one hand, from the resistance of the three services, which were reluctant to see any structural changes, and, on the other, from the armed forces' refusal to accept the existence of a single ministerial post, which they feared would jeopardize their service autonomy. These psychological and sociological reasons, however, did not eliminate the possibility of a more widespread recognition of the need for greater coordination within the armed forces' management.

In keeping with the objective of improved coordination, the preliminary clauses of the royal decree that established the Ministry of Defense contain two arguments: Its creation answered the armed forces' need for modernization as well as its wish to unify defense policy. Thus, through its new terms of reference, the Defense Ministry was to integrate the armed services to a greater extent than had those provisions it replaced. It was necessary, therefore, to bring together defense policy and military institutions and to put them in their proper context—namely, one of defense—while at the same time integrating the diverse military administration within a single ministerial department. The aim remained consistent: to bring about the unity of political responsibility at the highest level of management. Continued integration was achieved progressively, however, and it occurred in response more to the needs of policy and operational coordination than to the demands of a truly unified structure. The aim of complete unification has continued to be the ultimate objective of the Ministry of Defense since its establishment.

The structure of the Ministry of Defense has remained, until recently, one in which the minister has jointly held the three previous service ministerial posts. Within the Ministry, the development of a new horizontal structure, which was designed to achieve greater coordination and unity of management, was introduced—but only very slowly and rather insufficiently. The vertical structure, reflecting the military administration already in place, has lasted longer, even with a plurality of bodies. This has meant that certain people have long held the same responsibilities, and the result has been lowered efficiency in terms of wasted effort and wasted resources—the very opposite of what was being sought.

It was difficult for the minister of defense to carry out his task as long as the separation of the organization of the three services remained a political consideration. This is the reason why any real reform should aim at reorganizing the Defense Ministry's structures in order to give the responsible minister the means of actually being able to carry out his policies as elaborated and defined by the government. The defense minister's role is not to ratify military officers' decisions, but to have the latter apply the policies and decisions of the government. The absence of a truly effective means has meant that the minister of defense has had to change his role frequently to that of spokesman for the military rather than its political master. It has now become necessary to reform the organization of the military to allow the minister to gain the practical means of executing and exercising his proper role.

Since the creation of the Ministry of Defense, its whole structure has been organized on the basis of two principles. First, there is the separation of the military chain of command from the administrative branch; and, second, there is the differentiation between the active executive branches and those in a consultative capacity. On the practical level, the first of these two principles has never been carried out coherently or completely.

On a theoretical level, the principle of separation means the separation of the armed forces from the "administrative" group. "Armed forces" in this context refers to the organization of the army, navy, and air force. Their essential responsibility is the preparation and instruction of military personnel through the exercise of military leadership and command. The responsibility of administrative group (or civil service branches), on the other hand, is to deal with questions of pure administration, such as financial and budgetary matters, personnel policies, procurement, matters of litigation, and so on.

This theoretical differentiation, as specified by the law, has not been entirely reflected in reality. At the end of November 1983, the minister of defense announced the main outline of a project to reorganize his ministry in order to accommodate his organizational structure to the creation of the JEMAD. The envisaged reorganization was to allow for the existence, within the Defense Ministry, of two well-defined groups: a strictly military group placed under the authority of the JEMAD and the administrative group placed under the authority of the under-secretary for defense. Consequent upon this proposal, the JEMAD would carry the rank of secretary of state for defense and, as such, would be responsible for military policy in all its technical aspects; meanwhile, the under-secretary for defense would be responsible for all those political and administrative tasks within the Defense Ministry. The latter post has been, and remains, filled by a senior civil servant.

The envisaged reform claims to create the necessary conditions for the existence of a true Ministry of Defense, whose real authority was to be found, until today, in the hands of the headquarters of each branch of the armed forces. This reform hopes for the creation of a central management for personnel, which would bring together those responsible from the staffs of each branch of the services and coordinate their plans. We must note, however, that personnel matters were, until now, exclusively controlled by each service. Even so, in terms of the restructuring proposal, the minister of defense would have firm control over all purchases of equipment, foreign arms sales, and recruitments— all of which had previously been in the hands of the military. Other general management concerns—particularly the general management of arms and supplies, the management of information and public relations (DRISDE), and the Center for Defense Information (CESID), a section of the Spanish intelligence service—will remain within the Defense Ministry. As far as the impact of the reorganization is concerned, the headquarters of each of the services, under the command of its respective chief of staff, will have to relinquish to the administrative group certain of their previous functions. Most notable among these are the areas of armaments and personnel matters. Thus it is intended that conditions will be improved so that the minister of defense can carry out his functions fully and effectively, so long as there is public support.

Postscript

The reform of the central structures of Spanish management and administration of defense, which is still in train, takes place within a larger process of modernization of the machinery of defense and of the armed forces, with respect to their human, financial, and material resources. The Spanish leaders must face the challenge of modernizing the military machine in order to accommodate political developments and to complete its aim of greater operational efficiency. The next few years will show whether or not they will have succeeded.

Notes

1. See the laws for basis of national defense and military organization of July 1, 1980, in *Boletin Oficial del Estado* (*BOE*) of July 10, 1980, no. 165 (Madrid).

2. See Fundamental Law No. 4/81 of June 1 dealing with state of emergency, in exceptional circumstances, siege, and war, in *BOE* of June 5, 1981, p. 12341.

3. See paragraph II in "An Unfinished Reform," concerning the role of the Council for National Defense and the new outline of the role of the head of the state and the minister of defense.

4. See Decree-Law No. 11/77 of February 8, 1977, in *BOE* of February 9, 1977, p. 3135.

5. See Law No. 26/80 of May 19, 1980, in *BOE* of June 13, 1980, No. 142.

6. The JUJEM's role was modified through the reform of the Defense Law of July 1, 1980, and carried through in December 1983, the JUJEM having stopped being a collegiate body of command and having limited itself to an advisory role. See paragraph II in "An Unfinished Reform."

7. See Decree No. 3026/73 of December 23, 1976, in *BOE* of January 11, 1977, p. 522.

8. See Decree No. 9/77 of February 8, 1977, in *BOE* of February 9, 1977, p. 3133.

9. See Decree No. 3304/78 of August 25, 1978, in *BOE* of February 2, 1979, p. 2736.

10. See Decree No. 15518/77 of July 4, 1977, in *BOE* of July 5, 1977, p. 15035.

11
The United States

Karen A. McPherson

Bureaucracies demand functional specialization and expertise. Because modern Western societies have become ineluctably bureaucratized, any effort to understand the process by which decisions are made must focus on the specialized bureaucracies that have evolved to carry out the business of the society. One of the primary functions of any government must be to ensure the safety and security of its citizens from threats, both foreign and domestic. Thus, the bureaucratic entity that deals with national defense is a critical focus for analysis if one is to understand the priority that society places on its own survival and the values the government is prepared to defend.

Americans are essentially ambivalent about their military. Historically, they are heir to a powerful antimilitary tradition, but they are willing to support participation in a conflict if they feel threatened. They tend to ignore the military until they need it, at which time they expect it to rise to the occasion and keep them secure. In the past, the military responded to these demands and indeed maintained security. Even during the world wars, the prevailing state of transportation and communications technology provided the military with adequate time to achieve an acceptable state of readiness before confronting a direct threat to the nation's continued existence. However, it has become apparent that a future war cannot guarantee the same warning period. Thus there has emerged a growing interest in how the central organization for defense is structured in the United States, how it interacts with the other major actors in the defense decisionmaking process, and how well it can react to the demands placed upon it from abroad while still adhering to the basic tenets of a democracy that generally prefers the maintenance of its ideals even at the expense of its security.

I wish to acknowledge the assistance provided by Alan Ned Sabrosky, who read successive versions of this manuscript and provided useful suggestions for improving it.

Constitutional Framework

The constitutional framework within which the U.S. defense decisionmaking process operates is quite simple. It also has little relationship to the way decisions are made and policy is actually formulated. But it is useful nonetheless to examine the formal allocation of responsibilities that gave rise to the current system for defense decisionmaking.

The Constitution says little about the conduct of foreign affairs and of military activities. The Congress is given the responsibility for authorizing the expenditure of all moneys from the U.S. Treasury, including those used to support the military. The power of the purse is not an inconsequential one; policy is carried out through programs and with weapons and supporting equipment that must be paid for. A decision to pay or not to pay for something has direct implications for the ability of the United States to carry out the policy that the requested expenditure was to support. The Senate has additional responsibilities with regard to the appointment of ambassadors and the approval of treaties, to which the Senate has to give its consent. The Congress as a whole also has the power to declare war.

The president is given, in the Constitution, the title of commander-in-chief of the army and navy. He is also given general oversight responsibilities for the executive departments (not named in the Constitution) and the power to make treaties and to appoint ambassadors with the advice and consent of the Senate.

The Constitution says no more about security-related matters. The present defense establishment has grown up over the years and has been authorized by various public laws, but it has little constitutional base on which one might draw for an understanding of the way the system works. The Constitution provides a framework within which virtually any central organization of defense could have developed. It also establishes a network of interlocking responsibilities that would prohibit any one participant in the process from gaining an irrevocable position of prominence over any other participant. The president's responsibilities as commander-in-chief are not spelled out, but they clearly require the cooperation of the Congress, whose consent is needed at least for the expenditure of any money in the pursuit of the national interest.

Current Structure

The purpose of the Defense Department can best be described as the maintenance and employment of the military, as directed by the president through the secretary of defense and in response to the mandate of the Congress.[1] Thus there immediately appear to be two distinct functions for which the Department of Defense is responsible: maintaining and employing the armed forces. Over the years a dual

Figure 11.1   United States: Dual Chain of Command

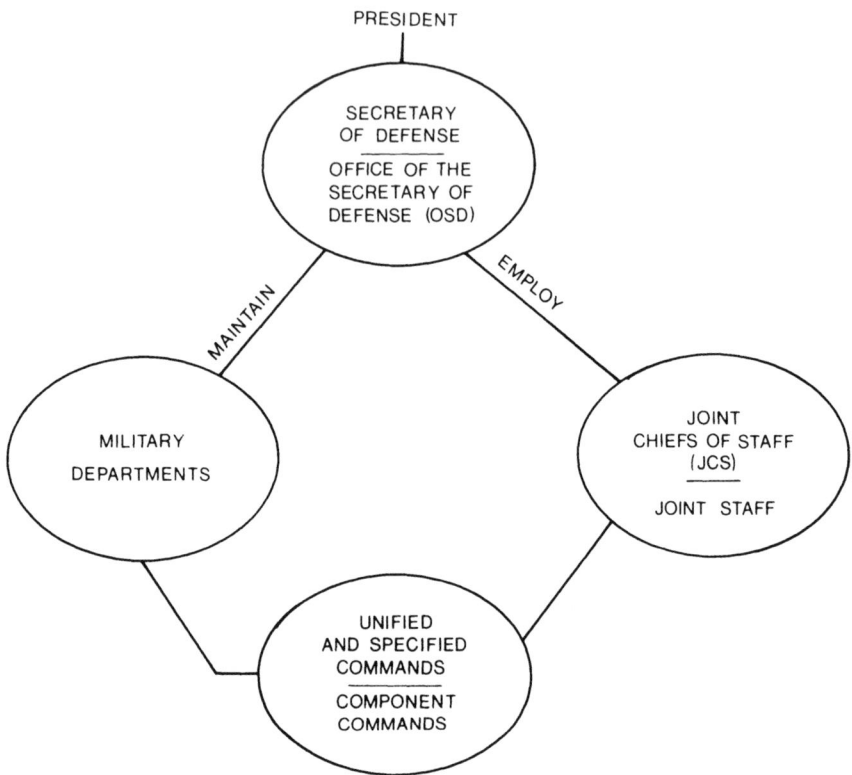

Source: H. D. Barrett, *Reappraising Defense Organization* (Washington, D.C.: National Defense University Press, 1983), p. 18.

chain of command has arisen in recognition of the two functional areas of responsibility. Figure 11.1 illustrates this dual chain of command. Maintaining the forces (which involves recruiting, training, and procurement functions) is directed by the secretary of defense and carried out by the military departments and the component commands. Employing the forces (which involves threat assessment; war-fighting capability; strategic, logistical, and operational planning; and command and control arrangements) is directed by the secretary of defense through the Joint Chiefs of Staff (JCS) to the commanders-in-chief of the Unified and Specified Commands (CINCs).

The last paragraph introduced several terms that may be unfamiliar; a slight digression to define them seems appropriate at this point.

Secretary of Defense. Presidentially appointed; member of the president's cabinet; senior civilian in the Department of Defense. Responsible for all aspects of the Defense Department's activities; all of the departmental functions are carried out under his authority, direction, and control. Staff support is provided by the Office of the Secretary of Defense (OSD).

Joint Chiefs of Staff. In the employment chain of command; composed of the chiefs of the four services and a chairman, who is a senior military officer charged with supervising the Joint Staff and acting as the spokesman for the JCS. The JCS has four main responsibilities: to act as principal military adviser to the president, the National Security Council, and the secretary of defense; to assist the National Command Authorities (the president and the secretary of defense) in the exercise of command; to prepare strategic and logistics plans to guide the overall defense policy and budgeting process; and to ensure congruence of service plans with the overall policy direction of the Department of Defense. Supported by the Joint Staff.

Military departments. In the maintaining chain of command; headed by civilian service secretaries and containing the four uniformed services responsible for providing for land, sea, and air warfare. Each service is headed by a service chief who reports to the service secretary; each service chief also serves as a member of the Joint Chiefs of Staff, in which organization he fills an employment role.

Unified and specified commands. In the employment chain of command; six unified commands (European Command, Pacific Command, Southern Command, Atlantic Command, Central Command, and Readiness Command); three specified commands (Aerospace Defense Command, Strategic Air Command, Military Airlift Command); exercise operational command over all forces assigned to them.

Component commands. Combine the employment and maintenance chains of command; maintain their forces through the service link and employ their forces under the CINCs.

Figure 11.2 presents a fully expanded illustration of the current (1984) Department of Defense organization. A number of things are made clear by this chart: the Department of Defense is a complex bureaucratic structure, there are numerous people who play multiple roles (the service chiefs of staff, for example), and the Office of the Secretary of Defense has control over most of the policy-oriented entities within the Department. It is useful at this juncture to highlight how the Department of Defense has evolved since its founding and to discuss the environmental changes that have brought about, or allowed for, this evolution.

Historical Development

The Department of Defense arose from the demands made upon defense decisionmakers during World War II. A *de facto* central organization emerged in 1942, with the organization of a Joint Chiefs of Staff. The National Security Act of 1947 formalized the Joint Chiefs of Staff as the chief military advisory body to the president, the National Security Council, the secretary of defense, and the Congress. More

Figure 11.2 United States Department of Defense

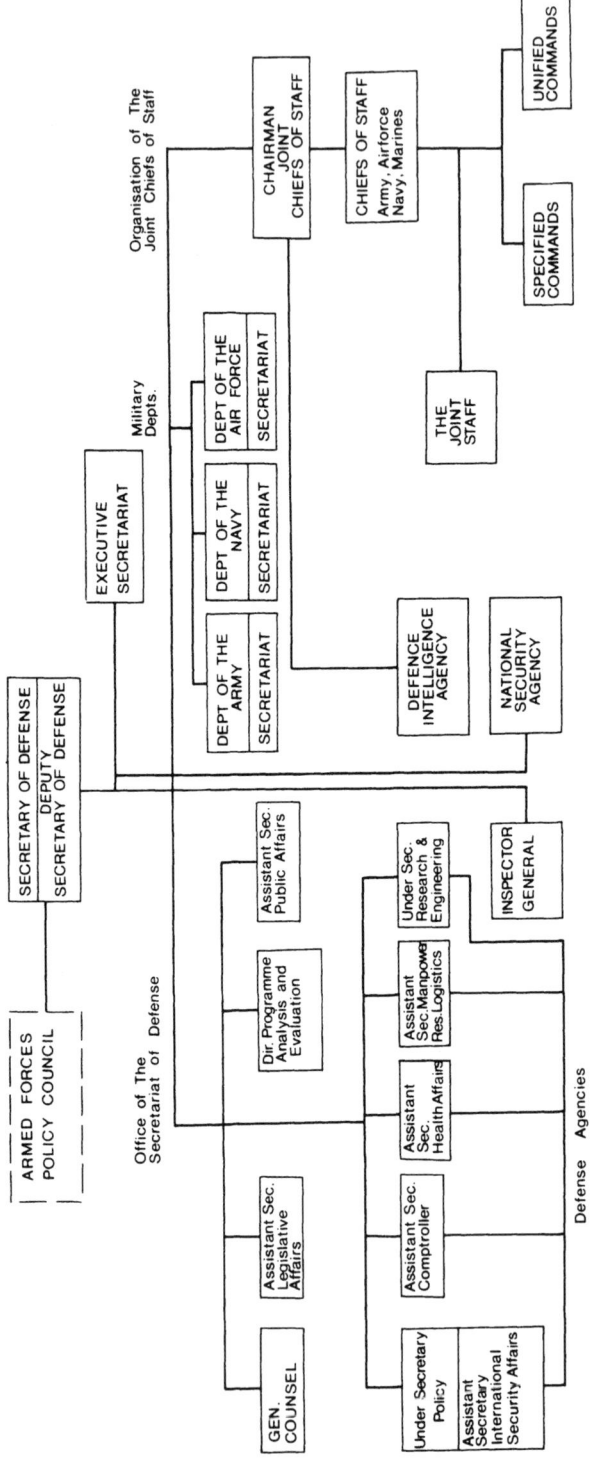

Source: U.S. Department of Defense.

Figure 11.3   United States: National Military Establishment (1948)

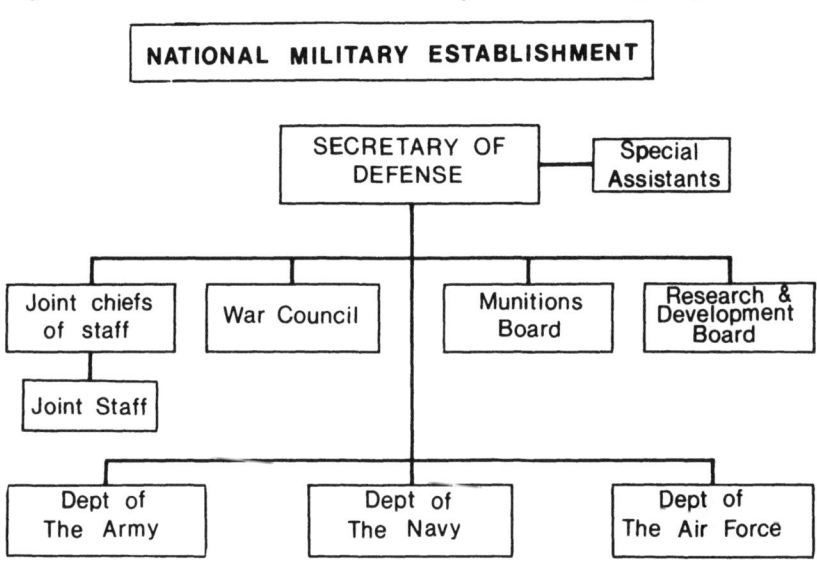

Source: *U.S. Government Manual* (Washington, D.C.: Government Printing Office, 1948).

significant, the 1947 Act created a Department of the Air Force and united it with the Departments of the Army and the Navy under a Department of Defense.

As Figure 11.3 illustrates, the original structure of the Department of Defense, or the National Military Establishment (as it was known then) was rudimentary. However, over the years the growing need for functional specialization within the Defense Department spurred organizational change; major organizational reforms occurred in 1949, 1953, and 1958, as the system began to function and the most obvious organizational flaws were highlighted and corrected. The goal of these organizational changes has been to rationalize the process by which defense decisions are made; however, as will be shown, organizational changes can address only at the margins problems that are not fundamentally organizational but rather are based on tradition, sentiment, and bureaucratic imperatives. Table 11.1 shows the major organizational changes that have occurred within the Department of Defense.

The role of the Joint Chiefs of Staff, the power of the secretary of defense, and the purview of the military departments have been the focus of the most important formal organizational changes that have occurred during the thirty-seven years of the Defense Department's existence. Overall, the process has been one by which the military departments have gradually but consistently yielded power to the secretary of defense, while the Joint Chiefs of Staff has been accorded

Table 11.1
Department of Defense Reorganizations

1949	Enhanced powers of secretary of defense; Established position of JCS chairman.
1953	Further strengthened authority of secretary of defense; Gave JCS chairman control over Joint Staff; Created six additional assistant secretaries of defense; Created general counsel; Included military departments in the chain of command.
1958	Established operational unified commands; Removed military departments from chain of command; Gave JCS chairman a vote; Made JCS chairman clearly subordinate to secretary of defense; Joint Staff integrated instead of being divided by service.
1977	Abolished one deputy secretary position; Established two new under secretaries for policy and for research and engineering.
1983	Established an assistant secretary for reserve affairs.

Source: Mark M. Lowenthal, *The Department of Defense: Organizational History* (Washington, D.C.: Congressional Research Service, 1978).

greater visibility and centralized control. The details of these trends bear examination.

Military Departments

The effect of past reorganizations has been to lessen the assigned responsibilities of the military departments, allowing them to be concerned almost exclusively with the maintaining function. For example, after having been specifically included in the operational chain of command in 1953, they were specifically excluded from that chain of command in the 1958 reorganization. In addition, the adoption of a department-wide Planning, Programming, and Budgeting System (PPBS) during the 1960s further diminished military department control over budgetary resources.

Office of the Secretary of Defense

The relationship between the military departments and the Office of the Secretary of Defense can almost be seen as a zero-sum game; what the military departments lost, the OSD picked up. In the 1958 reorganization, for example, the secretary of defense was authorized to reassign supply and service functions, assign combat forces, and designate which service would develop new weapons systems. According to one observer:

> The most widely recognized development in post World War Two defense organization has been the centralization of authority in the Secretary of Defense. From a position in 1947 in which the Services retained all powers not specifically delegated elsewhere, the Secretary of Defense has acquired complete responsibility for the management of the Department of Defense.[2]

Joint Chiefs of Staff

During World War II, the uniformed military, and more specifically the Joint Chiefs of Staff, operated with virtual autonomy to run the war effort. Because it was clearly outside the bounds of the U.S. constitutional framework for the Joint Chiefs of Staff to retain this preeminent position once peace was achieved, the initial organization of the Joint Chiefs of Staff under the 1947 Act gave it little latitude for activism. In 1949 a fifth member was added to the Joint Chiefs of Staff to serve as chairman. It was thought that a senior military man who was not simultaneously chief of staff of his arm of the military would be able to act in an unbiased fashion and facilitate JCS deliberations. Initially his role was largely ceremonial; he did not even have a vote. By 1953, his role was strengthened—although in that same reorganization the JCS as an entity was excluded from the operational chain of command. (A later Department of Defense directive provided that the secretary will transmit orders through the JCS.) Since then the prominence of the JCS has varied, depending on the desires of the president; the structure is in place, however, for the JCS to play an important role in the formation of defense policy.

Formal Role of Other Actors in the Decisionmaking Process

The Department of Defense is only one of the actors in the process of defense decisionmaking. Depending on the nature of the issue being considered, the president and the Congress play a greater or lesser role in the determination of U.S. policy. Under the American system of government, the executive branch consists of the president, his cabinet, the executive departments run by his cabinet (Departments of Defense, State, etc.), White House–based organizations (the Office of Management and Budget, National Security Council, etc.), and the president's personal staff. Throughout the following discussion, the term *executive* refers to these entities whose activities are directed by the president. The legislature consists of the Senate and House of Representatives. Throughout this discussion, the legislative arm in general is called the Congress.

When a budgetary matter is under consideration, the Department of Defense, calling upon advice from both its uniformed and its civilian employees, puts together a proposed budget. Because appointees of the president occupy important positions throughout the departmental structures responsible for making budget recommendations, it is likely that the wishes of the president, both publicly expressed and privately conveyed, will be reflected in the budget that emerges from the process. The process by which the budget is produced is called the Planning, Programming, Budgeting System (PPBS). It is neither possible nor appropriate to provide a detailed description of the PPBS in this chapter. The important thing to note is that the major Pentagon-based actors—the Secretary of Defense and his office, the JCS and its staff, and the military departments—have multiple opportunities to review the budget as it is formulated. This may sound like responsible policymaking—until one realizes that as a consequence those who would try to improve the defense budgeting process cannot let down their guard. Opponents of change, at any level, get several chances to scuttle reform.

Budget recommendations are next sent to the Office of Management and Budget (OMB) within the Executive Office of the President, where they are scrutinized and analyzed for their congruence with policies enunciated by the president and with budget requests from other departments. Once it passes the OMB hurdle, the budget is sent to the legislature, where both houses of Congress have a responsibility to deal with it in the light of their assessments of the national interest. Figure 11.4 depicts the process by which a budget bill is considered in the Congress.

Once it reaches Capitol Hill, the budget goes first to the House of Representatives, which has the constitutional obligation to originate bills dealing with the expenditure of public funds. In the House Armed Services Committee it is dissected and intimately analyzed by Committee staff members, as well as by members of the staffs of individual congressmen. While the budget is before the Committee, it is the subject of many hearings, in both the full Committee and the various subcommittees, to which witnesses are called to be questioned about the substance of the requested budget authorizations. These hearings usually go on for many months and may occupy weeks of time for key Department of Defense officials who are called to testify on the merits of the bill before the Committee. Key administration officials, outside experts, and academics are also called to testify about various aspects of the budget requests. After its deliberations, the Committee presents a revised version of the budget request to the full House of Representatives for approval.

In theory, the Senate does not begin its budget deliberations until the House is finished. In practice, however, the Senate begins work on the budget request at virtually the same time that such deliberation begins in the House. The Senate pattern replicates that of the House, as the Senate holds hearings at the Committee and subcommittee levels

Figure 11.4 United States: Congressional Decisionmaking Process

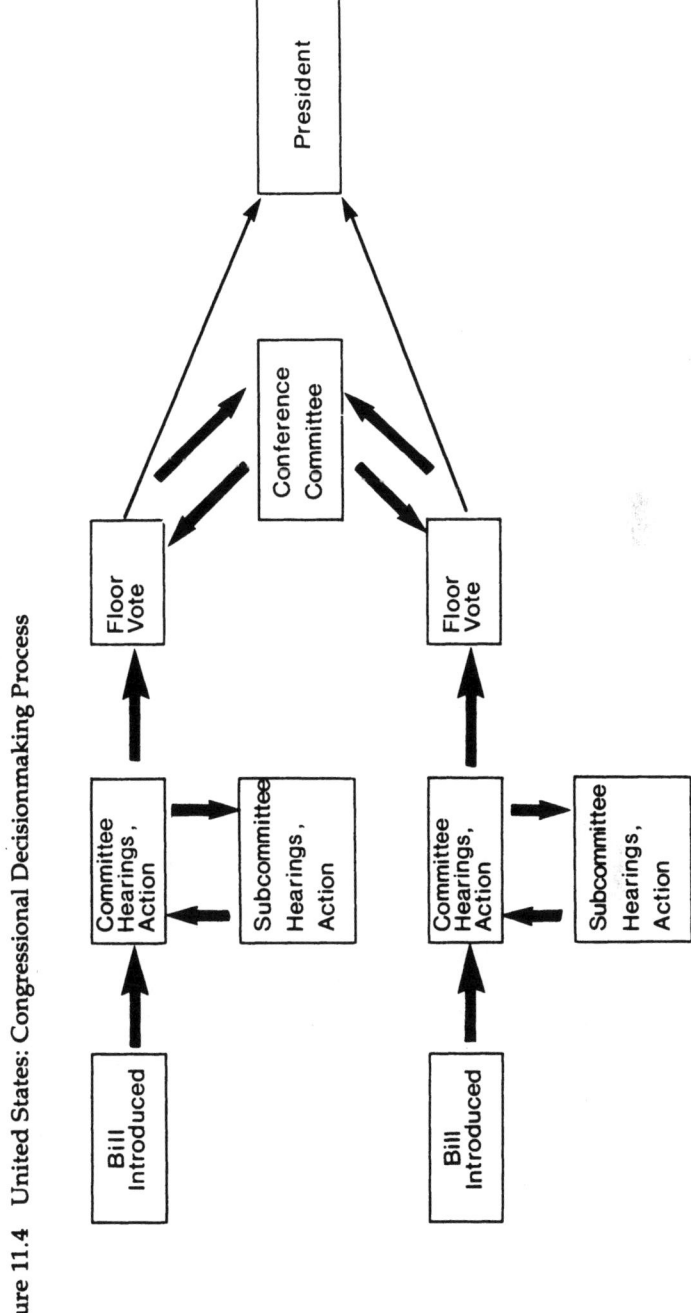

and prepares a revised version of the budget bill to be put to a vote of the full Senate.

At this point, the House and Senate versions of the budget might differ dramatically from one another, and neither may resemble the budget that the president sent to Congress for consideration. Assuming that the House and Senate both pass their defense authorization bills, the bills must somehow be brought into alignment so that only one defense authorization (budget) bill is sent to the president for his signature. This is done through the "Conference process": a Conference Committee is appointed for the express purpose of reconciling differences between the House and Senate versions of the budget bill. Selected members of both houses sit on this Conference Committee. Assuming that the Conference Committee succeeds in reconciling the two bills (as signified by each house's approval in full session of the compromise version produced by the Conference Committee), that compromise bill goes to the president for his signature.

A presidential signature on an authorization bill, however, does not mean that the process is complete. There is another major step and an entirely new set of committees that become involved at this point in the process. The authorizing committees (the House and Senate Armed Services Committees) have merely provided the authority to program money to be spent. The actual expenditure of money (whereby checks are written against the Treasury of the United States) requires the passage of an appropriations bill for each authorizing bill passed. Thus in each house a second bill, an appropriations bill, must find its way through the legislative process depicted in Figure 11.4.

This is how it would work in the case of the defense budget. Both the Senate and the House of Representatives have Appropriations Committees, whose subcommittees deal with the specific areas in which authorizing legislation is passed; the Defense subcommittees of the House and Senate Appropriations Committees deal with the defense appropriations bill.

At this stage, examination of the budget bill is usually more perfunctory than it was within the authorizing committees. There are two reasons for this. First, time is generally running out; a budget introduced early in the calendar year must be passed before the end of the fiscal year, which is September 30. Because the entire Congress (and often most of official Washington) takes a recess during the month of August, most of the substantive work on the bills must be completed by the end of July. If the authorization process takes up the amount of time it usually does, the appropriations committees are left with little time to examine the bills in depth. Second, the members of the appropriations subcommittees have generally not developed the same level of expertise on defense matters as have the members of the Armed Services Committees. Thus, they are not as well prepared to deal with the substance of the appropriations requested and are more likely to accept, rather than to challenge, the word of a witness who testifies that a given part of the appropriations bill is a necessity. But because the appropriations bills must be passed to allow money to be spent for the programs approved in the authorizing legislation, the scrutiny of the appropriations committees provides another hurdle that the budget must cross before it goes into effect.

If elements of the budget as authorized cause an inordinate amount of protest, it is possible for the appropriations process to allow the House and Senate a chance to reconsider the offending parts of the budget. Again, because the appropriations committees of the House and Senate proceed simultaneously but independently on the appropriations bills, it is likely that the two houses will come up with different bills. If this occurs, a second Conference Committee must be appointed to reconcile the differences between the two bills, and the House and Senate must each approve the compromises made by the Conference Committee. Only then can the appropriations bill go to the president for his signature, and only then can the Department of Defense begin to pursue the programs it began preparing budget justification for eighteen months earlier.

If the president objects to either the authorization or the appropriations bill as it comes to him from the Congress, he can veto the bill. His veto is not, however, absolute; it can be overturned by a two-thirds vote of both houses. If the veto is overturned, the bill becomes law without the president's signature; if, however, the veto stands, it is up to the Congress to continue consideration of the bill until agreement can be reached on provisions the president can live with or until resources can be marshaled to withstand a presidential veto. The president does not currently have line-item veto authority (although there is ongoing discussion of providing him with that authority). Thus, if the president objects to one item in the bill, he has no choice but to veto the entire bill. Presidents often threaten to veto authorization or appropriations bills as a way to pressure Congress to accede to their wishes; Congress frequently calls the president's bluff, thinking it unlikely that the president would be willing to call a halt to all Department of Defense activities because of his aversion to one item in a multibillion dollar budget.

Throughout the congressional process, the formal system does not require the Department of Defense to play an active role. The Department of Defense is ostensibly waiting to be told what to do with respect to the programs and expenditures authorized by the Congress. As the system has evolved, the Department of Defense plays an active role in providing information to the Congress, both openly through the hearing process and more informally through telephone and mail contact with individuals and committee members who have questions or comments about the budget. In addition, the presidential appointees within the Department of Defense engage in public relations activities—making speeches and appearing on television—to try to create a tide of public opinion in favor of the budget proposed by the administration. Recognizing that congressmen and senators are motivated by the need to be periodically reelected, successive administrations have assumed that legislators can be influenced by the appearance that their constituents are in favor of a particular piece of legislation.

When the issue to be resolved is one of policy rather than of budgets, the roles of the players in the process change significantly. The Congress plays at best a marginal, and at worst an obstructive, role in the determination of broad national security policy or in crisis management. Since the mid-1960s the Congress has made a concerted effort to play a more effective role in the policy arena. However, the 1973 War Powers Act (which placed limitations on the ability of the president to commit U.S. troops) and efforts to affect the amount of foreign and military aid given to various countries represent the extent to which the Congress has been able to influence this area.

Of much greater importance is the president and the organization around him—specifically, the National Security Council. The NSC has the responsibility to advise the president on the integration of domestic, foreign, and military policies. Statutory members of the NSC are the president, the vice-president, the secretary of state, and the secretary of defense. The secretary of the treasury is frequently present, and the chairman of the Joint Chiefs of Staff has been a regular participant in the meetings. In this capacity the JCS chairman is serving as principal military adviser to the president, not as a representative of the Department of Defense. The director of Central Intelligence is also a regular participant, as is the president's special assistant for national security affairs.

The primary policy functions of the NSC are policy coordination, advice, planning, crisis management, and serving as the focal point for ideas and initiatives within the national security community. The specific role played by the NSC is very much dependent on the personality and desires of the president whom it serves. The NSC meets routinely to discuss areas of concern, as well as on an emergency basis in the event of crisis. Specific policy guidance may be generated by these meetings; to whatever extent this guidance affects either the employment or maintenance arm in the Department of Defense, it is transmitted to the appropriate authority in the Department for implementation. Because the president is commander-in-chief, his directives, to the extent that they do not conflict with specific legislative requirements or constraints, have the force of law.[3]

The Department of State has primary, formal responsibility within the executive branch for the conduct of U.S. foreign policy; its role is probably best understood, however, if one recognizes that it is one of the smaller departments in the federal bureaucracy.[4] The Secretary of State is formally responsible for advising the president on foreign policy matters, supervising the State Department, and coordinating government activities abroad. Geographic and functional bureaus and offices handle most of the routine affairs of the State Department.

Over the years, the fortunes of the Department of State have fluctuated from administration to administration. For example, President John F. Kennedy chose to act as his own *de facto* secretary of state; the appointee he chose to fill that position, Dean Rusk, played a role clearly subordinate to the president. Likewise, President Richard M. Nixon initially chose to keep the locus of foreign policy decisionmaking within the White House, appointing Henry Kissinger as his national security adviser. It was only when Kissinger was formally appointed secretary of state during Nixon's second term of office that the Department of State was reestablished as an important center of power; this was clearly a function of Kissinger's incumbency as secretary of state rather than of a long-term resurgence of power in the State Department.

Myth Versus Reality

Department of Defense

Having to this point spent a great deal of time outlining and discussing the formal organizational structures through which defense decisions are made and implemented, I find it necessary to acknowledge that this formal organization has only a coincidental relationship with how policy is actually made. The academic literature that attempts to analyze bureaucracies goes to great lengths to untangle the many motivational skeins that explain the activities of a bureaucracy, but what really exists in the Defense Department might be more accurately termed a form of "organized anarchy" that inhibits efficiency and increases the likelihood of failure.[5]

The basic premises of an organized anarchy challenge the assumption that the policy preferences of elements in the bureaucracy, however defined, can be predictably observed in the policy outputs of the bureaucracy. Because of its size and complexity and the functional specialization that differentiates the responsibilities of one subgroup from another within the organization, the Department of Defense is a particular example of an "organized anarchy." Further complicating an already complex picture are outside forces that reinforce the military bureaucracy's anarchic character. These include the inherent ambiguity of the external environment, the existence of a variety of poorly defined and often inconsistent directions taken by the national defense policy, the nature of the structural channels through which problems flow to decisionmakers and decisions flow to actors, the fact that the system is overloaded and misloaded with information and demands, the lack of a real understanding of the processes by which the bureaucracy operates, and time constraints that preclude any really rational reconciliation of conflicting demands upon the bureaucracy.[6]

How can one relate the orderly, rational picture of Defense Department organization presented in the first part of this analysis to the organized anarchy image presented here? As should be clear from the earlier allusion to several efforts to mitigate through organizational reform the weaknesses of the bureaucratic structure of the Department of Defense, there is no real consensus as to what the proper roles of its civilian and military leadership ought to be. In spite of having been an ostensibly unified entity since 1947, the Department of Defense has never exhibited the degree of cooperative and integrated planning envisioned at its formation. Because the lines of authority are often unclear, the Office of the Secretary of Defense, the Joint Chiefs of Staff, and the military departments operate in a state of uneasy truce; the CINCs and the Component Commands are the uneasy recipients of nebulous and inconsistent guidance.

Office of the Secretary of Defense. The OSD has gained power over the years at the expense of the military departments—but to a greater extent on paper than in reality. It is undeniable that defense decision-making has become increasingly centralized as a result both of formal organizational changes and of informal changes in procedure. However, the ability of the OSD to exploit the potential of this centralization of power has been limited by the management approach through which OSD operates. Accusations of excessive micromanagement within the Defense Department coexist with accusations of inadequate attention to the need to establish a unified framework for the formulation and execution of defense policy. According to one observer:

> Adopting a more effective management approach will require correcting a number of weaknesses: ineffectual joint military participation in OSD policy formulation, insufficient delegation to operating levels of the Department, imprecise delineation of authority between the Office of the Secretary of Defense and the military departments, weak OSD evaluation capability, inattention to output measures such as joint warfighting or readiness capabilities in resource allocation decisions, and absence of cohesion and teamwork among constituent elements of the Department.[7]

Joint Chiefs of Staff. The major problem faced by the Joint Chiefs of Staff arises from the dual roles played by the members of the JCS. Only the chairman is free of service-related duties; the other members serve simultaneously as chiefs of staff of their individual services and as supposedly unbiased members of a joint organization responsible for integrating the requirements placed on the military and for developing a unified defense policy. However, because the allegiance of the chiefs of staff has been directed throughout their careers to their individual services, it is unrealistic to posit that they can set aside service-specific biases when called to serve in their joint capacity.

A second source of problems for the JCS is the fact that the chiefs owe their positions directly to the president; they serve at the behest of the president and can be removed from office by him at any time. This serves to politicize the Joint Chiefs of Staff to the point that their ability to render truly independent military advice to the president, and to provide truly professional military expertise in the process of formulating defense policy, is at least suspect.

The need to express consensus, to speak with one voice, also creates problems for the JCS. This drive for consensus impels the JCS to render opinions at a fairly high level of generality; only those ideas that manage not to offend any of the service-specific concerns of the members of the JCS will survive in JCS policy recommendations.

Finally, the absence of the JCS from the maintaining chain of command places it in the position of being responsible for the wartime activities of organizations over whose forces it has no day-to-day influence. The JCS has no ability to direct the allocation of resources for the training, recruiting, procurement, or general maintenance activities of the military services.

For these four major reasons, the apparently important place occupied by the JCS in the hierarchy of defense decisionmaking is illusory.

Military Departments. Ostensibly, the military departments serve only a maintaining role; they are not even in the employing chain of command. However, as earlier discussed, the inability of the JCS to play an effective role in directing the employment of the military forces of the United States allows that function to devolve onto the military departments. Thus, whereas the focus of formal organizational change over the decades since the founding of the Defense Department has been the diminution of the powers of the military departments, the effect has been largely cosmetic; service needs still dominate the process of defense decision-making.

Unified and Specified Commands. Formally in the employing chain of command, the CINCs share with the JCS an inability to control the organizations that they are to command in wartime. The CINCs are in "the unenviable position of having to face any contingency which may arise with forces whose size, structure, equipment, support, and readiness have been largely determined elsewhere by the individual Services acting independently."[8]

In addition, the CINCs suffer by not having a single military superior in the Pentagon whose responsibility it would be to synthesize their assessments of readiness and joint warfighting capability.

Component Commands. The Unified and Specified Commands were formed in order to provide joint, rather than service-specific, direction to the forces in the field. However, the Component Commands under them, by virtue of their role in the maintenance of their forces, play a more important role than that envisioned by the planners who established the Unified and Specified Commands. The Component Commands' links to the military departments bypass the joint focus of the Unified and Specified Commands and of the JCS; as mentioned earlier, the military departments have maintained a position in the hierarchy greatly disproportionate to their legal responsibilities. Therefore, the Component Commands share in that disproportionate authority.

Congressional Participation

An assessment of the actual, as opposed to the theoretical, relationship between the Department of Defense and the Congress also belies the tidy organizational structure and process presented earlier in this analysis. The fact that the two houses of the Congress deal with defense budget requests simultaneously rather than sequentially is of little fundamental importance; more important are the institutional relationships that affect budget deliberations.

Whereas it is true that the Congress has the ultimate authority to fund (or refuse to fund) budget requests from the Department of Defense, it is also true that the Department has several advantages that reduce the actual impact of the Congress. First, the Department of Defense sets the agenda for budget discussions; it is rare for major funding innovations to emerge from the Congress. The Congress generally reacts to the menu of spending proposals presented by the Department of Defense. Second, the size of the Department of Defense bureaucracy dwarfs the congressional staffs available to challenge the background work done in support of the budget requests. With rare exceptions, congressional staffs simply do not have either the time or the expertise to pose an effective challenge to the facts marshaled by the Defense Department employees whose careers may depend on successfully "selling" a program to the Congress. Third, the Department of Defense need concern itself only with defense matters; an already thin staff on Capitol Hill must try to provide some countervailing expertise in matters of defense while maintaining an awareness of other issues of national concern as well as of the political constraints that always affect what members of the House and Senate do.

Much has been made over the last decade of a purported congressional resurgence, of congressional recapture of power from the executive branch of government. The twin events of Vietnam and Watergate exposed the dangers of overweening and unchecked executive authority and elicited demands for greater participation by the Congress in the defense decisionmaking process.

The effects of these demands became evident in organizational changes undertaken within the House of Representatives during the mid-1970s. The waning of strong party loyalty on the part of both the electorate and the politicians (a phenomenon worthy of analysis in its own right but one that will simply be assumed here) and the passing of a generation of strong, long-term leaders of the Congress combined with the calls for organizational reform to dilute the influence of the chairman of the Armed Services Committee and to allow dissident opinions on matters of defense policy to be given much greater attention than had previously been the case. The increase in days allocated to hearings on the defense budget, and the increase in number of pages of testimony relating to its passage, add to the perception that the defense budget is subjected to greater scrutiny than ever before—that the days of its "free ride" through the Congress are over.[9] Evidence suggests that the Congress became more willing to cut the defense budget during the 1970s than it had been prior to that time.[10]

The question still remains, however, as to whether this increased congressional attention to the defense budget has had more than a marginal effect on the shape and direction of defense policy. The efforts that would have to be made to pursue rational rather than formula cuts in the defense budget are generally considered to be beyond the resources of the Congress.

Institutional and organizational changes that allowed greater scrutiny of defense budgets are not the only results of the post-Watergate, post-Vietnam "revolution" in relations between the Congress and the Department of Defense. Traditionally, it has been agreed that Congress's role in crisis decisionmaking was minimal; the president, as commander-in-chief of the nation's armed forces, was perceived as needing full authority to react in times of crisis. The experience of Vietnam (which was never a declared war and over which Congress could exercise only budgetary, not policy, control) provided Congress with evidence that giving the president (and the Department of Defense) too free a hand in the conduct even of crisis decisionmaking could lead to policies of questionable validity.

The Congress thus sought a role in crisis decisionmaking; the question came to be, what power should that role provide? The nature of crises requires rapid and often secret deliberations and decisionmaking; the Congress, in both design and practice, acts slowly and publicly. The specter of a president having to achieve consensus in a fractious House, for example, before being able to react to a crisis demanding rapid response raised questions about the feasibility of the Congress playing any role in crisis decisionmaking. One legislative attempt to place some controls over the president's freedom of action without completely tying his hands was the War Powers Act of 1973, which imposed upon the president the requirement to report to the Congress should he find it necessary to deploy U.S. troops in a combat situation. This act gave to Congress the authority to approve or disapprove such troop deployments within a certain (limited) period of time. Recent events in Lebanon suggest that the War Powers Act can be circumvented when the president feels that its invocation would too severely limit his flexibility as commander-in-chief; the kind of "legislative veto" involved in Congress's invocation of the War Powers Act has come under legal clouds, as well, through recent Supreme Court decisions. The proper constitutional role in the area of crisis decisionmaking has not been resolved.

One problem in attempting to limit the congressional role in crisis decisionmaking lies in what might be called the routinization of crisis. Transportation and communications technology has advanced to the point that events develop much faster than they used to and call for more rapid response than used to be necessary. In addition, Americans have an increasingly uneasy feeling that they no longer understand the world; they are frequently surprised by events in parts of the world that once seemed peripheral to their interests. By definition, crises are unanticipated events, with potentially critical outcomes, that demand rapid response. In today's international environment, events are more unpredictable, their outcomes are more threatening, and a response is required more rapidly. If crises, so defined, become routine, the policy areas in which congressional participation is seen to be legitimate would gradually decrease in number. Congress is unlikely to accept such exclusion from its co-equal role in the government.

Consequences

Department of Defense

The dual lines of authority within the Department of Defense and the disassociation of the joint elements of the Department from the day-to-day work of training, equipping, and supplying the forces mean that parochial service interests still dominate defense decisionmaking. The impacts of the Department's anarchic operational mores on strategy, force posture, and weapons acquisition are far-reaching and further undermine the ability of the Department to provide thoughtful overall policy guidance.

Rather, the rule seems to be to rationalize whatever exists regardless of its incompatibility with the external security environment, while asserting the need for ever-greater capabilities. That U.S. strategy is fundamentally incompatible with the force structure, for example, seems to go largely unnoticed. Weapons system acquisition seems to be driven by the rule that each service defines the threat in such a way as to guarantee that a mission over which it is the guardian must be accomplished with weapons that it controls. Thus the services are led to pursue weapons development programs that serve more to protect their share of the pie than to guarantee the nation's security.

The acquisition and promotion of the helicopter by the army, once it was determined that the air force "owned" all fixed-wing aviation, is difficult to understand in light of the vulnerability of that system to enemy fire. It can be understood only in the light of the bureaucratic imperatives that impel the army to protect its share of the defense budget. In the same fashion, the bureaucratic durability of the battleship and the aircraft carrier in the face of naval aviation and the combination of nuclear attack submarines and advanced missile technology has been remarkable. Similar assessments can be made of the air force's attachment to the manned bomber and the Marine Corps' faith in the large amphibious assault.[11]

The underlying problem of the Department of Defense, however, may not lie in its bureaucratic structure (or lack of same), but rather in the vague and contradictory guidance it gets from the political leadership whose guidance it is supposed to follow. If this is true, then organizational fixes will not address the problems of the Department of Defense. When the goals of an organization are ambiguous and nonoperationalized, as they tend to be in the Department of Defense, the connection between activities and goals is obscured and activity is pursued for its own sake.[12] Or stated another way, the Department of Defense may not be sure where it is going, but so long as the numbers look good, no one notices its wandering path. When this is coupled with the generally rapid turnover of both military and civilian personnel within the Defense Department, thus reducing accountability for actions, a situation of institutional drift is unavoidable.

Organized anarchy and institutional drift are undesirable in any organization. The mission of the Defense Department, however, exacerbates the problem. When operational failures result from the anarchic conditions, and both lives and prestige are lost unnecessarily, the situation becomes intolerable. One example of organized anarchy at its worst illustrates this point with grim clarity. The full story of Eagle Claw, the abortive attempt to rescue the U.S. hostages held in Iran, will take years to unfold, but startling insights into the reasons for its failure can be gained from viewing it in the light of bureaucratic politics in an organized anarchy. Logic and efficiency demand that a complex operation be undertaken by a small, tightly organized force; organized anarchy demands a "piece of the action" by all services so that the warm glow of success might be shared by all and the bitter fruits of failure ignored as someone else's fault. Eagle Claw was a multiservice operation, even though either the air force or the marines could have undertaken the operation alone, or at least with minimal support from the other services. Instead, all four services were called upon to provide personnel or equipment for an operation in which a single point of command was absent, the chain of command was unclear, and the effects of the ad hoc nature of the operation were all too evident when the unexpected occurred.[13]

Congressional Participation

The increased legislative focus on issues of national defense has increased public awareness of and attention to defense policy. This is what a democratic government should seek: activism and participation by an informed electorate. But given the basic U.S. ambivalence toward the military discussed at the beginning of this discussion, increased attention to defense matters means increased controversy, increased politicization of defense decisionmaking, decreased international credibility as Americans air their differences (loudly, of course—Americans never show restraint when they disagree), and a general perception of anarchy in the entire process of defense decisionmaking. Whereas it was once assumed that politics would stop at the water's edge, defense issues and international relations in general now play a prominent role in political campaigning in the United States. Perhaps the most obvious incident during the 1984 presidential election campaign to illustrate this point was candidate Jesse Jackson's trip to Syria to effect the release of a downed U.S. Navy pilot. The release of the pilot was welcomed, but the role played by Jackson in arranging the release deemed inappropriate for a political figure who had no official role in the government. The specter of candidates pursuing independent arms control negotiations, or making independent promises of military aid, should allow no thoughtful observer to rest easy.

Increased congressional scrutiny of defense budgets has also greatly increased the amount of time and energy the Department of Defense must devote to preparing, giving, and following up on testimony presented at budget hearings. All of this takes away from the time that might be spent in mitigating some of the worst effects of the anarchic decisionmaking process within the Department. Moreover, the Department becomes reactive rather than innovative.

Looking Ahead

The extent to which the myth of the defense decisionmaking process diverges from the reality suggests that corrective actions are in order. The issues to be dealt with are too important, and the consequences of failure too serious, to allow institutional drift to continue. As previous efforts at bureaucratic reform have shown, however, it is not easy to predict whether reforms will have the desired effects, given the organizational interests of the entities within the Department of Defense, on Capitol Hill, and in the White House whose positions in the hierarchy are threatened by efforts at reform.

Broadly speaking, there are three ways of attempting to address the problem of reform of the defense decisionmaking apparatus. One is to alter the organizational structure through which decisions are made; a second is to change the nature of the way the game is played; and the third is to change the character of the players in the game.[14]

The first of these options is predestined to fail. It is difficult to implement anything more substantial than incremental organizational changes within the Department of Defense for a variety of budgetary, institutional, and political reasons.[15] The relationship between the Department and the other actors is driven more by noninstitutionalized mores than by formal organizational structure; structural reform would have little impact on the mores that form the heart of the problem.

Another approach is to attempt to change the way the bureaucratic game is played—to affect the mores addressed in the preceding paragraph. Unfortunately, efforts to affect the fundamental nature of the way the Defense Department interacts with other players in the process would require the kind of systematic, long-range planning that the current practice of rapid turnover of high-ranking officials in the Department makes impossible. Changing the nature of the bureaucratic game as it is played within the Department of Defense is ruled out for much the same reason.[16]

The third possible course of action is to change the players in the game. Of course, merely exchanging old players for new, without changing the process by which they are selected or the criteria that make them eligible for selection, will ensure that no fundamental changes occur. Rather, Defense Department officials need to be chosen on the basis of their substantive knowledge instead of their political acumen, managerial proficiency, bureaucratic gamesmanship, and personal loyalty to the president. Likewise, members of Congress with responsibility for dealing with defense issues should be chosen because of their substantive knowledge of national defense policy, not because of their ability to secure defense contracts for contractors in their districts. Changes in the way officials in either the Department of Defense or the Congress are selected are not likely to occur.

It is therefore difficult to be optimistic about the chances for fundamental change in the way the United States is organized to make defense decisions. The three aforementioned major ways of implementing change have drawbacks that make their successful implementation unlikely. If there is no mechanism through which change can be effected, then change will not occur—no matter how compelling the need for change. The picture for the future does not appear to differ markedly from the past: organized anarchy, institutional drift, shifts with the political tide, in a reactive rather than an innovative posture. This was not the way the United States helped "win" the Second World War; but it is assuredly the way this country will help "lose" the peace.

Notes

1. Archie D. Barrett, *Reappraising Defense Organization* (Washington, D.C.: National Defense University Press, 1983), p. 17. The framework Colonel Barrett developed in his book was very helpful to me in the construction of this chapter. Discussions throughout the chapter of the dual chains of command that exist in the Pentagon borrow heavily from Colonel Barrett's analysis; I am indebted to his thought-provoking book.

2. Ibid., p. 42.

3. John E. Endicott, "The National Security Council—Formulating National Security Policy for Presidential Review," in John E. Endicott and Roy W. Stafford, Jr. (eds.), *American Defense Policy*, 4th ed. (Baltimore: Johns Hopkins University Press, 1977), p. 314.

4. Robert H. Trice, "The Structure of the National Security System," in B. Thomas Trout and James E. Harf (eds.), *National Security Affairs* (New Brunswick, N.J.: Transaction Books, 1982), p. 167.

5. Alan Ned Sabrosky, James Clay Thompson, and Karen A. McPherson, "Organized Anarchies: Military Bureaucracy in the 1980s," *Journal of Applied Behavioral Science* 18, no. 2 (1982):140.

6. Ibid., pp. 142–143.

7. Barrett, *Reappraising Defense Organization*, p. 5.

8. Ibid., p. 53.

9. Nancy J. Bearg and Edwin A. Deagle, Jr., "Congress and the Defense Budget," in Endicott and Stafford, *American Defense Policy*, pp. 341–342.

10. Ibid., p. 345.

11. Sabrosky et al., "Organized Anarchies," pp. 146–147.

12. William A. Lucas and Raymond H. Dawson, *The Organizational Politics of Defense* (Pittsburgh: International Studies Association, 1974), p. 16.

13. Sabrosky et al., "Organized Anarchies," p. 148.

14. M. Brecher, "Bureaucratic Politics in Foreign Policy," *Armed Forces and Society* (1976):2.

15. Sabrosky et al., "Organized Anarchies," p. 150.

16. Sabrosky et al., "Organized Anarchies," p. 151.

About the Editor
and Contributors

Robert H. Baker is currently lecturer in politics at the University of Lancaster, where he has taught a range of undergraduate and postgraduate courses specializing in the Soviet Union and Soviet defense policy. His research interests are in the area of Soviet politics, Soviet defense, and totalitarianism. His publications include contributions to *Arms Control, Royal United Services Institution for Higher Defence Studies Journal,* and a chapter on the Soviet Union in C. Clapham (ed.), *Private Patronage and Public Power* (Frances Pinter, 1982).

Wilfried Freiherr von Bredow is professor of international relations at the University of Marburg. He has been a research fellow at St. Anthony's College, Oxford; guest professor at the Institute of Political Science, University of Toulouse I; and Fulbright visiting professor at Manchester College, Indiana. His publications include *Moderner Militarismus: Analyse und Kritik* (1983); *Einfuhrung in die internationalen Wirtschaftsbeziehungen* (1981); and "The Peace Movement in the FRG," in *Armed Forces and Society* (1982). His research interests are in civil-military relations, East-West conflict, and West German defense and foreign policy.

José-Maria Comas is a member of the Centre d'Etudes et de Recherches sur l'Armée (CERSA), University of Toulouse I. His main research interests are in Spanish defense policy and military studies. His publications include *Le système militaire espagnol d'aujourd'hui (1939–1981)* (1982), *Deuxieme reconnaissances du système militaire espagnol* (1981), and *Poder politico y funcion militar en la Espana actual* (forthcoming).

Martin Edmonds is senior lecturer in higher defense studies and in politics at the University of Lancaster. He previously taught strategic studies and comparative politics at the University of Manchester and has been a research associate at Columbia University and a tutor in the graduate program in international relations at the University of Southern California. His publications include *War in the Next Decade* (coedited with Roger Beaumont, 1975); *International Arms Procurement,* a forthcoming volume on British military systems; and over fifty articles on defense and military studies in books and academic journals. He is editor-in-chief of a major new journal, *Defense Analysis.*

Reidar Lauritz Godø served with the Norwegian forces in the United Kingdom during World War II. In the postwar period Vice-Admiral Godø has held a number of key positions in Norwegian defense, including those of inspector general Coast Artillery, commandant of the National Defense College, chief of staff Defense Command, Norway, and deputy chief of Defense. During the period from 1976 to 1980 he served on the NATO Military Committee in Brussels as Norwegian Permanent Military Representative.

Virgilio Ilari is currently associate professor of Roman law at Macerata University. He has written *Gli italici nelle strutture militari romane* (1974), *Guerra e diritto nel mondo antico* (1980), and *L'interpretazione storica del diritto di guerra romano fra tradizione romanistica e giusnaturalismo* (1981)— and *Le Forze armate tra politica e potere (1943–1976)* (1979). He has published numerous articles on Italian military policy and history. In association with Lieutenant Colonel Ferruccio Botti, he has also written a study entitled *Il pensiero militare italiano dal primo al secondo dopoguerra (1919–1940)*, which will be published in 1985 by the Ufficio Storico of the Italian Army Staff.

Karen A. McPherson is currently an analyst for Science Applications, Inc., a large consulting company that does contract research for the U.S. Department of Defense. She has worked primarily in the areas of defense decisionmaking, military manpower, and civil-military relations and is currently involved in a major study for the Defense Department's Pacific Command to assess the United States' military posture in the Pacific.

Jean-Pierre Marichy is Chargé de Conference at the Institute of Political Science at the University of Toulouse I. His memberships include the Inter-University Seminar on Armed Forces and Society, the French Political Science Association, and the Centre d'Etudes et de Recherches sur l'Armée (CERSA), where he leads the research team in studies of French military systems and defense policy. He is author of *La Deuxieme Chambre dans la vie politique française depuis 1875* (1969) and editor of the volume *Le système militaire française* (1977) and has contributed numerous articles in books and journals on French civil-military relations, military discipline, and the evolution of French defense policy.

Masashi Nishihara is currently professor of international relations at the National Defense Academy, Yokosuka, Japan. He has taught in Kyoto Sangyo and Kyoto Universities and at the University of South Carolina and has been a visiting fellow at the Australian National University and the Rockefeller Foundation in New York. He is an associate of the Research Institute for Peace and Security, Tokyo, and a member of the International Institute for Strategic Studies, London. His publications include *The Japanese and Sukaro's Indonesia* (1976) and articles on Southeast Asian security, Japanese defense policy, and European-Japanese relations.

Gerald Segal is lecturer in the Department of Politics, University of Bristol. He has held similar teaching positions at the University of Wales (Aberystwyth) and the University of Leicester. He is the author of *The Great Power Triangle* (1982) and *Defending China* (1984); coauthor of *Nuclear War and Nuclear Peace* (1983); editor of *The China Factor* (1982) and *The Soviet Union and East Asia* (1983); and coeditor of *Soviet Strategy* (1981), *Soviet Strategy Towards Western Europe* (1984), and *Chinese Defence Policy* (1984).

Index